James the Apostle of Faith

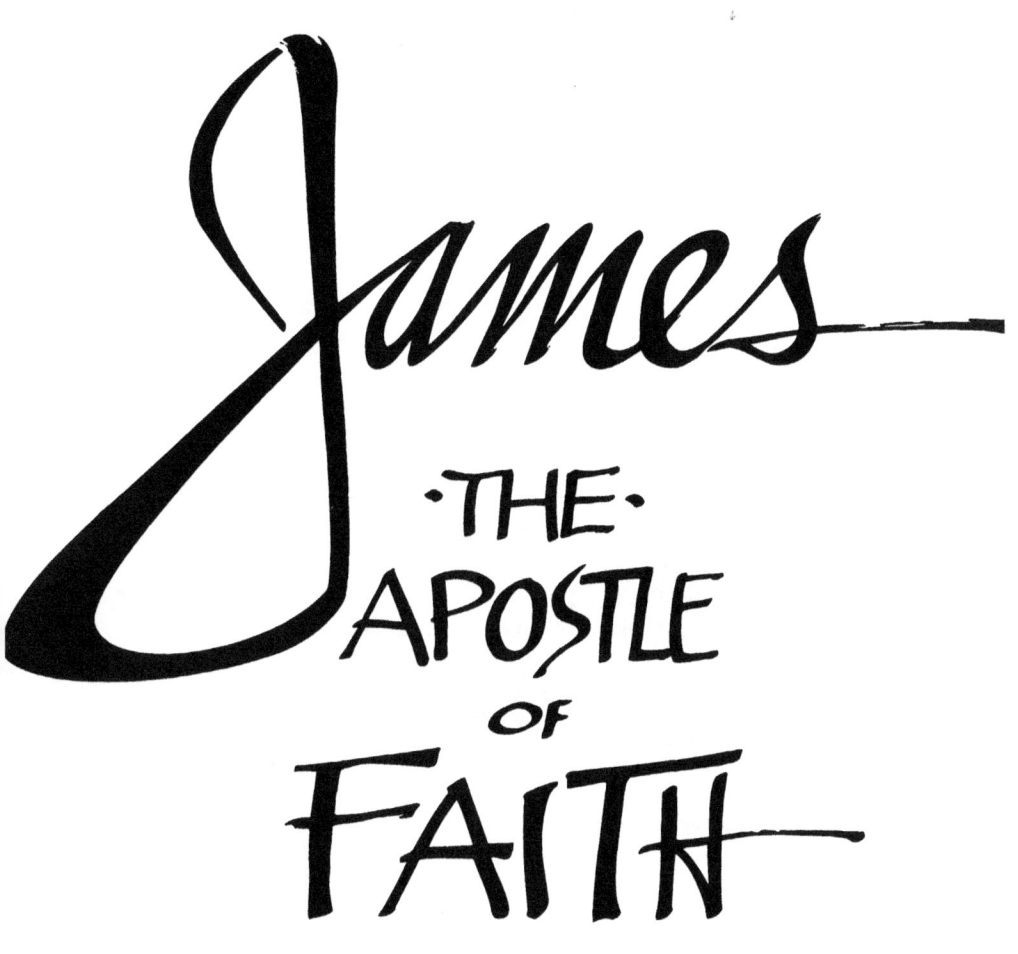

James the Apostle of Faith

A Primary Christological Epistle
for the Persecuted Church

David P. Scaer
Foreword by Paul L. Maier

Wipf & Stock
PUBLISHERS
Eugene, Oregon

Wipf and Stock Publishers
199 W 8th Ave, Suite 3
Eugene, OR 97401

James, the Apostle of Faith
A Primary Christological Epistle for the Persecuted Church
By Scaer, David P.
Copyright©1994 by Scaer, David P.
ISBN: 1-59244-990-5
Publication date 11/8/2004
Previously published by Concordia Publishing House, 1994

Unless otherwise indicated, the Bible text in this publication is from the Revised Standard Version of the Bible, copyrighted 1946, 1952, ©1971, 1973 by the Division of Christian Education of the National Council of the Churches of Christ in the U.S.A., and used by permission.

For
David, Stephen, and Peter

"But I saw none of the other apostles except James the Lord's brother."
Galatians 1:19

"And [Peter] said, 'Tell this to James and to the brethren.'"
Acts 12:17

"After they finished speaking, James replied, 'Brethren, listen to me.'"
Acts 15:13

Contents

Foreword	11
Preface	13
Acknowledgments	17
I. INTRODUCTION	19
Overcoming Luther's Legacy	19
The Attempt of Form Criticism	21
Opportunity for a Reevaluation	21
II. THE PERSON OF JAMES (1:1a)	23
III. ORIGIN, SETTING, DESTINATION, AND GREETING (1:1b)	28
IV. CHIEFLY A PASTORAL EPISTLE (1:2)	32
Organization in the Early Church	32
The Spread of the Church	33
The Church in Jerusalem	35
V. TEMPTATION, PERSECUTION, AND FAITH (1:2-8)	39
The Problem of Temptation for Jesus and the Church (1:2)	39
Suffering as the Result of Persecution (1:3)	40
Total Forgiveness in Time of Persecution (1:4)	41
Peter, Pastors, and Temptations (1:5-8)	42
James the Apostle of Faith: The First Defense	45
VI. THE PASTORAL OFFICE, THE LURE OF THE WORLD, AND CHRIST (1:9-18)	47
A Major Problem	47
A Preliminary Christology (1:9-10)	48
A Brief Exegetical Digression: James' Use of Isaiah 40 (1:10-11)	50
An Even Fuller Christology (1:12)	51
The Messiah, His People, and Stephen (1:12)	52
Original and Actual Sin (1:13-16)	55
Incarnation and Atonement (1:17-18)	57
VII. GUIDELINES FOR PASTORS (1:19-27)	63
Instructions for Preaching (1:19-20)	63
Baptism, Conversion, and the Final Salvation (1:21)	64
The Gospel as a Fulfilled Law (1:22-25)	66
Good Works and Judgment Day (1:26-27)	69

VIII. CHRIST'S POVERTY AND ITS IMPLICATIONS (2:1-7) — 72

- Jesus as God (2:1) — 72
- A Unique Understanding of Faith (2:1) — 73
- Synagogue or Church? (2:2-4) — 73
- The First Beatitude as Description of Christ and His Congregation (2:5-6) — 74
- An Allusion to Baptism (2:7) — 77
- The Church as Court: An Excursus — 78

IX. LOVE, SCRIPTURE, APOSTASY, AND THE TRIUMPH OF THE GOSPEL (2:8-13) — 81

- Scripture and Christ (2:8-9) — 81
- Adultery as Apostasy and Implications of Murder (2:10-11) — 82
- The Triumph of the Gospel (2:12-13) — 85

X. THE NEW TESTAMENT'S FIRST GREAT DISCUSSION ON JUSTIFICATION (2:14-26) — 87

- Faith and Works Seen from the Day of Judgment (2:14-17) — 87
- The Peace Ritual in the Liturgy (2:16) — 88
- Faith and Works (2:18) — 89
- Again to the Liturgy (2:19) — 90
- Abraham and Rahab: An Unlikely Combination of Examples of Justification — 90
- Abraham's Faith and Sacrifice (2:20-22) — 91
- James Introduces Gen. 15:6 into the Justification Discussion (2:23-24) — 93
- The Superior Faith of Rahab (2:25) — 94
- The Imagery of the Body and Breath (Not Body and Soul) (2:26) — 94
- James the Apostle of Faith: The Second Defense and Summation — 95

XI. AGAIN TO THE PASTORAL TASK (3:1-18) — 97

- Preaching and Doctrine (3:1-12) — 97
- An Addendum to a Most Difficult Section — 102
- Preachers Standing in Christ's Stead (3:13-18) — 104

XII. EXHORTATIONS AGAINST WORLDLINESS (4:1-17) — 109

- The Church Against Itself (4:1-4) — 109
- Correcting the Situation (4:5-10) — 111
- Putting Judgment in Its Proper Place (4:11-12) — 114
- The First Ending: A Gentle Rebuke (4:13-17) — 115

XIII. ADDENDA: (5:1-20) — 118

- A Condemnation of Unbelievers (5:1-6) — 119
- A Few Final Suggestions — 123
- Patience and the Parousia (5:7-11) — 124
- Careful Use of the Divine Name (5:12) — 129
- Personal Problems (5:13-18) — 130
- Correcting a Doctrinal Problem (5:19-20) — 134

XIV. EPILOG: AT THE DAWN OF THE NEW TESTAMENT	136
XV. LUTHER, THE LUTHERANS, AND JAMES: AN ATTEMPT AT A DEFENSE	138
Luther	138
The Lutherans	139
James	140
Notes	142
Bibliography	152
Index	155

Foreword

Controversy has swirled about the New Testament Epistle of James ever since the early church, when some denied it canonical status—through the Reformation era, when Luther dubbed it a "straw" epistle—to commentators today, who often deem it an unorganized collection of moralisms. Friends of the epistle have defended it and detractors attacked it—both for the wrong reasons. Its theology has been misunderstood as an anti-Pauline support for work-righteousness, while its authorship has been ascribed to any of the many Jameses who surface in the Gospels, or to unknowns using their names.

The time has come not only to correct centuries of misunderstanding of this epistle and to rehabilitate its author, but to weigh the possibility of its crucial early composition and probable influence on other writings in the New Testament canon. This volume is admirably suited for such a task. While many commentators achieve their radical reevaluations by a very arbitrary use of external criteria in judging their canonical subjects, David P. Scaer works his "revolution" in James interpretation by capitalizing on the rich internal evidences from the New Testament and the earliest church. Professor of New Testament and systematics at Concordia Theological Seminary, Ft. Wayne, Ind., Dr. Scaer is fully conversant with the mass of critical literature on James, and although he writes out of a Lutheran heritage, he disapproves of Luther's traditional disappointment with James. Indeed, an excursus at the close of these pages deals objectively with the great Reformer's disenchantment, showing how this was later modified both by Luther himself and his successors.

As regards authorship of the epistle, I was delighted to find Dr. Scaer's strong endorsement of James, the uterine or half-brother of Jesus, a son of Mary and Joseph after the birth of Christ. (Mary's status as "ever virgin"—despite Roman Catholic tradition and the fact that Luther still clung to it—simply will not stand against clear Biblical and patristic evidence.) I say "delighted," because this James is one of the most intriguing figures in earliest church history. During Jesus' public ministry he seems to have lurked outside His circle, and his unbelief then is very believable indeed: Put the case that your own brother today claimed to be divine! Converted by Jesus' special appearance to him after the resurrection, James quickly became the first "bishop of Jerusalem"—by faith and leadership, not nepotism. His strong authority at the time of the Jerusalem Council (Acts 15) is patent and uncontested, and his noble guidance of the persecuted first Christians is portrayed not only by the epistle which bears his name but by crucial testimony in *extra-Biblical* sources.

The first-century Jewish historian Flavius Josephus might almost be termed "the fifth evangelist" for all the tangencies with New Testament personalities he supplies. His *War* and *Antiquities* parade not only the various ruling Romans and Herods, but tell also of John the Baptist, Jesus Himself, and particularly James, whom he styles "the brother of Jesus," providing priceless data concerning his role in Jerusalem and his martyrdom by stoning in A.D. 62. For nearly 30 years after the resurrection, then, James was in charge of a Jewish Christianity centered in Jerusalem. Effectively, he and not Peter was the first "bishop" of the Christian church, and when the high priest and the Sanhedrin in Jerusalem stoned James to death in the *absence* of the Roman governor Albinus (who was so angry at this lynching that the high priest was deposed), it was a stunning parallel to Good Friday, which must be cited against all current attempts to rewrite the Passion story in the interest of exculpating the Sanhedrin.

James, then, occupies so fascinating and central a role in earliest Christianity that the church would be poorer for not having any documents from his pen. But, happily, it does have one: this crucial epistle!

As to dating, some scholars who see in the epistle a reaction to misuse of Pauline theology will find Prof. Scaer's placement of this epistle after the persecution of Acts 8 but before the Jerusalem Council (Acts 15) improbably early. But if Scaer's thesis holds, then this letter and not I Thessalonians becomes the *very first* writing in the New Testament canon.

The implications of this chronology are, of course, enormous. James then becomes a window into the life of the earliest church between Jesus and Paul, a segment for which we otherwise have precious little information. But more. James' discussion of justification, faith, and works becomes the earliest theology of these doctrines in the church, and Scaer locates probable dependence on James in much of the New Testament.

So far as the faith-works tension is concerned, "the memory of James is defamed if he is considered an apostle of works," Scaer writes. "He deserves along with Paul and even before him the title 'The Apostle of Faith.'" Hence the title of this book.

The other themes in these pages—James primarily as a pastoral epistle directed to the clergy, its message for a church under persecution, and James himself as an eschatological preacher in the mold of John the Baptist and Jesus—are advanced clearly and vigorously by a scholar who has mastered the languages and sources, and can use them creatively. He has also managed to catch the spirit of earliest Jewish Christianity before its systematization in Pauline vocabulary, its Gentile admixture, and its missionary vector to the northwest recounted in Acts. Fresh insights and original thought characterize the work throughout. Here is a rare looking glass into the fledgling church under duress, for which the author has provided the cleanest and strongest lens to date.

Paul L. Maier

Western Michigan University

Preface

Early in the 1970s F. F. Bruce, in a lecture at Wheaton College in Illinois before the 25th anniversary meeting of the Evangelical Theological Society, said that two periods of Christian history required special investigation: the time between Jesus and the rise of the first New Testament documents, and the time between the last document and the early church.

A teaching assignment at the seminary in the Epistle of James, at first a very reluctantly accepted task, provided me an open door into the period right after Jesus and before Paul. Fortuitously, my interest in Matthew's gospel provided an avenue for investigating James, as these writings are so similar in style. For years the students were commenting, rather complaining, that the Matthew course was one on James and vice versa. The problem was that one seemed to be the prolegomenon for the other. Since this could hardly be, which was really the first? The question of an oral tradition, raised so prominently by Bultmann, became important for understanding the relationship between these two books. Unless one was using the other—and this does not seem to be the case—both had to be drawing upon a common tradition. It was almost as if both were working from the same set of class notes, one to write a gospel and the other an epistle. Resolving this question of interrelationship would not involve Paul in the justification discussion.

A burden or an advantage of occidental Christianity is its Pauline heritage and near total reliance on him for its theology. This is true for its Roman Catholic, Lutheran, or Reformed expressions. Even Roman Catholicism, which has taken refuge more often in James than Protestantism has done, has never given James the high position accorded Paul. No one will theoretically deny that Christianity existed before Paul, but in reality it is nearly impossible to do Christian theology without the Pauline terminology.

James: The Apostle of Faith is one attempt to look at the church's theology after Jesus but before the advent of Paul as the theologically influential figure in the early church. A total de-Paulinization of theology for a western Christian is impossible, but at least the reader is made aware that a vibrant Christianity existed before Paul became prominent. Since Paul's writings are for western minds the most explicit expression of New Testament theology, he inevitably is brought into nearly each discussion.

The subtitle, *A Primary Christological Epistle for the Persecuted Church*, reveals the book's conclusion that James is a serious theological work for suffering Christians. This theology at all points revolved around a Christology which centered on the suffering of Jesus. If this is so, then Luther's demand that canonical books preach Christ has been more than satisfactorily answered in the case of James. Persecution and suffering were seen as more important and essential to church life in the earliest centuries than they are now. Today success is the mark of an acceptable Christianity. My esteemed colleague, Dr. William C. Weinrich, in his published doctoral dissertation, *Spirit and Martyrdom*, has shown that the earliest Christians not only had no inordinate fear of death but even looked forward to martyrdom as conclusive evidence that they were accepted by Christ. William R. Farmer in *Jesus and the Gospels* makes the point that our canonical gospels were selected because they proclaimed the suffering, martyred Christ—unlike the gnostic ones, which preached a glorified Christ.[1] James, by placing a suffering Christ before a persecuted church, satisfies this early-church criterion used in evaluating the gospels, incidentally also satisfying Luther's concern about preaching Christ.

At this point the question of the Spirit's inspiration comes into play. The same Spirit who assisted Christ in His suffering was working in the apostles and in their writings to proclaim and preserve His humiliation as the essence of the Gospel message.[2] These were distinguishable but not unrelated, independent activities of the Spirit. This Spirit who assisted Christ in His death was recognized by the early church as active in the death of saints. These deaths were considered as virtual sacramental signs of His presence.

The other criterion for both the early church and Luther was the apostolic authority of the New Testament writings. If the author is the same James whom Paul regards as apostle with Peter and John and calls the Lord's brother (Gal. 1:19; 2:9), the problem of canonicity resolves itself.[3] This is of course one of the burdens of this present book.

Apart from the question of whether any personal, theological, real, or imagined antagonism between Paul and James can be detected in the New Testament documents, Paul is pictured as deferring to James in a number of places. For Paul, James is apostle, the brother of the Lord, the recognized authority in the Jerusalem church, for whom he gathers offerings and whom he visits. Paul claims that James also received a resurrection appearance of the exalted Lord. As an apostle, the promise of the Spirit's speaking applies in a uniquely authoritative way to James's office and words. Together James and Paul suffered persecution as they preached the Gospel, and together they bore "the marks of Jesus" (Gal. 6:17).

References and refutations of Luther's criticisms of James are offered with only the greatest respect for the Reformer's memory and are really only permissible for one of his loyal sons. If Luther would have had the opportunity to look at James from a view which unveils a deeper Christological content, he would have seen this for himself. What is at issue here now is not defending a 16th-century figure or making apologies for his statements, but giving a forgotten and often misunderstood New Testament figure his due as an apostle.

The memory of James has rarely enjoyed this position of honor as apostle and preacher of the Gospel. When the Epistle of James is understood within its Christological framework, then both he and Paul are seen as similar in their understanding of Christology not as doctrinal abstraction but as a necessary suffering for and with Christ. James as much as Paul and Luther is a theologian of the cross. In him there is no trace of a theology of glory for the church.

James must be recognized as a theologian, no less capable than any other apostle, including Paul. Let it be said here: James is an apostle of *faith*; he is not the moralist he is so often portrayed as being. Moreover, James is at home in the Old Testament and is unsurpassed by any other epistle writer in using the language style of Jesus in addressing the problems of the early church. James is no less the pastor than is Paul. In his use of the Greek language he is surpassed perhaps only by the writer of Hebrews. All indications from Acts show that he was a recognized church leader and held the most responsible and honored position in the Jerusalem church for the longest time in the apostolic era.

In spite of all this, he has become a lost figure. Liturgical church calendars have set aside days for the Jameses who were the sons of Zebedee and Alphaeus, with whom he is frequently misidentified, but none for him. As a small compensation to overcome the centuries of neglect, this book has no other dedication but to the revival of the memory of that James who was the son of Mary and Joseph, the uterine brother of Jesus, the apostle chosen by the resurrected Lord, bishop of Jerusalem, recognized leader of the early church, author of the epistle bearing his name, and the one who wanted to be remembered as a servant of Jesus.

Soli Deo Gloria!

Acknowledgments

My assignment to Concordia Theological Seminary, then in Springfield, Ill., was primarily to systematic theology, with an accompanying responsibility in New Testament. In the early 1970s Dr. Lorman Petersen, then academic dean, assigned me to an elective seminar on the Epistles of James and Jude. Without this specific responsibility I would have ignored James, passed over it as offering nothing of any theological significance, and been content to let stand Luther's oft-repeated judgment about its being an epistle of straw.

Over the years the students at our seminary, now in Fort Wayne, Ind., challenged me constantly to reevaluate the traditional view that it was hardly more than a collection of moral admonitions for Christians. As the reader will soon discover, I learned that viewing James as a "how to do it book in Christianity" totally fails to understand him at all. To all those students who forced me to strain this epistle through the crucible of critical evaluation a word of thanks is due. They will know who they are. Our journey together through James may have been reluctant at first but was stimulating at the end.

My wife and three sons have been patient in letting the typewriter disturb the serenity of the beautiful Poconos in eastern Pennsylvania, where we are most at home in the summers. Their names were proleptic of what would be written on these pages. Dorothy and her name reflect God's gift (*dōrēma*) (James 1:17), and our sons each had at least one name of those early church theologians whose shadows are indelibly etched into the inner fiber of this epistle—David *Paul,* *Stephen* Charles, and *Peter James,* a double portion for the youngest.

Lois Rau, whom the Lord took so untimely from her family and her now pastor husband, first guided the rough draft into a more acceptable form. She will not be forgotten for her patient and generous spirit. This book must serve as a memorial to the industry of this saint of God. Tammy Raymer also served well from the beginning. Linda Newman not only helped with the final manuscript but instinctively knew what should have been said and proceeded to make the necessary adjustments. To my friend and colleague Prof. Dean O. Wenthe, whose loyalty to the confessional tradition has always instinctively known that this loyalty never was intended to exhaust the wider Biblical revelation, a special word of thanks for his encouragement and counsel over many years. Dr. Robert D. Preus, first as teacher, then as colleague, now as seminary president, and always as friend, continues to provide the intellectual climate where ideas meet and are refined.

Much of what is written here presupposes that the reader can put at his disposal other valuable resources with more detailed exegetical data. Three books, all in English, are particularly noteworthy; each makes a unique and immediately useful contribution. Joseph B. Mayor's *The Epistle of St. James*, nearly a century old, remains a classic in its abundance of Scriptural cross references, so necessary in seeing James in the totality of the New Testament canon. Peter Davids' *Commentary on James* in the *New International Greek Testament Commentary* (1982) provides the most up-to-date critical examination. Fair in setting forth opposing views in an easy-to-understand and stimulating way is Sophie Laws' *A Commentary on the Epistle of James* in the *Harper's New Testament Commentaries* (1980). Had Davids' and Laws' works been available at the time of the first writing, they would have provided opportunity for additional dialog. While many ideas put forth here find parallel in them, I only can take responsibility, especially for those ideas which at first may appear a bit startling.

If what is written here about James helps in any way to lead into the teachings of Jesus, especially as they are found in the Sermon on the Mount and the parables in Matthew's gospel, an important purpose will have been served.

Maundy Thursday
1983

David P. Scaer
Concordia Theological Seminary
Fort Wayne, Ind.

1/Introduction

Overcoming Luther's Legacy

No other book in the New Testament has suffered more than the Epistle of James in regard to the questions of its authorship, its place in the canon, and its content. It was omitted from several of the earliest canonical listings, and even those who supported its place in the New Testament mentioned the doubts that some had raised about its author.

A near-fatal blow was delivered by Martin Luther, who could find little good in the epistle. James, he thought, could not qualify as a writing of the apostles, as it came long after Paul and Peter. Since this epistle taught justification by works and not by faith as Paul had done, Luther did not consider it the work of an apostle. While Luther conceded that it mentioned the name of Christ, it taught nothing about His crucifixion and resurrection. Luther's most unkind criticism was directed at the total lack of organization of the epistle. He impugned the writer's ability both as theologian and as author.

"But this James does nothing more than drive to the law and to its works. Besides, he throws things together so chaotically that it seems to me he must have been some good, pious man, who took a few sayings from the disciples of the apostles and then tossed them off on paper.... In a word, he wanted to guard against those who relied on faith without works, but was unequal to the task."[1]

Those who respected the decisions of the early church to place James in the canon in spite of the recognized unanswered questions about its exact origin continued to follow Luther's assessment of its content as hardly more than a collection of wisdom sayings. Wisdom literature had surfaced in the Old Testament Book of Proverbs, remained popular in the hands of the rabbis in the intertestamental period, and found its way into James. Even Martin Dibelius, who with Rudolf Bultmann shares the title of the father of form criticism, saw no theology in James and called it paraenesis, which simply means "a text which strings together admonitions of general content."[2] Luther and Dibelius might have had entirely different views on the supernatural origins of the Scriptures, but they basically agreed that James had no theology and its chief value was a strung-out list of moralisms. What this view means is that James has hardly more value than Benjamin Franklin's *Poor Richard's Almanac*, with a slight doctoring up of the epistle in two places with the name of Christ to make it compatible for the Christian Bible. Though Luther's followers would not follow his radical suggestion of excising James from the canon, it was viewed suspiciously. Traditionally

James was called a "catholic" epistle, because it was seen as directed to an audience wider than just one church. After the Reformation this designation came to have a double meaning.[3]

Even where James was used in Protestant circles as a fully authentic and canonical writing, it was used as a counterbalance for any excesses in the preaching of grace as suggested by Paul's writings. To preach justification, one could go to Paul. For an antidote for the excesses of grace, a virtual warehouse of moral admonitions for Christian living could be found in James.[4] This is, of course, exactly the use Luther suggested. James was always a good excuse for a law sermon, if the preacher felt so inclined.

The antagonism between Paul and James, alleged by Luther, was not only put to good practical use by the homileticians in the evangelical traditions, but was perpetuated historically in the scholarly investigations of these two writers. So different were their theologies to most observers that it only stood to reason that one wrote to supply a corrective antidote for the other. But who was first? Even here Luther's assessment that James wrote to counteract the unintended libertinism of Paul's doctrine of salvation by grace through faith without works prevailed, with only a few exceptions, among most scholars until just recently.

But any view that sees James as a reaction to Paul's doctrine of free grace overlooks the fundamental fact that Paul rather than James has detailed instructions of behavior for the various groups in the congregation. Paul addresses nearly all the levels of society and the family and provides enough ammunition by himself for anyone who wants to construct a Christianity with moralistic overtones. The opposing view that Paul wrote to provide an evangelical counterbalance fails to note that to James belong such clear gospel expressions as God's promise of the crown of life to those who love Him. He also coined the phrase "the perfect law of liberty," a reference to the Gospel and not to the Law, as Luther thought.

The cross references and allusions common to James and Paul are obvious to most scholars, but the meaning of James remains hidden as long as the alleged antagonism between the two apostles is perpetuated as the one effective key to unlocking its meaning.

Simply because more of Paul's writings made their way into the New Testament, he became more influential. The controversy between the two apostles is thus always unfairly weighted in favor of Paul, whose preserved writings not only dominate the New Testament canon but also were specifically directed at the Gentile audience. It is no wonder that the Gentile descendants of a one time minority would find Paul more of an apostle to their liking. Even as early as the fourth century, when the canonical question was formally answered, the church had long been removed from the roots of its Jewish heritage. To this add Luther's rules for the game, which made Paul the norm for other early church writings. Paul became for Luther almost a canon within a canon. "In the first place it [James] is flatly against St. Paul and all the rest of Scripture in ascribing justification to works" (2:24).[5] It was almost as if James' alleged opponent, Paul, was also the referee. Though firmly placed within the canon, James is still either ignored or used for an occasional good threshing sermon of Law.

The Attempt of Form Criticism

Form criticism, popularized for New Testament studies by Martin Dibelius and Rudolf Bultmann, approached the Biblical documents atomistically. With its divisions of the Biblical texts into categories which were then tracked down to early church communities, form criticism paid less attention to theological organization and meaning. Form critics saw the gospels as collections of sayings, almost as Luther saw James. No wonder that Luther and Dibelius, who first detailed the form-critical procedures, came to nearly identical conclusions about James as a collection of wisdom sayings that had been Christianized here and there. Form criticism only perpetuated the widely held view that the synoptic gospels, that is Matthew, Mark, and Luke, contained biographical data about Jesus' life, and the epistles, especially Paul's, provided the theological substance which formed the real basis of what would become Christianity. The great treatments on faith, grace, Baptism, Lord's Supper, resurrection, and eschatology could be easily found in Paul rather than the synoptic gospels.[6]

One cannot escape seeing that in actual practice this was also Luther's view in the way he approached James. For him there was no theology here. For later scholars the gospels contained some biographical data about Jesus and preserved His teachings, which with the exception of John were seen as heavily ethical. Consider that the Sermon on the Mount, the most prominent in Matthew by pre-eminence of place and length, is valued for its ethical and not its Gospel content. Redaction criticism, without rejecting form criticism, took a more holistic view in assessing the organic unity and integrity of the Biblical documents.

Opportunity for a Reevaluation

While redaction criticism falters when it fails to appreciate and endorse the Biblical history as essential, it already has made major contributions in recognizing each of the synoptic gospels as self-contained theological treatises. This means that these gospels are not merely collections of the sayings and acts of Jesus, but are serious theological compositions, specifically written to preserve His sayings for the early church. Such an approach can only have positive benefits when it displays Jesus as *the* Revealer of Christian truth. He was a theologian in His own right, and His preaching was not a strung-out list of sermon illustrations, but actually theology. The impression is too often given that while Jesus in His death and resurrection is at the heart of the Christian message, it is Paul and not Jesus who is the best interpreter of these events. Redaction criticism is saying that the synoptic gospels, regardless of certain biographical details about the life of Jesus, are theological productions to be taken no less seriously than the epistles. Since the gospels place Jesus as the preacher of the message, they not only have the higher honor which the church has traditionally given them in its worship services, but also have the greater value theologically. The greater theological appreciation given to the gospels can have only positive benefits in interpreting James, which shares common expressions with Jesus as He appears in the gospels.

James is recognized as having a style closely resembling Jesus in the synoptic gospels, especially Matthew's Sermon on the Mount, but does not have what can be said to be direct quotations of these writings.[7] When the Jesus of the synoptic gospels can be appreciated as a theologian in His own right with a clear and *full* preaching of the Gospel—without comparing Him to Paul, then the way is open for seeing James chiefly as preacher and theologian. This is what he intended to be and what he in fact was. James must be understood within the context of the words of Jesus, especially as presented in the synoptic gospels, rather than judged by Paul. The historical winds put Paul in the prominent position and turned James into a preacher of the Law. Those who appreciated him too often did so for the wrong reasons.

Recent winds have been more favorable. More recent studies on this epistle have begun to appreciate James as a serious theological document with predetermined form, recognizable organization, and literary merit.[8] They have also begun to move away from seeing this epistle solely in terms of morals, ethics, or what is often called, in a somewhat theologically condescending way, practical rules for Christian living. The history of past interpretation does not make a total extrication from past views possible. The temptation is always to see James steeped in the thought world of the rabbis.[9] The answer lies in seeing James as thoroughly belonging to the tradition of the teachings of Jesus and thus having a distinct Christology, a view which to some might appear radical.

Only a thoroughly Christological writing could be expected to emerge from that age when the church lived with the vivid memory of Jesus and the hope of his imminent return. Christology was the totality of the early church's theology and not simply one part among many.[10] Each problem had its Christological implications for the early church. James wrote at the first crisis point of the church's history, even before the problem of the Gentiles and circumcision. Written less than one generation after the salvific events, James reflects the theological tensions of the early church as it lived between its still vivid memory of Jesus and its anticipation of His early return as the world's judge. Persecution came, as Jesus had promised, but His immediate return was delayed.

An additional problem came when the early Christians had to order their church lives without the personal presence of the apostles. This was a situation with potential for disintegration. Into this scene James steps with the first writing of what would later become the New Testament. For the first time the followers of Jesus had to deal with an authoritative document that did not belong to the Torah (the sacred writings of Moses) and the prophets. It was the dawn of a new and difficult age in the church. Into this situation James addressed his epistle.

II/The Person of James (1:1a)

1a James, a servant of God and of the Lord Jesus Christ...

The author of the first pastoral epistle is James the half-brother of the Lord. This view, not without some wide scholarly support, opens to us the world in which Jesus lived.[1] New Testament research attempts to isolate the earliest layers of tradition later incorporated in the gospels. The search for the earliest connections with the earthly Jesus would be resolved partially if the epistle were written by the uterine brother of Jesus. James, the brother of Jesus, is mentioned explicitly twice by the evangelist Matthew, 13:55 and 27:56. He is mentioned implicitly in 12:46 in a reference to the brothers of Jesus.[2]

The mentioning of James in Matthew's gospel could very well point to the fact that at the time of the writing the Lord's brother had already assumed a position of prominence in the early Jerusalem church. It could also indicate that James had surpassed Peter and become the first among the apostles and pastors in the early church. As Mary, Jesus' mother, is referred to as James' mother in Matthew's Gospel, James could already have penned his epistle and been established as the leader of the Jerusalem church as early as the end of the fourth decade.

The style of James throughout is hauntingly like that of Jesus Himself, especially in the Sermon on the Mount, but still the words of James cannot be said to be simple verbatim quotations from Jesus. Had Matthew's gospel already been written when James wrote, there might have been a tendency for him to conform his use of Jesus' teaching more closely to the extant written reports, which would have been increasingly regarded as more authoritative than the oral traditions. Thus the evidence points to the fact that the sayings of Jesus were still uncollected in our gospels and had not reached a definite form when the Epistle of James was written. This presents the best solution to the question of why James is so like Jesus in his style and theology but quotes Him directly in only a few places.

The Roman Catholic Church gives a lot of attention to the Holy Family. Jesus is the child, Mary is the mother and sole earthly parent, and Joseph is the guardian of Jesus and the consort of Mary, who officially for Catholics is ever a virgin. The New Testament gives importance to this earthly family, but offers a wider view of it. Along with Jesus, Mary, and Joseph, there are four sons, James, Joseph, Simon, and Jude, and at least two daughters, none of whose names have been handed down.[3] The author of the first epistle, the very first writing of the New Testament, is Mary's second and Joseph's first son. Jude, another son of Mary and Joseph, is the author of the New Testament epistle ascribed to him (Jude 1). According to Old Testament law, Jesus had become the legal heir of Joseph by his taking Mary as his wife while she was already pregnant. The naming of his first two sons as James and Joseph indicates that Joseph was interested in perpetuating his own family tradition through sons that were his by a blood relationship. English translations of the Bible cover up the fact that Joseph's father Jacob (Matt. 1:16) and Joseph's first natural son (Matt. 13:55) both had the same name. In Greek both were called *Jakobos*. His second natural son was named Joseph for himself. Jude, the name of another of Joseph's sons, reflects his consciousness of being Judah's descendant. It might go too far to suggest that Joseph looked more to James as his first son rather than to Jesus, whom he knew he could never completely claim as his own.

Certain recorded words of Jesus indicate that a small but detectable antagonism held sway in the relationships of this family over the mission of Jesus. Any claim that the family attempts to exercise over Jesus is repudiated by Him with the words, "Whoever does the will of my Father in heaven is My brother, and sister, and mother" (Matt. 12:50).

Later in the church's history James, the Lord's brother, would be deprived of any early prominence he enjoyed in the ministry of Jesus and the Jerusalem church by an evolving Mariology. Though the early church saw her and Joseph having their own children, she was later held to be a perpetual virgin. The real significance of the earthly family of our Lord was lost. Joseph and Mary gradually were regarded as the primordial celibate pair, and James and his full brothers and sisters had to be assigned to other parentage to safeguard their chastity. Even the thought that they were Joseph's children by a previous marriage is no longer tolerable according to this view. James, the Lord's brother, was relegated to the rank of cousin and was subsequently considered as one of the original 12 disciples, the son of Alphaeus (Matt. 10:2-3). The James who would later attain prominence in the early church was neither of the two disciples called James, sons of Zebedee and Alphaeus, but the James whose parents were Joseph and Mary.[4] The conception and birth of James dispels any docetic concept of the nuptial union between Joseph and Mary as an unnaturally sexless arrangement. It also assures us that Jesus was brought up in a home where natural sibling rivalries prevailed. Regardless of any competitive spirit among James and the other younger brothers, Jesus no more resented them than He resented His subjection to His parents (Luke 2:51).

Despite any animosities felt by James toward his brother Jesus, his relationship to Jesus as his half-brother would later serve not to hinder but to enhance his career in the church which was founded on and by Jesus. He would soon advance to the position held by Peter who is called the first of the apostles (Matt. 10:2). Though the incidents of James' conversion are not recorded, it seems to have occurred when he received a special visitation from Jesus after the resurrection but before the ascension (1 Cor. 15:7), as he is

The Person of James (1:1a)

already a Christian before Pentecost (Acts 1:14). Paul divided the appearances of Jesus into two categories. The first list is headed by Peter, includes the original disciples, and then a wider circle of at least five hundred. James heads up the second list, including a group identified as all the apostles and then finally Paul himself (1 Cor. 15:5-8). One might infer that, like Paul, James received a post-ascension appearance of Jesus, but this is ruled out by the mention of Jesus' brothers with the believers before Pentecost (Acts 1:14). Both James and Paul were converted by post-resurrection appearances of Jesus, but Paul seems to have been alone in having received a post-ascension appearance. Jude, brother of James and half-brother of Jesus, the author of the epistle with that name, seems to have been converted at the same time as James. Though converted after the resurrection, both James and Jude are placed at the wedding at Cana (John 2:12) and with the witnesses of the ascension (Acts 1:14). Thus they meet the requirements for apostleship of having been with Jesus from the beginning of His ministry to His ascension (Acts 1:21-22). Matthew comes close to suggesting the role of an apostolic witness for James by identifying Mary not as the mother of Jesus, as John does (19:25), but as "Mary the mother of James and Joseph" (Matt. 27:56). Identifying Mary by her relationship to her sons James and Joseph may show the prominent roles Jesus' brothers had at the time of the writing of Matthew's gospel. Up to this point Matthew refers to her as Jesus' mother, even when she is placed in the company of His brothers. When James wrote his epistle, Mary was still in Jerusalem. It is probable that she made her home with James and was associated with the house congregation for which he was the pastor or elder. For all three, James, Jude, and Paul, conversion meant apostleship also. When Paul wrote Galatians, considered to be one of his very first writings, he mentioned visiting James, the Lord's brother in Jerusalem (Gal. 1:19). Naturally Peter served as the first head of the church in Jerusalem (Acts 1:15; 2:14), but with his imprisonment and forced exile James surpassed any of the other remaining original 10 disciples and assumed the leadership (Acts 12:17), a position he maintained even when Peter returned for the Council of Jerusalem (Acts 15:13; 21:18).

It is not difficult to construct the personal characteristics of James. He was jealous and envious of others' successes (John 7:3-5), as is not uncommon with the second-born in families. His organizational ability was recognized in his promotion to the supervision of the early church. He was conversant in Jewish theology and Old Testament literature and wrote some of the best Greek style in the New Testament. He shared a world view identical to that of Jesus, as he also was brought up in the synagogue of Nazareth.

Herein lies the real clue to understanding his epistle. When James wrote, the church he headed was still Jewish in its customs, orientation, and language.[5] The great influx of Gentiles into the Christian church, brought about particularly through the wide-flung missionary journeys of Paul, had not yet happened. Missions in other parts of the Roman Empire were just in the launching stage. The reason for the decisively Jewish flavor of this epistle was dependence on the life of the Jewish synagogue, in which both

Jesus and James had been nourished. The religious and cultural life surrounding the Jerusalem temple remained a significant force in early Christian thinking (Acts 3:1). Any theory that sees the epistle as a production of a rabbi later touched up by a Christian who could not really forsake his roots in Judaism hardly does justice to the epistle's peculiar origin at the junction of synagogue and early church.

By the time James wrote the letter, James's sibling jealousy and doubting skepticism that caused him to question and even reject the Messianic credentials of his Brother had been replaced by a thoroughly integrated and rare blend of authority and humility. He could call himself simply James without further identification because he knew that the church was aware of who he was and of his authority. No trace of the lavish self-praise of his apostolic office so common to apocryphal writing can be found. Instead he could call himself a servant or a slave, *doulos*. James would have had every right to append to his name the titles of apostle and brother of the Lord, titles of high importance used of him by others. His previous lack of enthusiasm for his Brother's cause directed him to a self-effacing attitude. He had not accepted the Messianic claims of Jesus before the crucifixion, as did the original 12 disciples. James, a brother according to the flesh, had refused the first invitations of Jesus to become His brother according to the faith. His self-awareness of his own authority, position, and importance was tempered by his own penitent feelings for having rejected Jesus when others, who did not have that personal association with Jesus, were committing their lives to Him.

There is more in the title servant or slave, *doulos*, than first meets the eye. Of course there is the confession of humility, a major theme interlaced throughout the epistle. The title of servant is also a self-conscious attachment to the ministry of the Old Testament prophets and, more important, to that of Jesus Himself. The prophets understood themselves as God's servants, men who spoke only the message God gave them to speak and whose message could be as little ignored as if God Himself were present to do the speaking. In no other way did God speak to His people than through His prophets. The tradition of God's speaking through His prophets ceased with John the Baptist, but after Christ God's speaking was perpetuated through the apostles, who now called themselves servants. It was a position of honor, but shaded with Christ's humility.

The servant concept of self-sacrifice was foremost in the mind of Jesus as He spoke about His atonement (Matt. 20:20-28). For Jesus to be a servant meant giving His life as ransom for the sins of many (v. 28). This self-abjection practiced by Jesus is required of all those who attach themselves to Him to share in the benefits of that atonement. "Whoever would be great among you must be your servant" (v. 26). This was a theme developed by Isaiah. Paul sees the servant posture adopted by Christ as being required of all Christians (Phil. 2:5, 7). James calls himself a servant not only because of a keen awareness of the prophetlike authority belonging to him, but also because he is aware of the self-degrading attitude in which his Brother offered the atonement. James is now not only one who has accepted the results of the atonement by faith, but one who with Jesus has assumed the servant position.

The common understanding, also perpetuated by the translations, is that James is calling himself a servant "of God and of the Lord Jesus Christ." No one can question that the phrase "Lord Jesus Christ" is quite proper, but it is grammatically possible to read the epistle's first verse, "James the servant of Jesus Christ who is both God and Lord." Some might validly object by stating that the word "God" is generally reserved for the Father in the New Testament, but certainly this is not a hard and fast rule with no exceptions.[6] The Fourth Gospel could record the confession of Thomas to Jesus as "My Lord and my God." In the Jewish way of thinking designating Jesus as Lord is as gloriously honorific as calling Him God. Should James be calling his brother God and Lord, he would be matching the confession made by Peter (Matt. 16:16) that Jesus was the Christ, the Son of the living God. This confession James could make only after he had, like Paul, confronted Jesus in glory. Any feelings of rivalry toward Jesus during their days in Joseph's family were replaced by feelings of total subjection to that *Man* he dared no longer call just his brother but his "God and Lord." James is now servant, and Jesus is Lord. The older relationship between brothers is no longer valid in the new age.

The salutation of James with its reference to Jesus as God and Lord is the first of many statements in a very intricate and well-developed theology in this epistle. Jesus in His teachings, especially those recorded in the synoptic gospels, speaks more frequently of the relationship between the Father and the Son, with less attention to the Spirit. This same concentration on Jesus and His Father is also reflected in James, but there is here also a doctrine of the Spirit.

One of the major arguments used against the view that this epistle was written by the Lord's brother, or for that matter any other Palestinian, is its excellent Greek. This view was fueled by the central hypothesis of form criticism that the early church was divided into easily recognized Jewish and Hellenistic communities with each making its own contribution to the development of the New Testament. Though no one seriously debates the reality of nearly pure Hellenistic Gentile Christian communities, it is debatable whether purely Jewish communities remained untouched by Hellenization, even in Palestine. It is not improbable that first-century Palestinian Jews, including Jesus and James, were at home in the Greek language, as Hellenization had begun already three and a half centuries earlier with Alexander's conquest. Also not improbable is that Jesus may have preached in Greek, though this is not the point at issue. What is at issue is that, as many scholars are now pointing out, the argument of the excellent use of Greek may no longer be used as conclusive evidence against a Palestinian authorship.[7]

III/Origin, Setting, Destination, and Greeting (1:1b)

1b To the twelve tribes in the Dispersion: Greeting.

This first epistle in the New Testament is directed "to the twelve tribes in the Dispersion *(diaspora)*" (1:1).[1] There is no need to look endlessly for these people and their location. They are the first refugees of the first persecution of Christians from the city of Jerusalem (Acts 8:1), who have fled from the mother church in Jerusalem to the relative security and safety of the Judean and Samaritan hill country.[2] In retrospect those Christians would later learn that God was spreading His church through persecution, but then those first refugees fled for fear of their lives with little awareness that God was working in their history. In this sense the persecution of the church in any age is salvation history. The death of Stephen meant their fellow Jews were becoming their persecutors.

These persecuted Christians contained no Gentiles in their midst at this time. They were the heirs of Abraham, Isaac, and Jacob, not only by blood but by faith. In them the faith and the lineage of the patriarchs had been perpetuated. They had to be reminded that they were the 12 tribes of Israel and that persecution was in the tradition of their fathers. Nebuchadnezzar had driven their fathers from Jerusalem, and Antiochus Epiphanes had desecrated the city's holy places. The persecutions prophesied by Jesus (Matt. 10:17; 24-25) were fleshing themselves out in their history. Gentile Christians would later be taught to consider themselves sons of Abraham and God's true Israel, but these Jewish Christians felt quite comfortable with and entitled to the original and perhaps more primitive designation "twelve tribes."

This form of greeting helps us to pinpoint the circumstances and the date of this epistle. Until its writing the apostles and their fellow believers had remained in Jerusalem and its immediate environs. They were not without success in making an impact in a city with an estimated population of 25,000, according to Jeremias. "Those who were scattered" (Acts 8:4) engaged in the first large-scale missionary work outside of the city of Jerusalem. The word "scattered" *(diasperō, diaspora)* (Acts 8:1, 4; James 1:1) might have well become a technical term for those first Jewish Christians who fled Jerusalem from fear of persecution. Later it would apply to any persecuted Christian, Jew or Gentile (1 Peter 1:1).

During this first persecution Peter would leave Jerusalem for preaching in Samaria (Acts 8:14), Joppa, and Caesarea (Acts 10:23-24). James, the son of Zebedee and brother of John, shared in the leadership of the Jerusalem church, but only briefly (Acts 12:2). Peter's really permanent successor at Jerusalem was James, the Lord's brother (Acts 12:17). He would hold the post for nearly a quarter of a century and would soon be recognized as the patriarch of Jewish Christians.[3] Paul during this time had become converted and was quickly rising as a leader among Christians outside of Palestine (Acts 15:12), but still was not completely trusted by many Jewish Christians. It was to Christians who had left Jerusalem but who had not been noticeably influenced by Paul that James wrote his letter. Worshiping Christians were still gathering as a synagogue (2:2) and their confession in their church services was still the *Shema* of the Old Testament (2:19). These points must be explored in more detail below.

There is no hint in this epistle that these persecuted Jewish Christians, forced to flee from Jerusalem, had yet been faced with the Gentile problem. The setting aside of Jewish ritual regulations had not yet surfaced as it would later at the Council of Jerusalem (Acts 15:19-20). Though Hellenized Jews were included in the church, Gentiles were not. Some Jewish Christians might still have envisioned the entire nation of Israel as an instrument in God's hand for the conversion of the world. Their hopes might even have bordered on the Zionistic (Acts 1:6). If any held this hope, they were soon disappointed by the persecution.

James can be dated shortly after the persecution recorded in Acts 8 and before the preaching of Peter to Cornelius in Acts 10 and the Council of Jerusalem recorded in Acts 15. Plans for the wholesale missionary endeavors of the Antiochian church were still on the drawing boards (Acts 13:1-2). James' epistle is a valuable telescope into an often-forgotten period of the church's life. From our perspective we are more interested in learning how the Gospel went from a Jewish milieu to a Gentile one. The Council of Jerusalem (Acts 15) is the great watershed chapter for that problem. Our minds leapfrog over the problems of those Christians who still thought of themselves as Jews and who saw Israel as God's chosen nation. For us the church seems always Gentile and was never Jewish.

The Epistle of James reflects problems faced by Jewish Christians who were learning to disassociate themselves from the personal company of the apostles and from the city of Jerusalem, the city whose air breathed of religious ritual and the acts of salvation. As long as the early Christians remained in Jerusalem, none of the apostles would start writing those letters which later would be collected as our New Testament. The absence of the apostles required that the first New Testament writing come into existence. It is not unlikely that some of these first Christians had been converted by Jesus. Perhaps nearly all of them had actually heard Him preach. They may have been the unidentified faces in those crowds, mentioned with exceptional frequency in Matthew, whose curiosity was never sufficiently satisfied by the Rabbi from Nazareth, whom they called the Son of David and less complimentarily the carpenter's son. Some may have been witnesses of His crucifixion or in the mob that had called for His death.

The importance of the historical continuity between the Jews of Jesus' day and the Jewish Christians to whom James writes should not be underestimated. It is difficult to escape the notion that in certain places James is reindicting his readers, or those troubling his readers, for His death (5:6). With the Epistle of James so close to Jesus in time, place, and audience, there is no reason why the words of the Epistle of James and those of Jesus recorded in the synoptic gospels should not serve to interpret one another. Acts 1 and 2 tell us about how the disciples had to carry on the work of Jesus without His personal presence. This was the first crisis. The second crisis came when the responsibilities given by Jesus to the apostles had to be shifted to another generation. The Epistle of James will tell how they were to survive this.

The salutation to the readers is amazingly brief: "Greeting" (*chairein*). Striking is that only this epistle and the one whose contents are recorded in Acts 15:23-29, both attributed to a certain James, begin with the simple "Greeting." To base an entire argument for the authorship of the two letters on just the one word "Greeting" would, of course, be absurd, but in both cases the author is identified as James.[4] The word "Greeting" (or "Hail") is used by those who mocked Jesus as King of the Jews on the cross (Matt. 27:29) and used by Jesus in His resurrection appearance to the woman (Matt. 28:9). The word is not as theologically freighted as Paul's "grace," but in the early Christian community it carried the idea of that peace which was derived from the crucifixion and resurrection of Jesus. The custom of Christians wishing peace to their fellow believers is perpetuated most noticeably in some Communion liturgies, where the pastor still gives a greeting of peace to the congregation.

Some have noted the similarity between this epistle and the one whose contents are recorded in Acts 15:23-29, coming from the Jerusalem Council. The author of these two epistles was a recognized authority not only in writing such epistles but in circulating them in the church with his own authority and that of the other apostles. Apostolic authority is shared and not limited simply to one person. Letters in the very first decades of the church's existence were recognized as usual ways of exercising apostolic authority where the personal presence of an apostle was impossible. From this apostolic authority our entire New Testament later evolved.

It is better to date the Epistle of James earlier than the one recorded in Acts 15. The Epistle of James does not even allude to the Gentile problem, which would absorb the Jerusalem Council and which is the subject of the letter issued there by James. Both letters do show sympathetic concern for Jewish Christians. In the letter recorded in Acts, the Gentiles are excused from Jewish ritual but are asked not to offend Jewish sensitivities in the matter of the eating of meat with blood. Paul in his epistles gives far less evidence of this same degree of sensitivity towards Jewish feeling, since he preaches the Gospel in a situation which demands sensitivity to the situation of the Gentiles.

Both epistles attributed to James, with their simple greeting in the salutation, show no trace of the influence of Paul, even in the matter of justification. From a later perspective the two determinative theologians in the early church were seen to be Jesus Himself and Paul. The extensive salutations in the epistles of Paul are in themselves minitreatises on theology. Paul is probably responsible for this elaborate theological greeting, and the other New Testament writers, perhaps even Peter, were influenced to follow his style on this point. The two epistles of James show no traces of elaborate style in the salutation simply because the Pauline style and theological language had not yet become normative for the early church.

IV/Chiefly a Pastoral Epistle (1:2)

2 *... my brethren ...*

Organization in the Early Church

James' reference to "my brethren" informs us more specifically about the readers. The possibility that the letter, even in its original form, is addressed to non-Christian Jews must be categorically eliminated. There are indeed some portions of this epistle which may not be directed to the recipients of the letter themselves, but are diatribes, not an uncommon literary form in the ancient world, directed against absent unbelievers and enemies of the Christian community (5:1-6). This is, however, not unlike the lament of Jesus over Jerusalem (Matt. 23:37-39), which is not spoken directly to the intended audience.

The term "brothers" was not used as casually in the New Testament as it is today in church circles. It suggested that group which intimately shared the common faith. Jesus had said that His true brothers were those who did the will of the Father (Matt. 12:50) and not those who shared a close blood relationship with Him (Matt. 13:55), an important distinction in understanding the self-consciousness of James. After the resurrection it is used specifically for the disciples (Matt. 28:10), who are now entrusted with the message of salvation revealed in Jesus. The letter of James recorded in Acts is also addressed to "the brethren" (15:23). It leads us to the tentative impression that the audience in both cases consisted primarily of men who, like the apostles, were entrusted in a special way with the message of salvation, i.e., pastors. These were men who had been chosen by the apostles themselves to share with them in the pastoral responsibility of the church with its congregations (Acts 14:23). The New Testament writings may have been directed to the congregations through their pastors.

In this sense the New Testament epistles should be viewed as *pastoral* epistles at least in this limited sense. It is still proper protocol for denominational leaders, such as bishops and presidents, to address matters of general concern for congregations to and through the pastors. Churches with the custom of issuing pastoral or episcopal letters follow the protocol of the president's or bishop's letter being read to the congregation. It is expected that the pastor studies the letter. Many pastors who are in disagreement with the contents of such letters have been known to ignore the request to read the letter or to read the letter to the congregation without any enthusiastic comment. Such letters have always had implications of fellowship on a wider

Chiefly a Pastoral Epistle (1:2)

level. Without denying the general value of this epistle for all Christians at all times, James might very well have primarily directed this letter to pastors who were leaders of congregations in Judea and Samaria.

The Spread of the Church

With the persecution by Saul, Christians fled from Jerusalem to various communities throughout Judea and Samaria (Acts 8:1). The apostles, in order not to abrogate their claim as being the legitimate continuation of Israel, remained in Jerusalem. The apostles, as legal witnesses to the Lord's crucifixion and resurrection, a necessary function for their office, should remain as close as possible to those places where these sacred occurrences had taken place.

This first persecution in Jerusalem might very well have been the beginning of what we know as the pastoral office as distinct and separate from that of an apostle. Before the persecution the apostles had been the pastors of the church with its congregations, known as synagogues, in Jerusalem. House worship (Acts 2:46) could have been congregational assemblies in various parts of Jerusalem. With the mass exodus of Christians from Jerusalem, the Christians took with them the idea of congregational house or synagogue worship, a part of their Jewish heritage, but they did not take the apostles as their pastors. There were simply more congregations than apostles! For these congregations scattered throughout Judea and Samaria, pastors other than the apostles had to be assigned.

The organization of each of the individual congregations is not reported in Acts, but these congregations spread up to Galilee in a short time. Together all these congregations comprised the church (Acts 9:31). The pastors of these congregations outside of Jerusalem, together with the apostles in Jerusalem, met to act on such matters as missions (Acts 11:1) and doctrine (Acts 15:6), and in this way the church's unity manifested itself.

Along with the growth of church organization outside of Jerusalem, the seeds of denominationalism began to take root. Those denominational fruits are still with the church. A group called "the circumcision party" (Acts 11:2), who also seemed to be known as "the party of the Pharisees" (Acts 15:5), insisted upon seeing Christianity only as a sect or movement within Judaism instead of the sole claimant to the ancient Israel of the Old Testament.[1] In this movement Ebionism had its roots. During this period of a more elaborate church organization and the birth of denominationalism James rapidly gained the ascendancy (Acts 12:17).

Early church government seems to have been patterned after the Jewish Sanhedrin, whose members consisted of priests serving in Jerusalem and in the surrounding Judean countryside. Matters in the early church were first handled by the apostles themselves (Acts 1:15) and later by the apostles and other pastors operating in Jerusalem (Acts 12:17). The Council of Jerusalem involved not only the original apostles such as Peter and the local pastors, but also James, and also Paul and Barnabas, who were representatives not of the Jerusalem church but of the church in Antioch (Acts 15:2). This model of church organization seems to have been adopted in other churches; we notice, for instance, that a group of clergymen seem to be the church leaders in Antioch (Acts 13:1). Such a system of church government was also instituted by Paul and Barnabas on their first missionary journey throughout Asia Minor (Acts 14:23).[2]

A problem concerning the status of the Gentiles in a church that was almost entirely Jewish-oriented could not be handled simply by a local or provincial gathering of clergy. Such a problem would have to be resolved at a meeting with wider representation. Represented at the Council of Jerusalem were not only the apostles and pastors from Judea, Samaria, Galatia, but also Antioch. The presence of representatives from Antioch could very well point to the fact that in addition to Antioch other churches outside of Palestine were also represented. One might even suggest the presence of representatives from Egypt, Ethiopia, Asia Minor, and Damascus, as Acts records the presence of Christians in these places. They were still overwhelmingly Christians of Jewish background, who had come to recognize Jesus as Messiah. Remember that Pentecost means the conversion of Jews from all parts of the world and not Gentiles. The latter problem still had to be faced.

In regard to the council itself, two things should be noted for our purposes.

First, James was possessed with such personal self-confidence about his position as the leader of the church that he simply ends the council's deliberations by making his own decision normative for the church (Acts 15:13-21, esp. v. 19).[3] He summed up what he assumed to be the consensus of the group. James is pictured by Luke as one in control. With the church moving away from Palestine and with the impending destruction of Jerusalem, the importance of the church in that city would be short-lived. But in the earliest years of the church, Christians still regarded Jerusalem as important (Rom. 15:25-27). In that church James was the apostle who had to be reckoned with. Though Paul came to be recognized as the great apostle of Christianity, chiefly through the influence of his epistles, the center of authority remained with James and Jerusalem as long as James lived.

Second, it should be noted that brothers (*adelphoi*) is the usual greeting by which members of the council addressed each other. This is not to argue that this particular understanding of the word "brother" exhausts all New Testament usages of the word and that its every use demands this interpretation. Hardly! Still Peter (Acts 15:7) and James (Acts 15:13) address the Council of Jerusalem as brothers. The custom was probably of long standing in the church, as Peter addresses his fellow apostles after the ascension of Jesus with the same greeting (Acts 1:16).[4] The custom is not original with the Christian community, as Paul addresses the members of the Sanhedrin as brothers (Acts 23:1). Paul must have been associated with the Sanhedrin, if not as a member then as assistant to the group as a whole or to one of its members. Before his conversion he received letters from the high priest, the Sanhedrin's presiding officer, to persecute Christians worshiping in the

Damascus synagogues. Paul had been part of the Jewish religious establishment in Jerusalem. In James' letter recorded in Acts, the letter's senders who are described as "apostles and elders," call themselves and the letter's recipients brothers (Acts 15:23).[5] The Christian custom of addressing those who share the common task as fathers and brothers was Jewish in origin.

One of the real and significant clues to the interpretation of James' letter is recognizing that its first audience is chiefly pastors shepherding congregations without the opportunity of personally consulting the apostles in Jerusalem for each difficulty. Suggesting that the Epistle of James is in some sense a pastoral epistle should in no way indicate that its contents are unsuitable for all Christians, laity and clergy alike. The specifically recognized pastoral epistles of Paul contain much that is applicable to all Christians. Consider, for instance, 1 Tim. 2:4 with its clear statement of God's intent for universal salvation. On the other hand, epistles of a more general type often single out the clergy because of their special responsibilities and relationship to Christ. First Peter 5:1-5 is a special address for pastors. The passage from this pericope, "God opposes the proud, but gives grace to the humble" certainly has general applicability, though it was originally intended for the clergy, for whom pride can indeed be a problem. If certain of James' phrases are seen as having the clergy as their chief target, a change from the traditional interpretation may be required.

The Church in Jerusalem

Though the precise outlines of organization in the early Jerusalem church cannot be drawn, a certain reconstruction can be made from the references in Acts and parallels in the Pauline epistles. James did not write his letter for the Jerusalem church, but he did write it because of his position of leadership in that church, to those who had previously been resident there.

Larger congregations, common to Christianity from the middle of the first century, were a later development. The earliest Christians formed themselves into "house congregations," where attention was given to instruction in the apostolic doctrine, fellowship among believers, celebration of the Lord's Supper, and common prayer (Acts 2:42). The references to house (*oikos*) should be taken not merely to the ordinary residences of Christians, but rather to those residences which were regularly used for worship. English translations in referring to these simply as houses and households do not catch their inherent ecclesiastical nature. These house churches were chosen because of their proximity to where Christians were clustered together in the same neighborhoods and for their size. To say that these house churches were on every street corner would be an exaggeration, but they were strategically located throughout the city and its suburbs. On an average, perhaps only 20 or 30 people, at most 50, gathered at these house churches. The wealthier Christians with larger homes provided space for a gathering as large as 120 (Acts 1:15). The Council of Jerusalem probably made use of one of these larger residences. The house of Mary, the sister of Barnabas and the mother of John Mark, may have been the scene for all of these larger occasions. With more

Jews, especially among the upper class, becoming Christian, the choice of places for larger gatherings increased. As Jesus had gathered with His followers in their homes, the house congregations with their celebration of the Lord's Supper were seen as a continuation of His fellowship with them.[6]

It might be a mistake to regard the Christians in Jerusalem as a struggling minority. They may have been a minority, but they were making substantial inroads among the resident population. Joachim Jeremias estimates that Jerusalem's population during the time of Jesus was 25,000.[7] On Pentecost the 3,000 who were converted were not passing visitors in Jerusalem for the religious holiday, but foreign-born Jews who had taken up permanent residence (*katoikountes*, Acts 2:5) in their ancestral city.[8] The Jewish persecution of Christian synagogues which occasioned the Epistle of James was a recognition by the religious establishment that it was being seriously threatened. If by the time of persecution the Christians in Jerusalem had grown to 5,000, perhaps an overly conservative figure, this would mean that 20 percent of the population had associated themselves with synagogues where Jesus was confessed as the Jewish Messiah. With house churches numbering a membership even as high as 50 persons each, this would mean that there were at least 100 presbyters or pastors supervising the ordinary worship of the Christian population. The church was hardly a storefront operation! These Christians continued in the ordinary temple worship, but retreated to their house congregations for the Lord's Supper (Acts 2:46).[9]

The house congregations did not look upon themselves as separate administrative units, but as the church in Jerusalem over whom first the apostles and then others served as pastors (Acts 2:44-45). Though most Christians associated with one house, supervised by an elder, there was a high degree of mobility and they thought of themselves as part of the larger group. At first Peter and John were the recognized leaders, but others, for example Stephen and James, were established as official spokesmen. With the exile of Peter and the death of James, i.e., the brother of John and son of Zebedee, James the son of Mary and Joseph became the leader among the apostles and the other pastors (Acts 12:17, 15:13, 21:17-18), probably to the end of his life. There is no reason to distrust the extra-Biblical tradition on this point. Just how James ascended so rapidly within the organization of house congregations and their presbyters cannot be known with certainty.

By the time of Pentecost James had been converted, made an apostle by the risen Lord, and was recognized as a church member. He would presumably have assumed the leadership in one of the house congregations almost immediately, but not over the entire assembly, where Peter continued as undisputed leader. It can only be conjectured whether this house belonged to him or another Christian. As Mary, Jesus' mother and his own, was in Jerusalem at this time (Acts 1:14), she was not only residing with him but was worshiping with his house congregation. In fact his house may have attracted more attention just because of the fact that the family of Jesus was worshiping there. The early church had a greater awareness that the earthly

Jesus who had table fellowship with them before His crucifixion was continuing this fellowship with them on an even higher dimension after His resurrection, provided especially in the Lord's Supper. James, who had known Jesus intimately at table fellowship within His earthly family, provided a continuity such as no one else really could.

The church organization in Jerusalem may have reached a high stage of development during those early years. A large population would have demanded this. The pooling of the financial resources of the Jerusalem Christians for charity was sufficiently weighty as to necessitate appointing seven men just to handle these business details (Acts 4:32—6:6). The growing church with its more complex organization did not seem detrimental to further growth (Acts 6:7). At the Council of Jerusalem (Acts 15) were those same Christian leaders, now addressing a doctrinal concern that had risen in one of the outer provinces. James has unchallenged prominence at the Council of Jerusalem. This suggests a man recognized as so qualified to speak for the area church that he would also be recognized as qualified to address problems outside the area of his immediate responsibility.

The evidence seems to indicate that the Christians fleeing Jerusalem took with them the house church as the regular form of organization. The situation of many house churches forming one church was duplicated first in Damascus, then in Antioch, and then taken to Ephesus, Corinth, and Rome. At first the Christians fleeing Jerusalem because of the persecution were not in a position to form the same larger organization that was already in place in Jerusalem. Just as the Galatian Christians had looked to Jerusalem and James for a solution to the Judaizing problem, so in reverse James felt a responsibility for those Christians who had fled Jerusalem without a fully seasoned leadership. Older, larger churches still feel this responsibility for their smaller sister churches. Both the epistle and the council picture James as a man firmly in control of the situation and whose leadership remained unchallenged throughout his life.

Whatever antagonism Paul may later have felt against the Judaizers who had based themselves in Jerusalem, his concern for the Jerusalem church and its works of charity remained a priority with him (Rom. 15:25). Before going to Spain for mission work, he felt personally obligated to bring the money that had been raised for Jerusalem's poor. These funds were to maintain the system of charity there. Paul treats James with a respect in his epistles not accorded in each instance to Peter, whom he prefers to call by the Aramaic word Cephas.

It is not improbable that Paul knew the apostolic doctrine through personal contact with the Jerusalem apostles before his conversion. Perhaps, his persecution of the church was effective because he attended the house congregations. The Christian and purely Jewish synagogues were not all that dissimilar, at least in form. From personal experience he knew exactly which synagogues were Christian. "But Saul was ravaging the church, and entering house after house, he dragged off men and women and committed them to prison" (Acts 8:3). The houses entered by Paul were those used as house congregations. In the fluid ecclesiastical situation of Jerusalem the persecutors and the persecuted were well known to each other from previous religious association with one another.

By the second half of the first century larger congregations gradually begin to replace the house churches. This may have been necessary for doctrinal discipline in the face of heresy and to draw more clearly defined lines of demarcation between the church and external society. House churches seem to have been the rule in Corinth and Rome. If these churches were associated with Peter or others coming from Jerusalem, as seems the case, it is not improbable that a similar church organization was put in place there. First the house congregations were formed and then later the more embracing type of organization as was in place in Jerusalem was established. The rather complex and destructive beliefs in Corinth seem problems among the clergy meeting together, and not the laity. Though the office of the bishop as an administrative head does not seem in place in the early Jerusalem church, there is some support to suggest that the complexity of the church structure eventually required that one man, presumably the bishop, assumed the position of a permanent spokesman for the church and with it the larger and ever-growing administrative responsibility. The references to James in the Book of Acts seem to suggest that this process was already in motion in Jerusalem. There is no suggestion, however, that James acted independently of the presbyters as with the later-developed monarchial episcopate. James is always mentioned as operating corporately with the other elders or pastors.[10]

V/Temptation, Persecution, and Faith (1:2-8)

2 *Count it all joy, my brethren, when you meet various trials, for you know that the testing of your faith produces steadfastness. And let steadfastness have its full effect, that you may be perfect and complete, lacking in nothing.*

5 *If any of you lacks wisdom, let him ask God, who gives to all men generously and without reproaching, and it will be given him. But let him ask in faith, with no doubting, for he who doubts is like a wave of the sea that is driven and tossed by the wind. For that person must not suppose that a double-minded man, unstable in all his ways, will receive anything from the Lord.*

The Problem of Temptation for Jesus and the Church (1:2)

James immediately addresses the problem of temptation being faced by these novice pastors with their congregations. According to Matthew's gospel Jesus encountered temptations by Satan before He began His work among the people.

But what were these temptations faced by these early Christian leaders? Were they the internal desires of the flesh in the sense of physical gratification, or certain external difficulties, subtle but pervasive? The parallel prominent positions of the temptations in Matthew and in James are striking, even if the temptations of Jesus and those of the early Christians are not identical in each point. Satisfying physical appetites would hardly be considered an occasion for happiness, as James suggests, on the part of these Christians. Rather the temptation confronting these early Christians was the one of renouncing their faith in Jesus. They were experiencing the hardships arising from persecution. A model for the Christian's victory over the temptation to renounce the faith is the temptation of Jesus Himself by Satan in the wilderness. The last temptation involved surrendering faith in God for a pledge to Satan in exchange for the kingdoms of this world (Matt. 4:8-9). This final temptation of replacing God with Satan is a paradigm for all such temptations, including the situation confronted by the early church.

Behind each possible temptation to renounce the Christian faith is Satan himself, who desires to become the sole object of man's worship and devotion. He matches God's reward of eternal life with a life of constant pleasure and wealth. His reward is an eternity of a different type. The first Christians who had fled from Jerusalem because of their faith were constantly enticed and tempted to surrender their belief in Jesus and to return to the ordinary and regular services of the Jewish community. The enticement of the flesh is not the desire to engage in flagrant moral transgression, but to surrender the Gospel for the security of ordinary life. Even today in Moslem countries religion and culture form one unit, as also Jewish religion and culture have always (where possible) formed an indissoluble bond. For centuries Christian Europe bonded culture and religion together. It was difficult to distinguish life from religion for these Jewish Christians in the early church. They were not only beginning to feel increasingly unwelcome in the synagogues but were being ostracized by friends and even their closest family members. Paul's purpose in going to Damascus was to purge the synagogues of the Christian blight. Persecution can be subtle as well as explicit. The prediction of Jesus about the severing of the most intimate bonds because of faith in Him was fast coming true (Matt. 10:33-39). What made this Jewish persecution against the Jewish Christians more difficult to accept was that it was being conducted in God's name, which both groups equally held as sacred. This was the God whom both Jews and Christian Jews had worshiped together before the coming of Jesus and whom they were still worshiping together on occasion.[1] The one group saw in Jesus an imposter, and the other saw in Him the culmination of God's revelation. The persecutors conducted their persecution with religious zeal because they felt they were doing God a favor. Paul speaks of his religious zeal in his persecution of the church (Gal. 1:13). Christians could easily succumb to renouncing the faith because of the highly religious and persuasive claims of the persecutors, claims the persecuted could recognize. It was not a match of the secular against the religious, but the religious against the religious.

Suffering as the Result of Persecution (1:3)

Christianity knows of no concept of suffering for the sake of suffering. Monastic systems that brought unnecessary physical and mental torments to those who had taken the vows are certainly not embraced by the type of suffering James says will bring steadfastness and perfection. Sadistic joy brought on by pain is not encompassed within the boundaries of Christian suffering. There is no Christian value in suffering simply for the sake of suffering. Suffering's value to Christians lies in having faith encounter difficulties. Faith is then forced into a situation of having to listen more carefully to the words of God and take them more seriously. Suffering for Christ is ultimately suffering with Him. Christ understands His own suffering as an extension of the suffering of the saints of the Old Testament (Matt. 23:29-36). Many of the minor blessings of life, which make up the real fiber of life, are taken away in times of persecution, and the Christian, simply because of the circumstances, is left alone with God and His Word. Where previously he was impatient in not seeing more tangible signs of God's presence in His life, and especially impatient with the delay in the final revealing of God's glory, he learns that God's plan must first be carried out.

The Christian's time of tortuous waiting is that time when God is not only carrying through His plans, but is also bringing about changes in the Christian's personal life. Persecution strengthens faith because faith is forced to rely on God more and on itself and others less. Faith's strength does not come from itself, but from God. Through temptation God sorts out true faith from vestigial unbelief, which can never truly comprehend the real mysteries of Christianity. Faith that successfully resists temptation finally comes through a period of testing to its completion or perfection. Here James parallels Jesus' explanation of the parable of the sower, where abundant fruit is the final result (Matt. 13:18-23).

Total Forgiveness in Time of Persecution (1:4)

Faith, which is tested through persecution and endures patiently, reaches perfection and is said to be lacking in nothing. At first glance James seems to be speaking of sinlessness or at least some level of moral perfection. Most commentators lean in this direction, but miss the entire point. Within Christianity there have been movements to moral perfectionism. John, probably speaking to the Gnostics or their forerunners, who held to the possibility of reaching moral perfection in this life, said that claims to moral perfection were only examples of self-deception (1 John 1:8). Certain Christian groups have held similar beliefs and are often called perfectionists. Even if total sinlessness was not really possible for them, it was held up as a goal towards which believers could make progress. Without denying the atonement, they thought themselves to be more acceptable to God because of a certain internal moral good. Moral perfectionism as a goal among Protestants was prominently revived by John Wesley and is perpetuated among the holiness church bodies. The question is whether Jesus places moral perfectionism as a goal isolated from the totality of faith before His disciples as a quality to be acquired. "You, therefore, must be perfect, as your heavenly Father is perfect" (Matt 5:48). The perfection mentioned in the Sermon on the Mount is not the moral perfection which might be a legitimate goal of any ethical system. In the Sermon on the Mount, Jesus speaks of perfection as a quality shared by both the Creator and His creature. Perfection in this sense means not only being free from fault, but being free from finding fault in others. The Father's perfection is seen in that He continues to show goodness to both the just and the unjust, the good and the evil alike, without prejudice (Matt. 5:45). Perfection for the Christian is reached when he is able to understand and fulfill this commandment of loving enemies and praying for persecutors. In this way Christians are said to become perfect and the sons of the Father. Content with God's forgiveness for them and for the whole world, they find it impossible to take vengeance for wrongs done them.

Christian perfection, not in the sense of isolated morality but in the sense of sharing in the Father's forgiving attitude, is not only a possibility for Christians but a necessity. It finds its place in the Lord's Prayer in forgiving one's debtors as the Father has already forgiven His debtors (Matt. 6:12). It is exemplified in Jesus, who from the cross forgave His tormentors. Perhaps closer to the situation of these early Christians was the martyrdom of Stephen, who at the moment of death prayed, "Lord, do not hold this sin against them" (Acts 7:60). Requesting forgiveness for those responsible for one's death is reaching God's perfection. By his martyrdom Stephen, well known to these Jewish Christians, shared in Christ's death and lived out the petition of forgiveness in the Lord's Prayer. When the Christian is able to forgive perfectly all who have offended him, he then has reached the highest goal possible for a Christian here on earth. For this reason James can say that at this point of perfection the Christian is lacking in nothing. The Christian can never share in the perfection of God, since the Creator cannot give His divinity to the creature. Striving for participation in the divinity is not only wrong but the basis for all sin (Gen. 3:5).

In speaking of perfection as that totally forgiving spirit, James is moving into the arena of justification. The sins of all people against God, and hence also against all their fellow human beings, are already forgiven. Sins that people commit against one another are really sins conducted in God's arena, *coram Deo*, and hence against God, who has made man. When Christians realize that all sins against others have already been paid for and forgiven by their Creator, they will find it impossible to demand retribution for real or alleged wrongs against them personally. God has already justified the offended and the offender. All sins are forgiven.

Throughout this epistle there are strong evidences that the martyrdom of Stephen is a recent and still pungent memory in early Christian minds. The temptation is to renounce Christianity and thus avoid persecution, whether it be personal discomfort at the least or martyrdom at the most. From the outset of his epistle James no longer appears as simply a Jewish moral teacher in the Christian community but as a theologian who places the early church's problems within the context of a vibrant Christology and a meaningful doctrine of justification. James, speaking of the tested faith which forgives completely, is as close as possible in his understanding of faith to Paul and Luther. Faith for James here is hardly only head knowledge but a lively trust in the God who has made forgiveness a reality for that faith.

Peter, Pastors, and Temptations (1:5-8)

Some commentators point out that the description of a doubting Christian as a wave on the sea raises the possibility that the author is personally familiar with the Sea of Galilee. Nazareth, home for both Jesus and James, is not far removed from this good-sized inland lake. Just as storms on the North American Great Lakes can be more ferocious than those on the ocean, so a relatively small body of water like the Sea of Galilee can be the scene of violent storms. With the sea surrounded by mountains on all sides, the trapped winds bounce against the cliffs and quickly change, coming in from all directions. This is an apt description of a Christian who is caught between his commitment to Jesus and still is not willing to surrender friendship with the world. James is here not engaged in an abstract discussion on resisting temptation. He is speaking directly to Christians who are being lured back into the full communal life of the Jewish culture from which they have begun to be cut off abruptly by a persecution that reached a cutting edge with the stoning of Stephen. The Christian promise of a glorious life had unexpectedly brought death. Stephen's martyrdom was a contradiction for many, though death with and for Christ was part of the earliest Gospel message. At this point we have to ask whether James is making merely a general allusion with his reference to the wave or is there here a definite early church figure?

It is tempting to see that James here behind the imagery of the wave is pointing the finger at Peter. According to a very early dating for this epistle it was written soon after Peter left for exile outside the Jerusalem community (Acts 12:17). James had already assumed the position of leadership from Peter, but the person of Peter as the church's first leader and apparently first apostle to leave Jerusalem made a lasting impression on all. There is a resemblance between James' reference to the unstable wave and Peter's walking on the water in Matthew's Gospel.

Though the story of the appearance of Jesus to the disciples on the Sea of Galilee is found both in Matthew and Mark (6:45-51), the account of Peter's walking to Jesus on the water and the sinking of Peter is found only in Matthew (14:28-32). The terror in Peter's heart is caused by the wind (v. 30). Jesus responds to Peter's cry for help, but He also reprimands him by calling him a "man of little faith" and asking why he doubted. Peter's doubting (*distazein*) here does not involve the intellect but the emotions. Even in despair Peter still calls Jesus Lord. Doubt for Peter did not mean that he failed to recognize who Jesus really was, but he had not reached the point of putting perfect trust in Him. Similar was the attitude of the disciples to the resurrected Jesus. They grasped the fact of the resurrection but not its significance (Matt. 28:17).

The picture of the doubting man in James 1:6-8 fits the description of Peter in the pericope of his walking on the water. Desiring to give total loyalty to Jesus by following the command to walk on the water, Peter's faith turns into distrust. He becomes the "man of little faith." The doubting man in James is a believer, not an unbeliever, though doubt unchecked evolves into cynical unbelief. In the gospels Peter is designated as harvester of the Lord's harvest (Matt. 9:37-10:2), fisher of men (Matt. 4:18-20), and a rock man (Matt. 16:18). Peter's less courageous moments have also been recorded. For example he was also called Satan because of his failure to grasp suffering as part of Christ's mission (Matt. 16:23). The "double-minded man" who believes but with doubts and who resembles a wave pushed in every direction by the wind recalls Peter, whose goals shifted with the circumstances. To the early Christians, Peter was the fisher of men and also the man to whom his former career as a fisherman presented an alluring temptation after the Lord's resurrection (John 21:3). The reference to Peter as a wave moved by the wind would be immediately recognizable by the early Christians associated with the Jerusalem church. They all knew Peter, and the still-unwritten gospel preserved his unsavory moments along with his climb to prominence.

James is holding up Peter, the first of the Lord's apostles, as an example to all Christians to show that no one is exempt from the temptations of doubting and denial. Christians suffering for their faith frequently believe they are unique and are unaware that others have suffered and are still suffering. Perseverance is the only acceptable response demanded of Christians in temptation and sufferings.

One wonders if James, as Paul later does, here is indulging in a slight anti-Petrine polemic. At least James was not forced into exile from the Jerusalem church as was Peter. Though Peter was double-minded and doubted, he did in the moment of sinking call out to Jesus for salvation. He did put total reliance on Jesus, and his prayers were answered. The First Epistle of Peter is also a plea for perseverance among Christians. Commentators have noted the similarity between Peter and James on this point. Peter may have learned something from James. James writes to these early Christians not to confirm them in their doubts, but to warn them that persisting doubting will result in their destruction.

James' warning about the doubting that leads to self-destruction is part of the section on how Christians should ask God for wisdom with the assurance that it will be given. It would be easy to understand here in the sense of later Judaism, where wisdom is the application of a type of religious common sense to all areas of life. To this very day Jewish leaders are renowned for this earthly wisdom, a type of know-how that enables them to understand and penetrate life's practical dimensions. James, however, should not be categorized among the rabbinic writings. It does not belong to the tradition of wisdom literature, even though this is a common assessment. Such a view renders impossible a clear understanding of its essential theology.[2] Matthew's concept of wisdom can help us understand James' view on wisdom. Jesus describes His own preaching as wisdom superior to Solomon's (Matt. 12:42). In light of the early church's understanding that the message of Jesus was wisdom, it will simply not do to understand James' suggestion for a prayer to God for wisdom as a prayer for superior intelligence or secular know-how or even superior piety. For James the one who prays for wisdom must have total commitment—trust in the God to whom he addresses his prayers. Wisdom is needed to withstand the temptation of falling into apostasy.

James' invitation to pray for wisdom is addressed chiefly to pastors who have already been instructed by the apostles in the teachings of Jesus. Still lacking is the comprehension of the internal unity of these teachings and their application to their lives, especially the situation of suffering for the faith. These first pastors had become totally versed in the teaching of Jesus, but the Christian truth had not yet taken on its unified form in their minds. They were not unlike the apostles during their days of discipleship before the resurrection and Pentecost (Matt. 13:36). Embracing the words with their intellect but not comprehending the truth by faith can lead eventually to falling away from the truth (Matt. 13:21). Faced with the temptation of deserting the Christian truth in the hour of tribulation, they are to ask God for a fuller understanding of it (1:5-6). Since James' readers intellectually understood the message, it explains why he is not so clearly didactic as Paul, whose readers were far removed from Jerusalem and Jesus.

James the Apostle of Faith: The First Defense

In this section we encounter the first use of the word "faith," or "believing," and its cognates in this epistle (faith, belief: *pistis*; believe: *pisteuō*). This word, so prominent in the New Testament, was first penned by James. As will be seen below, James is not strapped down to any one use of the word "faith" in his epistle. For James it can mean simply intellectual assent to the truth or it can have the meaning of intellectual assent with trust, the one Luther promoted with dogged enthusiasm. Faith for James might mean the body of the faith, i.e., the church's doctrine. Possibly it might in one place refer to the faith which Jesus had. There are four possibilities in James. Each case must be decided individually. The versatility of his use of the word "faith" shows the type of complex theologian James was. He was hardly a collector of sayings.

Here where the readers are requested to pray to God in faith without doubting is the meaning later associated with Luther, who was influenced by Paul in coming to his Reformation understanding. Faith understood as total reliance upon God was a concept first set forth in writing by James, not by Paul, even though he would later standardize this particular meaning in his epistles for the church and receive the credit. James sees faith as involving knowledge of the true God and inner personal trust that this true God can indeed answer the prayers of the faithful. Rather than being simplistic in his definition of faith, James is as profound and multifaceted as any of the New Testament writers. Luther at the close of the section on the Lord's Prayer in the Large Catechism even quotes James favorably on his view of faith.

Mentioned above was the possibility that the wave of the sea that is blown around by the winds could be an oblique reference to Peter, whose professions of faith and denials were determined by the circumstances surrounding him. The man who asks in wisdom and receives might be an autobiographical reference to James himself. He is mentioned as having been within earshot distance of Jesus' preaching of the parables (Matt. 12:46—13:58) and apparently was acquainted with them. During Jesus' lifetime James had not been a recipient of the heavenly wisdom needed to interpret the teachings he heard. James could very well first have belonged to that wide group of people who recognized as valid the truth claims of Jesus' teaching but were reluctant to give their assent and trust. Rather than being abandoned by Jesus because of their initial reluctance, James and others could have been quickly won for His cause after the resurrection (Acts 1:14). Church history remembers James for his wisdom. The decree of the Apostolic Council (Acts 15) is a tribute to his wisdom. A cryptic signature for James, who is throughout self-effacing, would be appropriate. In the four gospels many can find such hidden self-references to the writers. It would not be impossible here.

The use of the divine names "God" and "Lord" in this epistle initially presents a problem not easily resolved. Finding a solution serves as one key to discovering the inner core of this epistle's Christology. This section has for its positive goal a prayer addressed to God (1:5) with the ultimate hope of receiving the request from the Lord (1:7). The rule of thumb in early New Testament theology is to interpret references to God as applicable to the Father and references to the Lord as applicable to the Son, unless there is clear contextual evidence to the contrary. It would seem, however, that the Father is referred to both as God (1:27) and Lord (3:9). Jesus is specifically called Lord (1:1 and 2:1). In this section on prayer (1:5-8) it might be best to consider the Father, God, as the one to whom the prayers are to be addressed and Jesus, the Lord, as the one who bestows these requested gifts on the church.[3] The distinction between the Father and the Son may at this point be unnecessary because these early Christians were as convinced of Jesus' identity with God as they were of His distinctiveness from the Father. The gifts of apostles, pastors, and other church workers and leaders were seen as the direct intervention of the Lord Jesus in the life of the early church (Eph. 4:11). There is no reason to contest that prayers in the early church were addressed to the Father; nevertheless Jesus was seen as the church's Benefactor in making the Father's blessings available to the church. If this is so, then even in the prayer life of the early church Trinitarian theology was coming to expression. While in our parlance "Lord" does not have a distinct meaning, it was for the early church a clear reference to Jesus and the most proper reference for Him especially in His glorified state.

VI/The Pastoral Office, the Lure of the World, and Christ (1:9-18)

9 *Let the lowly brother boast in his exaltation, and the rich in his humiliation, because like the flower of the grass he will pass away. For the sun rises with its scorching heat and withers the grass; its flower falls, and its beauty perishes. So will the rich man fade away in the midst of his pursuits.*

12 *Blessed is the man who endures trial, for when he has stood the test he will receive the crown of life which God has promised to those who love Him. Let no one say when he is tempted, "I am tempted by God"; for God cannot be tempted with evil and He Himself tempts no one; but each person is tempted when he is lured and enticed by his own desire. Then desire when it has conceived gives birth to sin; and sin when it is full-grown brings forth death.*

16 *Do not be deceived, my beloved brethren. Every good endowment and every perfect gift is from above, coming down from the Father of lights with whom there is no variation or shadow due to change. Of His own will He brought us forth by the Word of truth that we should be a kind of first fruits of His creatures.*

A Major Problem

This section with its warnings to rich and poor alike to be content with their lot is often seen as an address to two disparate economic classes in the congregation. This view could easily lead the reader to accept as valid the common interpretation of this epistle that the sections are simply a series of disconnected moralisms, a position popularized by Luther and rarely improved upon except by the most recent critics. There is no need, however, to see James' admonishing words as addressed to wealthy laymen, though they can always be most effectively applied to them. If, however, the thesis stands up that this epistle is directed primarily to pastors, then the inner connection between this section and the previous one becomes obvious. The previous section spoke about clergymen who were intellectually committed to the Christian faith but were reluctant to give their full personal trust. Those addressed in these verses are trusting in personal wealth rather than God.

The comparable section in the parable of the sower is the seed sown among the thorns. These are Christians who hear and believe the Word but soon succumb to this world's riches (Matt. 13:22). The parallel between Matthew and James is remarkable here in the matter of order. James speaks to the problem of persecution (1:2), as does Matthew (13:21), and then both proceed to the problem of riches in the Christian's life (Matt. 13:22 and James 1:9-11).

The admonitions against acquiring great personal wealth are directed specifically to the clergy, as Jesus also admonished His disciples. It is the disciples who were concerned with the acquiring of earthly goods and their own personal sacrifice for Jesus (Matt. 19:27). False is the impression that Jesus and the disciples comprised an unshaven, straggly group of itinerants. Peter and the others were as fishermen also businessmen. Jesus had rich people among His wider group of followers.

The devastatingly impoverished image of the clergy is of later invention. The wealthy and the poor brothers whom James addresses are pastors whose wealth or lack of it was becoming a bone of contention among them. James was reapplying to them the principles written down later in the parable of the sower.

A Preliminary Christology (1:9-10)

One of the complaints raised against this epistle is that its Christology is almost nonexistent. Even those who find a Christology in James limit it to those two passages where Jesus is explicitly mentioned. This negative opinion should be revised in light of the clearly explicit Christological language of vv. 9-10: "lowly ... exaltation ... rich ... humiliation." For a comparatively brief writing, these words are frequently used. All these terms are used in other New Testament references to Jesus, either by Himself or by others, to describe His humiliation and exaltation. Should it be demonstrated that James is using accepted dogmatic Christological terminology, then we must assume that it was not Paul who is responsible for a highly defined Christological dogmatic theology in the church, but Jesus. The use of such terminology by James would then indicate that the earliest Christians were already quite conversant in it.

Among the synoptic gospels only Matthew contains the self-designation of Jesus as humble or lowly (*tapeinos*), "I am gentle and *lowly* in heart" (Matt. 11:29). The verb form is used in Paul's great hymn to Christ's humiliation and exaltation, "He humbled (*etapeinōsen*) Himself and became obedient unto death" (Phil. 2:8).[1] The words of Jesus, "Whoever exalts himself will be humbled, and whoever humbles (*tapeinōsei*) himself will be exalted" in Matt. 23:12 reflect the same combination of humility and exaltation as does James 1:9. "Let the lowly (*tapeinos*) brother boast in his exaltation." Though the words of Jesus in Matthew about humbling and exalting are intended as guides for the Christian, especially during times of duress, both passages embrace a well-formulated Christology. Jesus was the One who humbled Himself by crucifixion so that God could exalt Him by resurrection. His humiliation becomes model and motivation, especially for the rich in the congregation. The words, "Let . . . the rich [boast] in his humiliation" silhouette the humiliation of Jesus. Paul uses the same theme in describing Christ's humiliation: "Though He [Jesus] was rich, yet for your sake He became poor, so that by His poverty you might become rich" (2 Cor. 8:9). James' urging the poor to boast in his exaltation and the rich in his humiliation takes its formative shape against a Christology made more explicit by Paul, but implicitly present in his own writing. James thus links the teaching of Jesus and the preaching of Paul. Understanding James' terminology as being Christologically freighted thus rescues this epistle from the common opinion which consigns it to a type of moralistic, rabbinic literature.

The genius of both the style of Jesus, especially as handed down through Matthew, and that of James is that their theology and its application are combined into one form. James is as little interested in humility as an isolated virtue as is Jesus. Humility for the Christian is the extension of Christology into living. In speaking to the Gentiles, Paul more carefully distinguishes theology from its application, the revealed abstract truth from its incorporation in church life, or if you will, the message of justification from sanctification. The failure to recognize this style common to Jesus and James has been one of the chief reasons that the theological treasures of both Jesus and James have not been fully appreciated.

After his specific address to the rich and poor pastors, an address built upon the scaffolding of a specific Christology involving humiliation and exaltation, James punctuates his message with an eschatological warning. The style here is not unlike that of Psalm 1, which speaks about those who continue in God's Word and thus have no need to fear God's judgment and about those who have disregarded that Word and must face that judgment. They are penalized by disappearing like the chaff. In Old Testament theology eschatology is presented in agricultural terms. John the Baptist takes advantage of these images and portrays Jesus the eschatological Judge as a farmer sweeping clean his barn floor to divide the wheat from the chaff (Matt. 3:12). In the parable of the sower the agricultural imagery persists. The seed whose plant is destroyed by the scorching sun represents those who believe and then fall away when faced with persecution (Matt. 13:5-6, 20-21). James sees the sun destroying the rich. These early pastors were faced with the temptation of surrendering their Christian faith in order to gain some financial advantages. Pursuit of riches for their own sake is vain and leads nowhere. Even real financial gain is ultimately illusory. But for the Christian there is an even more disastrous element in seeking wealth. Those who give allegiance to Satan by going after riches must face a verdict of eternal condemnation. The beauty of the flower, which symbolizes the rich man, is said to perish. The verb for "perish" (*apollumi*) is the technical term for those who are consigned to the pangs of hell (Matt. 10:28).

James makes frequent reference to the rich. Identifying these rich is basic to understanding his letter, but it does not seem that each use of the word refers to the same group. The rich, in the first case, seem to be believing members of the church who are in danger of losing salvation. Some of the clergy were personally rich (1:10), as other members of the congregation obviously were (2:2). Christians who are rich are always tempted to identify with rich people in general and not with other Christians, especially if they should happen to be poor. The diatribes against the rich (5:1-6), though not directed to rich members of the congregation, could very well be a not-so-subtle warning to Christians that the fated doom of the unbelieving rich can become the fate of Christians who in abundance of wealth have deserted Him who became poor for their sakes. The rich Christian is not merely to be frightened by the judgment day, but he is given the model of Jesus, who surrendered wealth for the poverty of human existence. Following this model, the rich Christian can receive those riches, that is, salvation and all its concomitant blessings, which can never be taken away from him. The poor rejoices that in Christ he shares in God's wealth.

A Brief Exegetical Digression: James' Use of Isaiah 40 (1:10-11)

Is. 40:6-8 is quoted in near completeness in 1 Peter 1:24-25 and partially in James 1:10-11. It appears that Isaiah 40 belonged to those collections of the Old Testament Scriptures of which the early Christians made frequent use,[2] as Is. 40:3 is used in all four gospels to introduce John as the forerunner of Christ (Matt. 3:3; Mark 1:3; Luke 3:4-6; John 1:23). The sections of Isaiah 40 quoted in the gospels have to do with introduction of the voice and with that voice's authority from God. Is. 40:6-8, the message of the voice who comes speaking in God's stead, is quoted only in 1 Peter 1:24-25, and only an allusion is found in James 1:10-11. The voice's message from Isaiah is not quoted in any of the gospels. The uses to which the passage is put in 1 Peter and in James differ from each other, but their meanings are complementary. The emphasis in the Petrine passage is rebirth through the Word of God, which is immune to perishing. In James the same passage from Isaiah is used to indicate the transitoriness of human existence. James later discusses regeneration (1:18), as he continues to use the agricultural imagery with his reference to the firstfruits. While James stresses the preparatory repentance in connection with his use of the Isaiah passage and Peter the later regeneration, both writers have a developed doctrine of regeneration involving a renunciation of earthly perishing things as prerequisite for rebirth through the Word of God. This is recognizable as the pattern for Baptism. This pattern in 1 Peter is a reason offered by some scholars for seeing in it a baptismal homily.

The early Christian writers saw the Isaiah 40 passage as one of the links between the Old and New Testaments. As mentioned, all four gospel writers include the account of John the Baptist and explain his role by the use of Is. 40:3. The person of the Baptist plays no role in the epistles, since the church, with the coming of Jesus as the Christ, has moved successfully from the prophetic to the apostolic period. The prophetic task of the Baptist has outlived its usefulness with the fulfillment of the prophet's promise in the coming of Jesus. Though the person of the Baptist has outlived its usefulness, still his message is normative for the church. Everyone attaching himself to the Kingdom must still submit to the penitential requirements outlined in his message. The person of John the Baptist continued to make an impression upon the entire Palestinian populace even after his death (Matt. 21:23-27). His spartan existence was eloquent testimony against the opulent life. He pointed out the vanity of human life in its unattached and autonomous existence and showed that this human life had eventually to face an accounting before God (James 1:11; Matt. 3:7-12).

The person of John the Baptist serves as the link between the Old Testament people of God and the church of Jesus Christ, and thus he is the greatest among those born of woman (Matt. 11:11). James does not introduce the person of John the Baptist because these Christians have heard and believed his message and already have accepted Jesus as the Christ. The Baptist's Messianic heralding of the nearness of the Kingdom, repeated by Jesus, is a once-and-for-all-time function, incapable of repetition. In Christ's death and resurrection the Kingdom has come. The Baptist's message of contrition and acceptance nevertheless has a necessary validity for all who come to faith. His proclamation of the coming Messianic kingdom has, however, lost its force, since the Kingdom is no longer a future possibility but in Christ has become a present reality.

Peter has the longer version of the Isaiah 40 section; he includes vv. 6-8, with only a few minor alterations. There is reason for Peter's longer version and James' abridged version. Peter's audience is decisively Gentile and has not heard the Baptist's message. James' audience is not only Jewish, but their introduction to Jesus in many cases was through the Baptist's preaching. As Gentiles come to Christianity without prior acceptance of Judaism, the person of the Baptist is not reintroduced by James or Peter, but the Baptist's message of repentance must be confronted by all.

An Even Fuller Christology (1:12)

James continues with his Christology in speaking of the blessed man, 1:12: "Blessed is the man who endures trial, for when he has stood the test he will receive the crown of life." It reflects a mode of speaking that can be traced back to Ps. 1:1, "Blessed is the man," a phrase similar to each of the Beatitudes, especially the last two (Matt 5:10-11), where reward follows persecution. The plural of the Beatitudes is replaced by the singular in James. Also striking is the use of that word by Jesus as He applies it to Peter, who has made the Messianic confession (Matt. 16:17). The question in James is whether this is a specific reference to one particular person or to any number of persons. Who is the blessed man who endures trial? Could James have intended a deliberate multiple application of these words? The problem is intensified by the use of *anēr*, the Greek work for a male and not any human being in general.

Understanding Psalm 1 as Messianic may provide the key to understanding both the Beatitudes and this passage in James. At this point the Beatitudes and James appear interdependent or share a common source. To regard Psalm 1 as solely Messianic in the sense that other applications of it are rendered a priori impossible will prevent the full intended meaning of James and the Beatitudes from being developed. The ideal man who spends day and night meditating on God's law is the Messianic man recognized by God as king in Psalm 2.[3] The Messiah was so closely connected with His people that the Jew believed he shared in all the benefits the Messiah earned. As the Jew read in Psalm 1 about the Messiah, that one ideal Jew, he also saw described in those words what God wanted him to be and what he would become in the Messiah. Without the Messianic interpretation Psalm 1 can too easily be understood only as moralistic injunctions. The Beatitudes without a primary Christological understanding suffer the same moralistic doom. When Psalm 1, and for that matter the other related psalms, are understood in a wider Messianic sense, then the Beatitudes and the James passage become clearer. Using dogmatic terms, Christology and sanctification constitute a totality.

The great blessings promised in the Beatitudes belong to Christians because they have shared in Christ's work. Even the last beatitude (Matt. 5:10-12) has its application to Christians only in connection with persecution endured for Christ's sake. The use of the singular in Ps. 1:1 and James 1:12 and the plural in the Beatitudes is significant in showing that the Messiah's work has its meaning only in relation to His people. His people have their life only in relationship to the Messiah. The Messiah can be isolated from His people as little as they can be isolated from Him.

The Messiah, His People, and Stephen (1:12)

V. 12 has a curious combination of the singular and the plural that reflects the Messiah's intimate connection with His people. It can be read in several ways, with reference to Jesus or to Peter and not simply to all Christians, as generally understood. The man who endures trial is singular, but the promise of eternal life is made to those (plural) who love Him.

The blessed man who endures trial may very well be Jesus Himself, who endured Satan's temptations (Matt. 4:1). James used the Greek word *anēr*, a male, and not *anthrōpos*, a human being. It is thus more probable that his reference here is to one man. While the temptations of Jesus certainly included those recorded in Matthew 4, His entire ministry, including His crucifixion, was plagued by constant Satanic temptations to renounce the Messianic tasks entrusted to Him by the Father. The man referred to by James has not yet received the ultimate reward, which still lies in the future. This at first glance suggests that the reference is not to Jesus, who has been glorified by God, but to all Christians in general. As every Christian must go through trial in order to reach the ultimate goal of the crown of life (Rev. 2:10), Christians in general are being promised that crown by James. Since Christ continues to suffer with His people, He might still be the subject of this verse. In the appearance to Saul, Jesus says of Himself, "I am Jesus, whom you are persecuting" (Acts 9:5). The man in James is also still undergoing persecution (*peirasmon*). We need not distinguish between the suffering of Jesus and that of His church. Jesus shares in the church's suffering in that the acts performed against the church are really done against Him. While Christ is already in glory with the Father, the final step in the process of glorification has not yet taken place. All things still must be made subject to Christ (1 Cor. 15:24-25). On the last day the final crowning of Jesus shall take place. Right now it still remains in the future. All those who have shared in His persecution here on earth will receive the crown of life.

It is tempting to see here in the phrase "blessed . . . man" a cryptic reference to Peter. Of all the apostles only he is singled out by Jesus as blessed (Matt. 16:17). His personal difficulties first in denying Jesus and later in his exile from Jerusalem left a deep impression on the early church. Regardless of the failures of all Christians, they succeed in Christ and are entitled to be called blessed with Him. A double sense is deliberate.

James seems to be the first of the apostles to use the term "crown" as a reference to eternal life. Other writers of the New Testament, Paul, Peter, and John (2 Tim. 4:8; 1 Peter 5:4; Rev. 2:10), would later follow James' lead in understanding the term "crown" as a metaphorical expression for eternal life. It is not found in the gospels. If James is not using oral tradition, unincorporated in the gospels, then he originated this use of the phrase.

As mentioned, this epistle was written shortly after the persecution which led to the death of Stephen and the exile of Peter from Jerusalem. The memory of the martyred Stephen was still fresh in the minds of Christians. This general persecution was the very cause of their exile, the problem now addressed by James. Perhaps these early Christians had at first not considered martyrdom, predicted by Jesus, as a serious possibility. Now they knew otherwise. The reference to the crown of life as a theological term applying to eternal life could have taken on special significance, since Stephen in Greek means crown. James might have been making a deliberate play on Stephen's name. The proportionately large amount of space given to Stephen's martyrdom in Acts 8 indicates that even nearly a generation later, when Luke penned the Book of Acts and others had died for the faith, the martyrdom of Stephen was still prominent in their minds. He was the first to endure the ultimate trial. He confessed the faith without denial and had been given the crown of life.[4] James is indeed writing a theology which is eminently practical, but he weaves into the fabric the duplicity of a wavering Peter and the constancy of a steadfast Stephen. Others would suffer martyrdom, as Jesus had promised, but the initial shock of the first martyr, Stephen, would leave the most lasting impression. The death of James, the son of Zebedee, the first apostle to be martyred, is mentioned only in passing. Stephen's death became the standard for Christian martyrdom.

The giver of the crown of life is not absolutely clear. Some manuscripts have attempted to put in God, and others the Lord, as the subject of the verb "promise." Who is the One who promises the crown of life to those who love Him? The parallel in 2 Tim. 4:8 can be helpful. There the crown of righteousness is given to all who love the appearing of Jesus as Lord rather than God as Father. Love in James and the Johannine writings is a synonym for Paul's "believing" or "having faith." The promise of eternal life is made to those who have faith and not to those who have earned it by fulfilling moral prerequisites. The alleged work-righteousness of James, as seen by Luther among others, simply is not so and is without support. Quite the contrary is true. James, like Luther, sees faith as the hand that grasps the promises. The person who has promised eternal life is that blessed man, that is Jesus, who is suffering along with His church. The crown of life, which Jesus receives from the Father, Jesus in turn gives to all Christians to share. Those who love Jesus receive the crown of life.

James has a Christology which understands Jesus as the divine Lord. Salvation is for those who place their faith in Jesus as the Messiah who has undergone humiliation and exaltation. Far from being a disconnected series of Jewish moralisms, as some have alleged, James represents the church's first real theological treatise. So profound is the connection between theology and life in James that any moralistic interpretation totally distorts his message.

It cannot be conclusively shown when, where, and under what circumstances the promise of the crown of life alluded to by James first originated. As mentioned, it may be associated with the martyrdom of Stephen. It could be a logion of Jesus unrecorded in the Gospels.[5] In Rev. 2:10 Jesus as the glorified Lord makes the promise of the crown of life to those who are "faithful unto death." The phrase had become part of the church's treasury of piety. The words in Revelation are contained in a letter sent to Christians who face persecution through imprisonment, not unlike the situation addressed by James. The threat of imprisonment by Saul was real, even for those Christians who had left Jerusalem (Acts 9:1-2). To these dispersed Christians, facing imprisonment and death, James addresses his letter.

There is no record that Jesus before His crucifixion made the promise of eternal life using the words "the crown of life." But eternal life as a present reality in the believer's life does, at least, have its roots in the preaching of Jesus. John's gospel in particular has promises of eternal life for the believers who love Him. John's use of the word "love" in his gospel (8:42; 14-15) as a synonym for "faith" is paralleled in James. Though the concept of love as a substitute for faith, used by James and John, can be traced to Jesus, the exact origin of the concept of "crown of life" still presents difficulty. As pointed out, James does use the word *zōē* for life, which is also the technical term for eternal life in John (3:16). The logion may have originated with Stephen's death, but it may have been suggested by certain metaphors of Jesus, even if He did not use the term itself.

The use of the word "crown" may easily have grown up in the early church in connection with the concept of Kingdom membership. The first of the Beatitudes says that the kingdom of heaven belongs to the poor in spirit (Matt. 5:3), and the disciples are promised thrones from which they will judge Israel's tribes (Matt. 19:28). The metaphor of the crown could easily have come into use with such other Kingdom metaphors as throne and judge, used by Jesus.

Another real possibility is that these words were spoken directly by Jesus to James after the resurrection in connection with his conversion. Rev. 2:10 specifically attributes the promise of the crown to Jesus in His glory and not in His humility. The promise is intended for a church under persecution. The crown of life is for those faithful unto death. It was the Lord in glory and not in humility who called His brother James into the apostleship. If James is the real brother of Jesus, his conversion occurred by an appearance of Jesus to him during the 40 days following the resurrection. James may have heard the words then. Regardless of the phrase's precise origin, it became and remains a popular phrase in the church.

The commentators discuss how some manuscripts have substituted either "God" or "the Lord" for "He" in the phrase "which [crown] He has promised to those who love Him." The substitutions seem to have been made to avoid the obvious suggestion that eternal life is promised by the man who has endured the trials, Jesus Himself. Grammatically the identity of the blessed man is capable of more than one interpretation. The reference to Jesus fits best.

Original and Actual Sin (1:13-16)

Two views have traditionally dominated the Christian concept of sin. The differences between these two views found classical expression in the fifth-century controversy between Pelagius, a British monk, and St. Augustine, an African bishop. Pelagius saw sins as a series of disconnected acts without one affecting the other. Man was born in a state of moral neutrality and had the freedom to perform either morally good or evil acts. St. Augustine saw individual sins as a result of man's inborn sinful nature and held that each person had no choice except to sin. From an Augustinian perspective a condition of moral neutrality was impossible. Only after conversion did good works become possible for the believer, and then only in a limited sense. Paul and Luther are recognized as having Augustinian views of sin. James is often seen as espousing a legalistic Jewish morality, and thus fitting into the Pelagian category. A legalistic morality is Pelagian in outlook because it is based on the premise that man is capable by himself or with some divine aid of fulfilling God's requirements. If James is viewed as writing a collection of moral imperatives, even in a somewhat Christianized sense, then he would have to be listed in the category of Pelagian or at least semi-Pelagian writings.

A careful examination of this section (1:13-16), however, shows that James is strongly Augustinian in his view of man, his nature, and his inborn sin. Attributing sin to internal desires hauntingly reminds the reader of the approach of Jesus, who saw behind even apparent acts of righteousness an innate sinfulness (Matt. 5:28; 7:21-23; 15:19-20). Sin for James is caused not by a person's associates or environment, but by an internal condition. It is inherent and intrinsic.

James' anthropological discussion of man's nature is brief but hardly lacks depth. Though his theology is applicable to Christians of every time, he is speaking to those first Christians who were succumbing to occasional apostasy to avoid persecution. The temptation was to renounce Jesus to spare themselves suffering. James wants his readers to be aware of the real source of their problem. The sinner confronted with his own failure to overcome the sin of apostasy first wants to shift the burden of guilt from himself to someone else. That someone is most conveniently God. Looking for an outside cause of sin, but never in oneself, is the ever-present Pelagian motive. It is the easiest course in resolving guilt and the moral dilemma. It was the course taken by Adam when he attempted to shift the responsibility for his sin to God, who had created the woman for him (Gen. 3:12). The possible accusation by these persecuted Christians that God might be the real cause of sin gives James an opportunity to set forth his diagnosis of their sin and apostasy.

God Himself is morally good in His essence and has no choice but to oppose all evil. Evil is to be understood as anything opposed to God. Tribulations experienced by Christians do not originate with God. Sin arises through the interaction between man's sinful nature and the world's hostility to God's purposes. The petition of the Lord's Prayer, "Lead us not into temptation" (Matt. 6:13) is a request for God to equip the Christian to overcome temptation.

But is there a contradiction between 1:2 and 1:13? In the first citation temptation is viewed as an opportunity for joy, in the second as an opportunity for sin. Temptation, though always evil in origin and satanically inspired (Matt. 4:1; 6:13), is of positive benefit in the Christian's life if it forces increased reliance on God and less reliance on self. The Christian overcomes the temptation, Satan is conquered, and Christ is victorious in His saints. This, like Easter, is occasion for joy. Completely disastrous are the results when the Christian tries to resist the temptation with his own resources. Then Satan's victory is assured. God is neither the inventor nor the cause, direct or indirect, of those external circumstances which are called temptations. God's invariableness, a topic of the following pericope, allows Him no participation in the cause of evil. James will say of God that with Him "there is no variation or shadow due to change" (1:17). Luther also saw that God uses Satan and evil to strengthen the Christian in his faith. This Luther handled in discussing *Anfechtungen,* satanic inflictions from God in Christian lives.

Sin for James comes into existence and takes form when man's internal desires respond to the external enticements. Man's desires are internal emotions, inherently sinful, looking for external expression through personal gratification (Matt. 5:28). Sometimes the Greek word for desire can have the purely neutral meaning of a wish (Matt. 13:17), but in a moral connection desire refers to the inborn human longing to participate in sin (Rom. 1:24). James borders on the flowery in describing the sinful desires at work in a person as luring and enticing (RSV), dragging away and enticing (NIV), drawing away and enticing (KJV). Allurement into sin involves both the will

Pastoral Office, World, and Christ (1:9-18)

and the emotions. No part of human existence can refrain from participation in sin.

James' graphic description of the development of sin within the Christian is unmatched by any other New Testament writer. Not even Paul, the Augustinian without peer in the New Testament, does a better job. Sin's progress is compared to the conception of a child, its birth, and finally the full development of an adult human being.[6] Sin takes shape because our internal desires have been successful in their unrelenting drive to conceive sin within us. The conception-birth imagery reflects "that which is born of the flesh is flesh." The conception of sin by our own desires allows for no abortion in its development. After birth, sin eventually evolves into death. On this point James would later be paralleled by Paul, "The wages of sin is death" (Rom. 6:23). For James the death which is the end result of desire conceived into sin is eternal death and not only the termination of human life on earth. Counterbalanced with the prospect of death for the sinner is the reward of the resurrected life for believers (1:18). Paul has a similar formula in Rom. 6:23, "The wages of sin is death, but the free gift of God is eternal life in Christ Jesus our Lord." On this point, as with many others, James has anticipated Paul's more explicit theology intended for Gentiles or Hellenized Jews away from Palestine.

The admonition in 1:16, "Do not be deceived, my beloved brethren," is placed by the RSV and NIV as the first sentence of the following section. The Nestle text, however, places it as the conclusion to the previous section. As a warning, it seems more appropriately applied to those who had forgotten that sin had its origin within themselves and had begun to accuse God for their sin. As the following section (1:17-18) is one of promise, the admonition or warning of v. 16 really has no place there.

The admonition seems to be primarily addressed to the clergy as regards their official preaching and teaching. The phrase "my beloved brethren" is not addressed to all Christians in general but singles out a particular group within the church. The deception involved here is doctrinal error. James' concern is not only that they believe the right things but that they teach the right things and refrain from teaching falsehood (cf. 3:1-2; 5:19-20). The concern for pure doctrine must not first be associated with a later development of the church system of government emerging at the time of the Pauline pastoral epistles. It appears as early as the Epistle of James.

James does not permit the threat of eternal death, whose progress from conception is described, to stand as God's final word against the sinner. The description of the process resulting in eternal death is matched by the description of a divine activity which comes to completion in eternal life.

Incarnation and Atonement (1:17-18)

Paul uses the word *dōrēma*, endowment of salvation (Rom. 5:16). Here James definitely has it referring to something which God gives in regard to salvation. James is not referring to the benefits of creation. In the New Testament the word group revolving around the word "give" (*didōmi*), in a theological sense, describes God's giving Himself in Christ for atonement. God so loves the world that He gives His Son (John 3:16). Jesus gives His life as a ransom for many (Matt. 20:28). Rather than taking this as a reference to many divinely bestowed gifts, this gift from God is to be taken as a reference to the one perfect Gift of Jesus Christ in His atonement.

The phrase "Every good endowment and every perfect gift is from above" is most frequently understood as a reference to God's general goodness as extended to all of His creatures, the brute and rational, believer and unbeliever alike. This interpretation fits the view that the Epistle of James is a *Jewish* writing in the rabbinical style which has undergone a slight Christian renovation. This opinion is unsatisfactory for a number of reasons. Set between sections on original sin and on regeneration, such an interpretation just does not fit. More important, the language is strongly freighted with Christological terms.

The English translations are not agreed on how this section should be rendered, even though there is general agreement among the commentators about its being understood as a reference to God's creative goodness and hence also His providence. The Greek's "every good gift (*dosis*) and every perfect gift (or endowment, *dōrēma*)" is merged by the New International Version (NIV) into a singular subject with two adjectives, so that it reads "every good and perfect gift." The RSV is more faithful to the original in rendering two subjects, but maintains the singular verb "is," because it must see the plural subject as having a single sense. Both translations detect that James is only referring to one gift or one kind of gift and not several gifts.

The vocabulary of this section with its strong Christological terminology and salvific expressions indicates that James is speaking of God's plan of salvation in an abbreviated way. It could be paraphrased in this way: "The one perfect and good gift of salvation has already come down from heaven." This would of course be God's work of incarnation and atonement in Jesus Christ. Since this suggestion may to some be startlingly new, it must be carefully delineated.

What is the "every good and perfect gift"(NIV)? Must it refer to many gifts or could it possibly refer to simply one gift which can be beneficial in any number of situations?

The two Greek words translated as "gift" (*dosis* and *dōrēma*) have overlapping but still distinguishable meanings. *Dosis* carries the meaning of gift, and *dōrēma* the idea of generosity.[7] Paul uses the latter word for God's generosity in giving salvation (Rom. 5:16). *Dosis* is derived from *didōmi*, (to give) and, as mentioned, is frequently used of God's giving of Himself in Jesus Christ for the world's salvation. The Greek words for "all" (*pasa* and *pan*) stress the gift's wholeness, totality, and purity, which can be individualized for a particular situation.[8]

The words "good" (*agathē*) and "perfect" (*teleion*) add still another dimension. Most appropriately "good" refers to God Himself (Matt. 19:17). The gift is good because it originates with God and carries with it God's own qualities. James has moved beyond the ethical, moral, or philosophical goodness of God to the themes of incarnation and atonement. The perfection of the gift is not chiefly its freedom from moral blemishes but its meeting God's requirements. A cognate for the word "perfect" is used by Jesus in announcing the end of His suffering (*tetelestai*, "It is finished," John 19:30). The gift given by the Father has satisfied all of His condemning judgments against man.

The adverb "from above" (*anōthen*) and the verb "coming down" (*katabainon*) further describe the peculiarity of this gift. "From above" is used of the regeneration process by John (3:3,7). It also describes the incarnation (the process through which the Son of God shared in human existence) and it points to His inherent authority over all things. "He who comes from above (*anōthen*) is above all" (John 3:31). "Coming down" is the theological term in the New Testament to describe the incarnation. "No one has ascended into heaven but he who descended (*katabas*) from heaven, the Son of Man" (John 3:13).[9]

The similarity here to the Johannine incarnation terminology is striking. Terms easily recognized as *peculiarly* those of the Fourth Gospel in describing the incarnation of the Word (*logos*) are used in the Epistle of James. *Agathē*, good, attaches to the gift an attribute associated with God Himself (Matt. 19:17), and *teleion* is the attribute of completion, in the sense of satisfying God's just requirements. James here is bringing together incarnation, deity, completion, and overabundance. The word "gift" (*dosis*) in the phrase "every good gift" (KJV) may carry with it the concept of sacrifice. While the usual term for the sacrificial gift is *dōron* (Matt. 5:24), both *dōron* and *dosis* are derived from *didōmi*, a verb which carries with it sacrificial overtones, especially when God is described as the Giver (Matt. 20:28). Taking this data together, the "good and perfect gift" (NIV) which "is from above, coming down from the Father" is the Father's giving of His Son in incarnation and atonement for the benefit of man's salvation. James is dealing with the heart of the Christian message. The present tense of this sentence emphasizes the continuing reality of God's salvific activity among men.

At this point James launches into a discussion of God's invariableness. The phrase "the Father of lights" is without parallel. Light in the singular can be used of salvation (Luke 2:32), but with the plural James has something else in mind. The phrase "no variation or shadow due to change" points to an astronomical image. God's steadfastness is like the stars, whose position in the heavens is consistent and whose steady positions can serve as guides for travelers. James, who seems at home with nautical and agricultural illustrations (1:6,9-11; 3:4, 12, 18; 5:4, 7, 18), might have had some acquaintance with the science of determining distances and locations according to the stars. The word for err and error, especially doctrinal error, *planaō* and *planē* (Matt. 24:4-5; 1 John 4:6), is the basis for the English word "planets," wandering stars, whose course is unsteady. It is used by James in 5:19. Jude 13 indeed makes this comparison between stars and planets. For him false teachers are wandering stars or planets whose course through the heavens is not as easily charted as the stars. God remains constant not only in Himself, but in the Word He reveals to men. The truthfulness of His Word is only a necessary reflection of what He is in Himself. Having first discussed sin and then incarnation with atonement, James now is ready to speak of regeneration. The order is quite logical.

The phrase "Of His own will He brought us forth by the Word of truth" (v. 18) is a specific reference to the Christian's regeneration. James uses the same words for the regeneration of the Christian as for sin giving birth to death (1:15, *apokuō*). There is no clue as to why James prefers *apokuō* to *gennaō*, which with its cognates is used by other New Testament writers in describing the process of regeneration. A hesitancy to give verbatim quotes from Jesus may be the answer. James' use of *apokuō* would indicate an unusually creative literary mind. First Peter 1:23, a clear parallel, also attributes regeneration (*anagennaō*) to the Word of God. First Peter has been recognized by some as a treatise or homily on Baptism. With the similarity between James 1:18 and 1 Peter 1:23 so evident, it could very well be that James is alluding to the baptism of his readers. The great regeneration chapter, John 3, specifically attributes regeneration to water and the Spirit (v. 5). The background for this section is the preaching of John the Baptist, who required baptism of those desiring to enter the Kingdom. James calls God's regenerating element "the Word of truth" because, as His truth, this Word shares in His invariableness.[10]

James' theological and literary genius and uniqueness lie in his ability to blend theology into the immediate application. He does not first have to lay down theological principles from which he draws applications. Like Jesus, James in stating the application is at the same time putting forth the theological principles. This way of writing and thinking, that weaves principle and application together, is difficult to grasp for those not acquainted with the Old Testament way of thinking.

With his description of the Christian's birth from God by the Word, James is touching the doctrines of the sacraments, the Holy Spirit, and authority. This act of birth in their baptism is at the foundation of his readers' lives. Through God's act of begetting in baptism they have come into a new relationship with Him. This new relationship brings life and not death as did the older birth in which desire brought forth sin. The new relationship demands faith, which James also calls love for Jesus. Those who love Jesus are promised the crown of life. They have been reborn by the Father's Word of truth.

James' doctrine of the Holy Spirit exists as a shadow in his letter, but it's there. The early church, so close to the person of Jesus as the manifestation of God, concentrated on Christology. The Spirit was reality, but it was left to later generations to develop what was nevertheless early set forth in the New Testament. In the early church those who were born again and had been baptized were those upon whom the Spirit had worked (Acts 2:38). New birth and the Spirit were coordinate thoughts for the New Testament.

James' phrase "the Word of truth" might also be interrelated with his concepts of the Gospel and Holy Scripture. It can be paraphrased as the Word which is the truth. Is this a reference to the Gospel, Baptism, Scripture or even Christ Himself? James does have a specific concept of the Holy Scriptures. He sees Scriptural passages as evidences of the truth, and Old Testament allusions are so comfortably and delicately interwoven into the fiber of his message that it becomes difficult to distinguish James' message from that of the Old Testament. God's Word as the Gospel, whether it be in the Scriptures, which demonstrate the truth of a matter, or whether it be in Baptism, by which people are rescued from error, always has the quality of being the truth.

There could also be here a statement of Christology. The phrase "the Word of truth" seems to anticipate the Fourth Gospel, where Jesus is identified as "the Word" (1:1) and "the Truth" (14:6). It is not improbable that John in developing his unique understanding of Jesus as the incarnate Word and the Truth may have been influenced by James. The influence of James on the Fourth Gospel should not be discounted.

In no way can James' concept of salvation be regarded as synergistic. Christians are Christians because of God's will and not man's. "Of His own will He brought us forth." The rebirth from above happens at the Father's good pleasure. Luther's strictures against James appear even more regrettable when it is realized that James shares with Paul, Augustine, and Luther himself a view of salvation that sees a depravity in man so severe that self-salvation is impossible. God is the only cause of salvation.[11] Here in embryonic form is also the Pauline doctrine of predestination. No mention is made of any contribution that man makes to becoming a Christian. The cause of salvation does not lie in man or in any of his accomplishments but, as James says, in God's will. Matt. 11:27 and Luke 10:22 present interesting parallels. According to these citations the Father has committed to the Son the authority to choose who should receive God's revelation. Receiving the revelation (Matt. 11:27) and being reborn (James 1:18) are metaphors explaining the same phenomenon of becoming a Christian. The Father, who gives birth, and the Son, who reveals the Father, work conjointly to achieve this goal. James' discussion on rebirth parallels John 1:13, where Christians are also described as being born by God's will. The parallel is even more striking as both writers put the concept of the Word in a prominent role.

Because of God's act of regeneration, Christians enjoy a special place in the totality of God's creation. They have now become the firstfruits of creation. James here is speaking of the total restoration of the entire creation and not merely the redemption of the human race. This doctrine of universal restoration finds its classical expression in Paul's discussion of the corruption of the creation on account of man's sin with the promise of its future restoration with "the redemption of our bodies," Christians being the firstfruits of this cosmic restoration (Rom. 8:18-23).

Theologically understood, the concept of the firstfruits carries with it the promise of the resurrection (cf. 1 Cor. 15:20, 23). Envisioned by James is not a universal salvation, but a universal restoration in which Christians are the catalysts. In one brief sentence James has moved from a concept of grace and predestination to baptismal regeneration made effective by God's Word, then finally to a resurrection involving universal restoration of the creation. Paul, of course, discusses these matters at greater length (Rom. 6:4; 8:22-23) than James, whose brevity should never be understood as lacking depth. To say that James knows nothing of the concept of the resurrection is deceptive. He knows of Christians' sharing in a future glory. He also knows of a Jesus Christ who by the resurrection has already passed through death to a state of living glory (2:1).

VII/Guidelines for Pastors (1:19-27)

19 *Know this, my beloved brethren. Let every man be quick to hear, slow to speak, slow to anger, for the anger of man does not work the righteousness of God. Therefore put away all filthiness and rank growth of wickedness and receive with meekness the implanted Word, which is able to save your souls.*

22 *But be doers of the Word, and not hearers only, deceiving yourselves. For if anyone is a hearer of the Word and not a doer, he is like a man who observes his natural face in a mirror; for he observes himself and goes away and at once forgets what he was like. But he who looks into the perfect law, the law of liberty, and perseveres, being no hearer that forgets but a doer that acts, he shall be blessed in his doing.*

26 *If anyone thinks he is religious and does not bridle his tongue but deceives his heart, this man's religion is vain. Religion that is pure and undefiled before God and the Father is this: to visit orphans and widows in their affliction, and to keep oneself unstained from the world.*

Instructions for Preaching (1:19-20)

This section has been used as a general prohibition against jocular speech, that levity in language is off limits. If this would mean that James is laying down rules for use of language in general, then perhaps his epistle rightly deserves to be judged as moralistic. But, rather than giving guidelines for the use of language in general, James is laying down guidelines for Christian preaching. The epistle here singles out a group identified as "my beloved brethren," similar to the use of "brethren" for clergy in Jerusalem and Antioch (Acts 15:22-23).

Further evidence for considering this section as consisting of guidelines for preaching is suggested by the use of the word *laleō* for speaking instead of *legō*, which refers to any type of general expression.[1] *Laleō* used without modifiers refers to an authoritative speaking in the name of God. This word is roughly equivalent to teaching (*didaskō*), as Paul can substitute one for the other (1 Cor. 14:35 and 1 Tim. 2:12). The admonition of being quick to hear is a warning to pastors and preachers to give more attention to the study of the Scriptures and the apostolic doctrine before engaging in Law preaching which fails to grasp the real mission of Jesus and thus unnecessarily condemns the congregation.

This suggestion is supported by v. 21, where the readers are urged to "receive ... the implanted Word." This can hardly be a demand for personal conversion, as these readers are addressed as Christians by the phrase "my beloved brethren." The readers are not unbelievers, but those who have already been born of God and have accepted the love of God in Christ Jesus! These readers are being directed or rather redirected to a Word with which they are already acquainted. This is an admonition with a warning to pay more attention to what God has spoken. The combination of the hearing and the doing in v. 22 suggests that the hearing of v. 19 is a hearing of the Word.

It can also be noted here that the combination of hearing and doing the Word concludes the Sermon on the Mount: "Everyone then who hears these words of Mine and does them will be like a wise man who built his house upon the rock; and the rains fell, and the floods came, and the winds blew and beat upon that house, but it did not fall, because it had been founded upon the rock" (Matt. 7:24-25). Jesus in the final verse of the Sermon alludes to a coming persecution, which has now materialized in the church situation James is addressing.

Attention to the Gospel had become even more important now that the church was dispersed from Jerusalem and was forming into congregations that did not enjoy personal apostolic supervision. Persecution has made their situation critical. Attentiveness to what Jesus said about persecution is suddenly important, as at this time the gospels had not been penned. What these pastors knew about Jesus was limited by their memory. They are admonished to pay attention to the oral tradition which under apostolic supervision was normative for these early Christians (cf. 2 Thess. 2:15).[2] In no way can James be considered an activist pragmatic churchman with no interest in theology. Quite to the contrary! Although he condemns those who heard but did not respond (1:22), his first warning is not about proper response but about careful listening to God's Word.

Following the admonition to listen with care to God's Word are two admonitions requiring hesitancy in speaking and in wrath. Here James is not requiring hesitancy in all types of vocal expression. "Slow to speak, slow to anger" is an admonition for preachers against that type of Law preaching which forgets that believers in Christ have already been saved from God's anger. The preached Word is not one of soul-scorching damnation but the one which is able to save souls (1:21). Such condemnatory preaching does not actualize God's righteousness in Christian lives (1:22). It is not difficult to determine the reason why their preaching had degenerated into legalism.

All of these first Christian pastors were brought up in Judaism, a religion which in Jesus' day had deteriorated into a Law preaching which taught the possibility of actually living up to its own demands. Jewish legalism had infiltrated the early church and continued to require of Christians adherence to various ceremonial laws (Acts 15:5).[3] Some of these preachers might have been preaching God's displeasure over the failure of some to fulfill these ceremonial obligations. There are indications that the preachers themselves had fallen into error and were preaching it (3:1). The admonition to give more careful attention to the Word was directed to those who had brought such error into their preaching. If "the anger of man does not work the righteousness of God," the question that must be asked is what then does work that righteousness of God! It is certainly not Law preaching!

Any type of preaching that leaves the reader condemned under the anger of God without chance of rescue by the Gospel must fall into the category of false doctrine because by omission it obliterates the atonement. Not only does man's anger not work God's righteousness, it destroys it. God alone has the right of indignation over the breaking of His law, but He has resolved His anger in the atonement. Preaching the Law without the Gospel gives a false picture of God. Preaching anger so that the hearer is left in despair is a right which even God has surrendered because of Christ's death. James' admonition against anger resembles Jesus' warning against anger towards the brother in the Sermon on the Mount: "But I say to you that everyone who is angry with his brother shall be liable to judgment" (Matt. 5:22). The one who works God's righteousness is not man but God Himself. The alternative to the false righteousness worked by man's anger is already contained in the phrase "the righteousness of God." This is the righteousness which considers the sinner righteous for Christ's sake.

Baptism, Conversion, and the Final Salvation (1:21)

The exhortation to put away evil and to receive the implanted Word is freighted with baptismal imagery.[4] Before receiving Christian baptism the individual must renounce Satan and his works. John the Baptist in his preaching called for this radical conversion from evil to good. As sin continues to reside even in the Christian, it continually beleaguers him. The word "put away" (*apotithēmi*) is the New Testament's theological term for renouncing the sinful nature remaining in the Christian even after conversion. Rom. 13:12 finds in this nature "the works of darkness," and Eph. 4:22 calls it "the old man" (KJV). First Peter, recognized by many scholars as an epistle on Baptism, contains an exhortation to do away with evil (2:1) in terminology similar to James. It is difficult to avoid the suggestion that 1 Peter develops themes of James in certain places.

Certainly all types of evil should be avoided by the Christian. The specific evil here is a supposed righteous anger towards those who have offended us. Cursing other people, not merely in the sense of using foul language but passing a real judgment of God on them, is intolerable because the one who curses has assumed God's rightful position of passing judgment. Man has become judge in God's place over sins which God has forgiven. This is wrong on all counts.

The phrase "receive with meekness the implanted Word which is able to save your souls" on first glance seems to be a self-contradiction because it exhorts the reader to receive something which is already part of his nature. Receiving what is already possessed refers to the continual efficacy of Baptism in the life of the Christian. The word "receive" is already used by Jesus (Matt. 10:40) as a term for faith and can be used for those who already have some attachment to the Kingdom. James here is not admonishing unbelievers to come to faith, but rather he is urging believers to take spiritual advantage of what they already possess. "The implanted (*emphuton*) Word" suggests that the Word (*logos*) has already become an organic part of the Christian's life through a previous action. This past action of the Word on the Christian remains efficacious—and is still able to save souls.

As James has a broad understanding of faith, so he also uses the word "save" (*sōzō*) in a variety of ways. Faith without works is incapable of saving (2:14). God saves (4:12). Prayer saves the sick person (5:15). A person who turns a sinner from his way saves him (5:20). Saving embraces the whole concept of salvation including rescue from damnation to the final glorification through resurrection. The reference here in 1:21 to receiving "the implanted Word which is able to save" closely resembles 1 Peter 3:20-21, a baptismal pericope. Here the salvation of eight souls through the water of the Noahic flood is compared to the salvation brought by baptism. God is always the One who saves, though faith, prayer, and Baptism are all said to save.

The saving Word is the message of salvation, which has already become ingrained in the life of Christians. Nevertheless, it is tempting to see James' concept of the Word (*logos*) as resembling John's incarnate Word. Regardless, behind this baptismal Word God is still acting faithfully.

The admonition to humility stands in connection with the reception of salvation. It contrasts man's anger as an obstacle with God's righteousness coming to fulfillment in the lives of others. The humility of the Christian who receives the implanted Word is a Messianic quality, found first in Jesus, then in the believer. In Matthew the quality of meekness is an attribute of the Messiah. Jesus says of Himself that He is meek (11:29 KJV), and the Messianic King comes into Jerusalem meek, riding on a donkey. The Beatitudes see spiritual poverty, i.e., total dependence on God, as the primary characteristic of those who belong to Him (Matt. 5:3).

The Gospel as a Fulfilled Law (1:22-25)

The admonition to "be doers of the Word and not hearers only" can too easily and falsely be understood merely as encouragement for the sanctified Christian life. It is this kind of understanding that has prevented this epistle from being understood to its fullest dimensions. The Word of which James is speaking should not be understood as the Law with its regulations and condemnations, but rather as the Gospel, i.e., the totality of the revelation which God has provided in the person of Jesus Christ. The Word which Christians are to do is the same implanted Word which is able to save their souls. This is hardly a reference to the Decalog![5]

James' imagery of the man looking in the mirror and forgetting what he looks like is startlingly similar to the Sermon on the Mount's concluding parable of two men building houses, one on the rock and one on the sand (Matt. 7:24-27). In both the Sermon and in James, the hearing of the Word comes first and is followed by doing. In the Sermon on the Mount, Jesus identifies these words as His own. In James it is simply "the Word," without any definite article. In the Sermon the refusal to do the Word brings eschatological disaster (Matt. 7:27). James also distinguishes between the doers and the nondoers of the Word, as does the Sermon. However, he lacks the Sermon's finality. The one who hears and does not do the Word is admonished to take the Word seriously and presumably avoids the disaster. James' admonition to spiritual self-introspection resembles Jesus' warning to take the beam out of one's own eye (Matt. 7:3-5). This can only be done by looking at oneself in the mirror of God's Word.

Some attention should here again be given to define more precisely what meaning James intends with his use of "Word." In v. 21 the Word has the ability to save. Within the context of the present section "the Word" is synonymous with "the perfect... law of liberty" (v. 25). This of course gave Luther great difficulty, because he saw the Law as offering only punishment and slavery. James' "law of liberty" is the Gospel and not the Law as condemnation and punishment. Paul seems to develop James' concept of "law of liberty" in Rom. 8:2, "For the law of the Spirit of life in Christ Jesus has set me free from the law of sin and death." For both Paul and James this new law is God's revelation available in Jesus Christ.[6]

"The perfect... law of liberty" might be paraphrased as: "The law which has now been perfected by Christ's atonement releases Christians from the fear of condemnation by it in their fulfilling it." Since Christ has taken away the sting and condemnation of the Law, the Christian may live according to the Law without any fear of coming under the Law's condemnation, now made defunct by the cross.

The words "Law" and "Word" are interchangeable with both James and Jesus. In the Sermon on the Mount the doers of the Word are called those who do the will of Jesus' Father (Matt. 7:21). Those who do not carry out the will of the Father are called evildoers (Matt. 7:23), literally those who work against the Law (*hoi ergazomenoi tēn anomian*). The Sermon is not speaking about general lawbreakers, but specifically against those opposed to the Gospel, i.e., God's revelation in Christ.

This is the only New Testament reference to "Law" as perfect. Here again James is grossly misunderstood if this is seen as a reference to the lack of imperfections in the divine law. This is not a hymn praising God's written revelation. The word for perfect (*teleios*) and its cognates suggests bringing something to perfection or completion, as discussed in connection with James 1:17. James in all citations (1:4, 17, 25; 2:22; 3:2) is consistent in understanding perfection as bringing something to completion.[7] For James the perfect law carries with it the concept of Christ's fulfillment of God's requirements through His holy life and His atoning death.[8] The Law has been fulfilled not through a divine sovereign act of arbitrary abrogation but by Christ's satisfying the divine requirements of the Law with its demands. Thus the Law is not presented to the Christian with its demands only, but also with the fulfillment of these demands. To the non-Christian the Law appears revealing the wrath of God because he has not yet recognized Christ as the Law's perfect answer. But to the Christian the Law appears with Christ as its perfect, completed answer. Christ has absorbed the accusations of the Law together with its wrath into Himself, and the Law without its threats appears to the Christian as providing guidelines for His life. In traditional dogmatic theology this is called the third use of the Law. In Christ the tension between the Law's threats and the Gospel's promises is resolved.

The Law now answered and fulfilled in Christ is not only called "the perfect law" but also "the law of liberty," since the Christian is free from the Law's accusations even when he fails. The Christian's failure is already resolved by Christ's fulfillment of the Law's demands by His life and His payment of the Law's penalties by His death. Christian freedom means a certain recklessness in doing good. Without the fear of the Law's accusation in his life, the Christian becomes uninhibited in accomplishing what God wants done in His law. The Law without Christ is constricting and burdensome, but with and in Christ a new positive dimension is opened. It is really a different kind of law. Christ has made it radically different.

The references to the doers and nondoers of the Word are to be understood within the context of the Christian congregation. The distinction made here is not between Christians and pagans but between those who have true faith and those who do not. This same distinction is also basic to Matthew, where it is made in an eschatological setting (Matt. 25:31-46). The concluding pericopes in the Sermon on the Mount—the narrow gate (Matt. 7:13-14), a tree known by its fruit (7:15-20), the judgment (7:21-23), and the two foundations (7:24-27)—all revolve around the distinction between a proper and an improper understanding of the words of Jesus. Without denying the strong ethical implications in both James and the Sermon on the Mount concerning the doing of the Word, the more profound and deeper dimension of doing is real accepting of what Jesus has said. The problem is not the intellectual failure to understand what Jesus has said, but accepting as true for oneself what He has said, i.e., receiving God's Word in faith. In the parable of the two foundations, both men have heard what Jesus has said but only one follows His directions. The other, who disregards them, meets destruction. Similarly in James the problem is not that some are unaware of what the Word requires of them, but rather that it makes no lasting impression on them. The glance in the mirror to find personal defects must be replaced by a life which continually finds itself embedded in God's revelation in Jesus Christ. That person and that person alone receives the eschatological blessing: "He shall be blessed in his doing."

So v. 25 sums up the life of the Christian and gives him a blessing that shall be of value to him in the coming life. It might be paraphrased in this way: "The one who peers into and remains in the law which has been completed in Christ's atonement and who has been given the freedom to live up to its already fulfilled requirements shall be recognized as belonging to Christ as he does it. This promise applies not to the person who hears but fails to believe, but only to the one who actually accomplishes what God requires." The message here resembles that of the parable of the sower (Matt. 13:18-23),

Guidelines for Pastors (1:19-27)

in that not everyone who is associated with the outward dimensions of the church shall be found acceptable on the Last Day.

The word "blessed" (*makarios*) ties Messianism, the church, and eschatology together. The person in whom the Word reaches its designated goal is blessed not *because of* what he does, but his blessedness is recognizable *in* what he does. The thought is rooted in Psalm 1, where the righteous brings forth fruit in his season as he is expected to (v. 3), and is furthered by the Beatitudes, where the blessed are again recognized by what they do. After they have died, the blessedness of the Christians is still recognizable on earth by what they have done (Rev. 14:13). Here again it would be easy to fall into the trap of seeing the blessedness of Christians as compensation for their moral perfection.[9] Their blessedness is seen in that they resemble God in refusing to pass condemnation over sinners with whom God is no longer angry. They forgive as they are forgiven. They are the ones who refrain from passing judgment in God's stead and are receiving God's salvation with the meekness of Christ (1:21).

Good Works and Judgment Day (1:26-27)

These verses concerning bridling the tongue, deceiving the heart, obligations to widows and orphans, and avoiding worldliness have been seen as further evidence for a moralizing approach to Christianity, falsely attributed to James. One recent commentator sees concern for orphans and widows as a virtue among the rabbis which would be rewarded in the afterlife. But it is here that James must be shown to be very unrabbinic.

The immediate background for these verses seems to be the problem of the distribution of charity among widows in the early church at Jerusalem. The Hellenized Jewish Christians were complaining that their widows were not receiving the same attention as were those Christian widows who were native to Palestine (Acts 6:1). Thus it seems that, from the very beginning of the church organization in Jerusalem, charity was handled not in a haphazard way but according to strict organizational procedures. The complaint may have been lodged against the apostles themselves, as they ask that this task be transferred to seven men chosen by the congregation. These seven men, among whom were Stephen and Philip, sometimes called deacons or ministers, may have been the first clergy in the church who were not apostles. This is a widely held view. It cannot be overlooked that the clergy or those associated with the clergy had the administrative responsibility for charity.

As the church spread out from Jerusalem into the rest of Palestine, the pastors in what certainly seemed small congregations also were the administrators of the funds. The word "to visit" (*episkeptesthai*) suggests more than a type of social visit, but rather a visit with authority, concern, and relief. It is used in the song of Zechariah, the Benedictus, "Blessed be the Lord God of Israel, for he has *visited* and redeemed His people" (Luke 1:68).

The connection between the bridling of the tongue and the visitation of the needy does not seem obvious. Seeing this as admonition to refrain from a foul mouth is hardly adequate. Rather this seems to be an admonition against a heavy preaching of the Law, leaving the congregation with the erroneous impression that God is chiefly a God of wrath in making requirements and exacting punishments and not a God of love who comes to the aid of His people. The preachers, addressed by James, were deceiving themselves into believing that their preaching of the Law was giving the people the proper perspective on God. In doing this they were disqualifying themselves as God's servants. This kind of religion was futile and without substance.

Standing behind this pericope is the final judgment scene in which Jesus as King and Judge rewards those who have been considerate to the needy (Matt. 25:31-46). One of the commended virtues is visiting the sick and imprisoned (vv. 36, 43). The virtue in charitable work is not in the works themselves as some sort of detached humanistic ethic, but it rests in being able to identify Christ in the sufferer and coming to His assistance (v. 45). Still such a view of charity seems to be only a small improvement on performing charity simply for charity's sake.

The first charity embarked upon by the Jerusalem church was care for widows. It is inconsequential that Acts makes no reference to orphans as does James. The disruption of the family through the death of its chief financial supporter was seen as a tragic evil which the church was necessarily compelled to address. But why this particular problem and not another? God's first paradise, where the family unit was unthreatened, was destroyed by death. Now the church as God's reconstruction of His paradise was obligated to alleviate as much as possible the evil consequences brought by death. The sharing of the wealth among Christians, a temporary social experiment (Acts 4:34-37), was an attempt to remove the line between the rich and the poor, a prototype and prelude to the final days when all evidences of evil would be removed. This is the thought of Mary's song of praise, the Magnificat, "He has filled the hungry with good things, and the rich He has sent empty away" (Luke 1:53). In the Sermon on the Mount the meek inherit the earth (Matt. 5:5).

Jesus appeared as the One who was lowly, humble, and poor. The dishonored poor man mentioned in 2:6 could very well be a reference to Jesus. On this more must be said later. Throughout the gospels Jesus is described as poor and is associated with the poor. The rich have a disadvantage in getting into the kingdom (Matt. 19:23-24) which the poor do not. Jesus' association with the poor and needy is a necessary result of His humiliation. He shares in the deepest and lowliest degradation known by men. The widows and orphans are deprived because of death. Those who are the most deprived are most like Jesus in His humility. In the least of His brothers Jesus can be found (Matt. 25:40). On this account James says that the religion acceptable to God and the Father is the care of those who have lost all visible means of earthly support. Though bereft of earthly fathers, God has become their Father in a special way. In their affliction they became totally dependent on

Guidelines for Pastors (1:19-27)

Him. Through the church God is removing their affliction and showing evidences of what the final times will be like.

The admonition of keeping oneself spotless from the world, if detached from and lifted out of this pericope, would seem hardly more than encouragement for morally clean living. Important as that thought is, James is referring to the Christian's total detachment from the concerns of this world (*kosmos*), a concept developed in John. Again, it is difficult to avoid the conclusion that John is dependent on James for many of his fundamental concepts, including the dualism between God and the world. Throughout Matthew, especially in the Sermon on the Mount (6:25-34), Jesus warns His disciples about concerns for ordinary existence, i.e., the things of this world. This is of course James' message also. Such concerns are evidences of unbelief still residing in the Christian after conversion.

The Christian's commitment to charity, especially among those who are suffering within the church, cannot be hindered by concerns to share in more and more of the world's goods. Attachment to the world means the failure of Christians to carry out their obligations to Christ as He is found in the poor.

VIII/Christ's Poverty and Its Implications (2:1-7)

1 My brethren, show no partiality as you hold the faith of our Lord Jesus Christ, the Lord of glory. For if a man with gold rings and in fine clothing comes into your assembly, and a poor man in shabby clothing also comes in, and you pay attention to the one who wears the fine clothing and say, "Have a seat here, please," while you say to the poor man, "Stand there," or, "Sit at my feet," have you not made distinctions among yourselves, and become judges with evil thoughts? Listen, my beloved brethren. Has not God chosen those who are poor in the world to be rich in faith and heirs of the kingdom which He has promised to those who love Him? But you have dishonored the poor man. Is it not the rich who oppress you, is it not they who drag you into court? Is it not they who blaspheme the honorable name which was invoked over you?

Jesus as God (2:1)

The reference to holding "the faith of our Lord Jesus Christ, the Lord of glory," is one of the most challenging sections for interpretation in the entire epistle, as it speaks of faith and the person of Christ. The RSV and the New King James Version repeat the word "Lord," so the phrase reads: "Our Lord Jesus Christ, the Lord of glory." Some have suggested that it should read, "Our Lord Jesus Christ, who is the glory," i.e., the *shekinah*, the glory which is God Himself.[1] There is no quarrel here. James is clearly making a reference to the deity of Christ, especially in the context of the final judgment. Rather than repeating the word "Lord," it might be best to favor the translation, "our Lord of glory, Jesus Christ." It could have been adopted by Paul in 1 Cor. 2:8, where he says of Christ that the rulers of the world would not have killed Him if they had known that He was the Lord of glory.

James' phrase evidences a well-developed explicit Christology on his part, not recognized by all. It is a confession about who Jesus really is. He is not only the one whom the Old Testament prophets anticipated, i.e., the Anointed, the Messiah, the Christ, but He is also the manifestation on earth of everything God is. Jesus is the incarnate God Himself. Since a high Christology was seen as missing in the rest of the epistle, it has been suggested it was added later. This is hardly necessary, as the entire epistle is Christological.

Christ's Poverty (2:1-7)   73

A Unique Understanding of Faith (2:1)

At first it seems more natural to take the phrase, the *faith* of our Lord of glory, Jesus Christ, as a reference to faith which finds its object in Him. If this is so, then James rather than Paul should be credited with developing what later was understood as the evangelical understanding of faith.[2] But here it is possible to understand faith as a reference to the teachings and attitude which Jesus Christ Himself had. They must believe and have the same attitude Jesus had. The admonition to hold to the faith of our Lord Jesus Christ without impartiality reflects Christ's lack of discrimination (Matt. 22:16). Though He was the Lord of glory, He showed no favoritism to the rich but regarded all men alike. From this faith no deviation is allowed.

Synagogue or Church? (2:2-4)

The synagogue where the Christians are to show no impartiality is the early Christian congregation. In the early days of the church Christians may have been recognized by their fellow Jews as offering a particular form of Judaism. On their part the Christians understood themselves as a movement within Judaism given the obligation of bringing it to a recognition of who Jesus really was. Their assemblies were recognized as synagogues by other Jews, and they had no hesitancy in calling these assemblies synagogues. Only the sharp division between Christianity and Judaism caused Christians to forsake that word and even to use it later in a totally pejorative sense (Rev. 2:9).[3]

James is hardly laying down rules of worship etiquette for those Jewish synagogues which had not recognized Jesus as the Christ. At a time when Gentiles were not members of the core congregation in Jerusalem, Christians in the rest of Palestine, to whom this epistle is addressed, would continue to call their worshiping assemblies synagogues. The order of worship in the Christian synagogues probably differed little from their counterparts among the Jews not accepting Jesus. In the Christian synagogues the clear confession was made that Jesus was the complete answer to all of Israel's hopes. Among Gentile Christians their worshiping assemblies were called churches and not synagogues.

A problem in these early Christian congregations was the paying of more attention to those who made it clear by their appearance that they were wealthy than to those whose clothes identified them as society's poor. It is easy to understand such behavior, for the rich person would be seen to be in a better position in providing help to fulfill the Christian obligation to the needy. Actually, though, because of their similarity to Christ in His poverty, the poor held the preferred position.[4]

The reconstruction of the worship rites of the early Christian congregation is not as important as realizing that such flagrant discrimination was a direct contradiction of the faith which the Lord Jesus had given them. While He treated all men alike, the early Christians were contradicting what He said by what they did. They were assuming that wealth was a sign of

God's approval. In despising the poor they arrogated to themselves the prerogative of judgment which belongs to God alone. The poor they considered objects of their contempt by having them assume a position as a stool for their feet. Such contempt for the poor was in fact disregard for Jesus' own poverty. They were rejecting those whom He had accepted. He Himself had been the poorest of men.[5] He criticized those who grabbed the best places for themselves and held that the rich could enter the Kingdom only with the greatest difficulty.

The First Beatitude as Description of Christ and His Congregation (2:5-6)

The principles for the proper attitude to the poor are found in this section. V. 5 puts it all together. "Has not God chosen those who are poor in the world to be rich in faith and heirs of the kingdom which He has promised to those who love Him?" The resemblance to the First Beatitude, "Blessed are the poor in spirit, for theirs is the kingdom of heaven" (Matt. 5:3), is striking.

Who are the poor chosen by God? Again, James and the First Beatitude seem dependent on a common tradition. Curious is James' switch from the plural to the singular. After describing the blessedness of the poor (plural), James adds, "You have dishonored the poor man" (singular) (2:6). Would it not have been more consistent for James to have used the plural and said, "You are dishonoring the poor ones," since the congregation's behavior against the poverty-stricken was a continuing affront? James seems to be referring to one specific act in the past by his use of the aorist (past tense) and singular object. It may be that the poor man is a generic reference to all poor men, but why is there no generic reference for the rich man? The use of the singular in v. 6 and not the plural is unnatural, unless James is referring to one poor man in particular. The designation best fits Christ, whose self-impoverishment was a mark of His servanthood.

The Beatitudes, which are the first recorded preaching of Jesus in the Sermon on the Mount and the Gospel of Matthew, begin by speaking of the blessedness of those who are "poor in spirit." No unified understanding on the nature of the Beatitudes exists. A correct understanding of the Beatitudes is important for any proper understanding of James, who seems to be applying the First Beatitude to a specific problem among the early Christians who are openly favoring the rich over the poor. The "poor in spirit" for Matthew and the "poor in the world" for James are those who have put their total reliance on God and who do not place their confidence in anything this world has to offer.[6] They are the ones God has chosen to share in the final glory with Christ. The poor are associated with the coming of the Messiah.

In answering the imprisoned John the Baptist, the final convincing proof that the Messianic reign of God has appeared in Jesus is neither the alleviation of physical disease nor even the resurrection of the dead, but that the poor have the Gospel preached to them (Matt. 11:5). The ones for whom God had intended the Kingdom have finally received it.

As in so many places, James is close to Matthew again here. The poor whom the Christians are despising are the very ones whom God has designated to be heirs of the Kingdom. Right here James appears as much the apostle of grace as Paul. The choice for salvation is made by God. The poor are called heirs not because their poverty has entitled them to salvation or earned it for them, but because God has designated it for them. This evangelical concept of salvation is furthered by the use of the word "promise" (*epaggelizō*). The Kingdom is not earned, but promised. The Lutheran Confessions speak of the Gospel as promise.

In the parable of the murderous tenants in the vineyard the heir is Christ and the inheritance is everything promised to Him by the Father (Matt. 21:38). Though the heir is killed (Matt. 21:39), He is alive as the son for whom the father-king gives a banquet in the parable of the wedding feast (Matt. 22:1-13). The inheritance is shared by the heir, who is Christ, with those chosen by God as heirs, Christians. In the final judgment scene Jesus invites those who have shown mercy to the needy to accept the inheritance God has prepared for them (25:34).

Characteristic of both Matthew and James is that one designation with a Messianic meaning can apply both to Jesus and to His church. What belongs primarily to Christ can be attributed to Christians through faith. The poor in the world are called "rich in faith" because they have become "heirs of the Kingdom" (2:5). In both Matthew and James the co-heirs of Jesus are recognizable by their acts of mercy to the poor. In such compassion Christians resemble Christ. The connection between Christ and His church must be more closely drawn. The question is whether the poor in the First Beatitude and the poor man in James are chiefly Christological references. The data points in this direction.

The Beatitudes do not refer to different categories of people, but each Beatitude is better understood as speaking of the same persons. Those who are poor in spirit are the same ones who mourn, hunger, and thirst. Those who were called poor in spirit, destined to receive the Kingdom, are in the Third Beatitude designated as the meek, to whom the earth has been promised as their inheritance. The kingdom promised in the Beatitudes is delivered in the final judgment scene (Matt. 25:34). The similarity of these Matthean sections to James 2:5 is unmistakable.

In the New Testament poor (*ptōchos*), meek (*praus*), and humble (*tapeinos*) form a constellation of words referring to Christ in His humility. Jesus invites people to come to Him because He is meek (*praus*) and lowly (*tapeinos*). Though Christians may be regarded by God as poor, meek, and humble, they possess these qualities only as they are in Christ and Christ in them. It would not only be inappropriate but obviously hypocritical for any Christians to say about themselves that they were poor, meek, and lowly, because such designations refer to Christ's humiliation for sinners' sake. A Christian is not to look for these virtues in himself, but is to let God find them and reward them at His time. Though the Beatitudes speak of the meek (plural) inheriting the earth, only Christ can say, "I am meek and lowly in heart" (Matt. 11:29 KJV).

JAMES: THE APOSTLE OF FAITH

Paul developed this poverty theme in his Christology by seeing Christ as rich, but who impoverishes (*eptōcheusen*) Himself so that Christians can become rich in Him (*ploutēsēte*) (2 Cor. 8:9). Christ's poverty (*ptōcheia*) is beneficial for Christians. Paul also sees Christ's humility (*etapeinōsen*) in His submission to death by crucifixion (Phil. 2:8). Poverty, meekness, and humility find their central focus in Christ. Christians are recognized as belonging to Christ by reflecting these attitudes in their lives, and they share with Him in being abused. With Him they are reviled, persecuted, and satanically slandered (Matt. 5:11; 12:24).

The Christians in the first congregations by discriminating against the poor in their social behavior had lost their awareness of Christ's organic connection with His people. Their offense against the poor was dishonoring Christ, who forsook His riches and for their sake had become poor. Their behavior was destructive of Christianity at its core, as their despising of the poor showed they were unaware of Christ's humility. Equally important was their own failure to see that they were one in Christ with those whom they were so shabbily treating. They themselves also were targets of the contempt of the rich. James uses rich almost as a synonym for enemies of the Gospel.

James' reference to the poor as heirs of the kingdom which God has promised finds a reflection in Gal. 3:29: "And if you are Christ's, then you are Abraham's offspring, heirs according to promise." Any suggestion that James teaches a righteousness of works seems increasingly inappropriate, especially as the strong parallelism between James and Paul becomes clearer. If James is really the earliest extant New Testament writing, then it is probable that a fledgling apostle like Paul would have relied on James, the recognized leader of the church, to develop his own theology.[7] Paul did hold the Jerusalem church, with James its leader, in high honor.

The kingdom which is promised is eschatological,[8] but not in the sense of a far-off goal but a reality which is breaking in upon Christians now. The preaching ministry of Jesus is summarized by Matthew as a proclamation of the nearness of the Kingdom (4:17). Through crucifixion and resurrection the Kingdom of God had appeared on earth. In the realest sense Jesus embodies the Kingdom in Himself. The Kingdom is revealed in Jesus, but its total glorious manifestation still rests in the future (Matt. 25:34). In one sentence James designates the heirs of this kingdom as "those who are poor in the world," "rich in faith," "heirs of the Kingdom," and as "those who love Him" (2:5).

Love as a synonym for faith or belief is associated with the Johannine writings, a matter previously mentioned. In James 1:12 in a similar phrase "the crown of life" is promised "to those who love Him." There, as mentioned, the "blessed ... man" could be a reference to Christ, who "has stood the test." In 2:5 the kingdom is promised "to those who love Him." The most obvious referent is God. Is this to the Father or to the Son? In 1:27 God seems clearly to refer to the Father, but 2:5 is part of a section focusing on Jesus as the major person. He, who is called our "Lord of glory," Jesus Christ, could also be the God whom the heirs of the kingdom love. This is, of course, the mystery of the incarnation and humiliation, that the Lord of glory, God Himself, became also the poorest of men.

The oppressive attitude of the rich over the poor is not simply a general social observation that the rich have certain legal advantages over the poor or even over Christians. James is addressing a specific problem in the early church which had spread from Jerusalem throughout Palestine. The Jews were given far-reaching powers by the Romans over their own communities not only in Palestine but in other parts of the eastern empire. They were now using this power to eliminate or purge those synagogues where Jesus was acknowledged as the Christ. It has been pointed out that Stephen was put to death by a religious tribunal legally constituted and recognized. Paul before his conversion was legally empowered to exercise this authority in Damascus (Acts 9:1-2). The persecution that disrupted the Jerusalem church and caused the dispersion of congregations or Christian synagogues outside of that city had followed the persecuted Christians into exile. Christians were sought out in their own synagogues and as they participated in the worship services of other synagogues. Jews who did not recognize Jesus as the Christ blasphemed His name and called upon the accused Christians to do the same. Christians returning to the regular synagogues were required to say, "Jesus be cursed!" (1 Cor. 12:3).

An Allusion to Baptism (2:7)

The reference to "the honorable name which was invoked over you" could very well be an allusion to Baptism. According to Acts, Baptism was carried out in the name of Jesus and the baptized Christians bore His name.[9] Offending against Jesus was also a direct offense against all baptized Christians, because all bore the name of Christ through Baptism. By this time the custom, begun in Antioch, of calling the followers of Jesus Christians may have become widespread. Baptism meant an indissoluble union not only between the baptized and Christ, but among all those who had been baptized.[10] The poor against whom the Christians were discriminating in their worship services were also one with Christ and themselves. The rich Jews to whom they catered were oppressing them, the poor, and, before that time, Christ Himself.

Among the Jews the "name" was a reference to the God of Israel. With the early Christians it took on the added dimension of a reference to Jesus. At the final time all creatures will bow at the name of Jesus, as it is "the name which is above every name" (Phil. 2:9). James comes close to Paul's ode to Jesus' name by referring to it as the beautiful name (*to kalon onoma*).

Matthew's gospel, coming out of the same milieu as James' epistle, develops the conception narrative around the naming of Jesus, an act seen as fulfillment of the Is. 7:14 prophecy. The name "Jesus" means "the Lord saves" and in Jesus God truly becomes Emmanuel, i.e., "God [is] with us" (Matt. 1:21-23). The promise of Jesus to be with His church, "Lo, I am with you always, to the close of the age" (Matt. 28:20), brings the Emmanuel prophecy and the name of Jesus to their fullest dimensions.

The name of the Triune God given in Baptism is the guarantee of God's presence in the church for the salvation of His people. Christians are absorbed into Christ's name by Baptism, and all churchly activity is carried out in His name. Healing and preaching were carried out in the name of Jesus (Acts 3:6; 4:7). The name was considered the answer to salvation: "For there is no other name under heaven given among men by which we must be saved" (Acts 4:12). The Christian "receives forgiveness of sins through His name" (Acts 10:43). Both the first sermons of Peter in Jerusalem and the Epistle of James come roughly from the same level of early church development. Early Christians would easily understand "that worthy name by the which ye are called" (KJV) as a reference to Christ's work in their lives, that intimate connection by which Christ was reflected in them.

Conversion, calling, church, Spirit, Christ, Father, and Baptism were seen in the early church as closely connected. The one who was called was also baptized, became a member of the church, and shared intimate relationship with the Triune God. "There is one body [i.e., the church] and one Spirit, just as you were called to the one hope that belongs to your call, one Lord [i.e., Jesus], one faith [i.e., one standard of truth], one Baptism, one God and Father of us all" (Eph. 4:4-6). The name of Jesus, by which these early Christians were called through Baptism, remained their permanent possession through faith.

In the light of Matthew's gospel, which shares with James a clearly Palestinian origin, there is evidence that infant baptism was being carried out in the Jerusalem congregation, from which James was writing. Jesus refers to receiving a child in His name (Matt. 18:5), i.e., the child who has become Jesus' possession and through Baptism bears Jesus' name as his own. For James the prophets preached by the authority of the name of Jesus (5:10) and the pastors cared for the church's sick (5:14), matters to be discussed below.

The Church as Court: An Excursus

A recent commentator, Peter Davids, challenges the usual interpretation of *sunagōge* as a church service and follows the suggestion of W. B. Ward that this is a reference to a church court.[11] It is argued that for a worship service the rich and poor man would not have to be directed to their seats. The suggestion is intriguing, since 2:6 speaks specifically about the rich dragging the poor into courts and v. 8 makes references to the royal law. It is difficult to deny that the language reflects a judicial environment. On the other hand, James, very much like Paul in 1 Corinthians, is throughout his letter addressing liturgical concerns of the worshiping congregation, particularly the matter of pastoral conduct and preaching.

Perhaps the solution is that disputes between members were handled as part of the regular worship, more particularly as part of the confession before the celebration of the Lord's Supper. The admonition in 5:16 to confess sins could very well be a reference to mutual confession as part of the worship service. In the case of James 2:1-7 the congregations in settling disputes were giving preferential treatment to the rich in the manner in which the dispute was discussed. While the rich person was given a place of honor, the poor by having to stand or sit on the floor was virtually prejudged as the offender even before the case was heard. This behavior was an offense against Jesus Christ, who showed no partiality in His treatment of others (2:1). Those giving the rich the advantage in the church courts made themselves guilty of offending the Law (2:9) and were sinning, perhaps even against Christ Himself (2:6). The words of 2:12-13—"So speak and so act as those who are to be judged under the law of liberty. For judgment is without mercy to one who has shown no mercy; yet mercy triumphs over judgment"—are fitting for those entrusted with making decisions between men.

The idea that the church or congregation would have certain judicial functions may be strange to us, but was not to the Jewish world in which the church was springing up. The distinction between religious, civil, and criminal offenses was not as important as it is now. The mentioning of murder, adultery, and offense against the Law in 2:10-11 suggests that the congregation was acting on a broad number of cases.

Support for the view that the church acted as a court may be found in 1 Cor. 6:1-8, particularly vv. 5b-6: "Can it be that there is no man among you wise enough to decide between members of the brotherhood, but brother goes to law against brother, and that before unbelievers?"

In Corinth, instead of resolving disputes among themselves within the context of the congregation, Christians were going to secular courts. People destined to judge the world and angels on the Last Day acted as though they were incompetent to handle what Paul calls trivial lawsuits. While in James it does seem that certain rich persons were in certain cases resorting to the secular courts (2:6), the problem is that the church courts themselves were conducted inequitably in favor of the rich. It is difficult to determine from 1 Corinthians where in the church's life these legal disputes among Christians were to be settled, a question raised in connection with Davids' proposed understanding of James 2:2-7. Still it is difficult to escape the idea that disputes in Corinth were settled as part of the worship service.

In 1 Corinthians the immediately preceding section (ch. 5) addresses the problem of immorality in connection with what seems to be the Lord's Supper (vv. 6-8). Such an immoral person cannot be part of the worshiping congregation (vv. 12-13). The whole tenor of 1 Corinthians tends towards liturgical instruction for the worshiping congregation.

Though there might be support for the view that worshiping congregations in the early church in some cases acted as a court in handling disputes among members, the question of theological justification for the practice remains. Simply to say that it was a custom carried over from the synagogue into the early church may provide a historical but not a theological explanation for it.

The theological motivation for settling disputes within the worshiping situation may be found in the Lord's Prayer, "And forgive us our debts, as we also have forgiven our debtors" (Matt. 6:12), with a specific formula provided in Matt. 18:19-20. J. Duncan M. Derrett suggests that this pericope should be separated from the previous one and that it contains Jesus' procedure for handling disputes within the church. It does fit with the following pericopes of forgiving the brother each time he repents (vv. 21-22) and the unforgiving servant (vv. 23-35). In Derrett's view Matt. 18:19-20 does not refer to God's always responding to the specific requests of two or more Christians in prayer but to the presence of Jesus in settling disputes between members. Derrett reconstructs the situation in this way: Two Christians, failing to settle a dispute between themselves, each appoint a fair-minded representative to thrash out the difficulty. If this also fails, the two representatives appoint a congregation member with a reputation for impartiality. Where two disputing parties come to reconciliation within the congregation, Christ is present. Derrett offers this translation:[12]

> Again I tell you that if two individuals (literally, two of you [Christians]) arrive at an accord on earth concerning any (literally, any and every) claim that they may be persuing it shall be allowed, ratified (literally it shall succeed, 'come off') on the part of my heavenly Father. For where there are two or three convened in my name, there I am amongst them.

All three pericopes (Matt. 18:19-20; 1 Cor. 6:1-8; and James 2:1-7) are similar. The topic is the handling of disputes among members within the context of the church. These disputes were not limited to religious or doctrinal matters. In Matthew Jesus is said to be present in resolving the disputes, and in James He is present in His identity with the offended poor. James 2:1 is an admonition that those who decide should do it with the same impartial spirit that Jesus had. Paul brings in the Christological motif at the eschatological level. Their judging the world and angels can only be understood as an activity carried out with Christ. In all three Christ is involved—as the present Reconciler, the accused poor, and the Judge.

It is still difficult to escape the conviction that all three pericopes have their central focus within the context of the celebration of the Lord's Supper in the early church. Confession of sins and reconciliation before the celebration has always been practiced. The Lord's Prayer was prayed in connection with the Lord's Supper specifically for the purpose of reconciliation of Christians with God and with one another. The current handshaking ceremony is only a first attempt to restore the ancient custom. Reconciliation between Christians was done under the larger reality of God's reconciliation with all sinners. This seems to fit James 2:1-7. The church was a court not to determine guilt but to make reconciliation effective among believers. In doing this they were like Christ the divine Reconciler (James) or Christ the Reconciler who was present (Matthew).

IX/Love, Scripture, Apostasy, and the Triumph of the Gospel (2:8-13)

8 *If you really fulfill the royal law, according to the scripture, "You shall love your neighbor as yourself," you do well. But if you show partiality, you commit sin, and are convicted by the law as transgressors. For whoever keeps the whole law but fails in one point has become guilty of all of it. For he who said, "Do not commit adultery," said also, "Do not kill." If you do not commit adultery but do kill, you have become a transgressor of the law. So speak and so act as those who are to be judged under the law of liberty. For judgment is without mercy to one who has shown no mercy; yet mercy triumphs over judgment.*

Bearing the name of Christ through Baptism means for the Christian incorporation in Him (Rom. 6:3-4). With this understanding of the beautiful name borne by Christians, it is not difficult to see why James sets forth the principle of love of neighbor as requiring first of all impartiality towards all and secondly refraining from sin. "You shall love your neighbor as yourself" (2:8) is called the royal law by James. This command is said by Jesus to be second in importance to loving God, and together both commands constitute the substance of God's revelation through the prophets (Matt. 22:37-40). The congregations to which James addresses his epistle are aware of the same tradition which Matthew incorporates in his gospel and thus know of this obligation. Throughout James, the firm impression is given that the audience addressed is fully knowledgeable in the Christian religion. Their problem is understanding their religion in the light of the new situation of persecution. They do not have a problem with knowing and loving God, but with comprehending that this involves loving one's neighbor, especially the poor in the congregation.

Scripture and Christ (2:8-9)

The command to love is called "the royal law, according to the Scripture." James' phrase "according to the Scripture" (*kata tēn graphēn*) is close to Paul's "according to the Scriptures" (*kata tas graphas*) (1 Cor. 15:3-4). Though the reference to the law of love is from Lev. 19:18, the failure to mention a specific reference suggests that James sees the principle of love as the central understanding of the entire Old Testament and not merely one passage.

Rather than seeing a fully evolved doctrine of the Scriptures as emerging in a later period of church development, it would be better to recognize that from the beginning the church had a clear-cut, definite view on the nature of the Scriptures as setting forth God's will, especially as intended for the Messiah.[1] Paul in the citation quoted from 1 Corinthians 15 sees Christ's crucifixion and resurrection as happening according to what the Scriptures have prescribed. Jesus sees the events of His own life in the same light (cf. Matt. 26:54, 56). James also wants his readers to understand that his message about a fuller reflection of Christ's attitude in their lives has its real foundation in the Old Testament. It is not an invention of Christianity, but belonged to the older religion of the prophets. Love is the thrust of not one passage but of the entire prophetic revelation.

The command to love the neighbor, grounded in the Old Testament with the words "according to the Scripture," is also called "the royal law," i.e., the law issued by the King for His kingdom. James has spoken of the poor who inherit the kingdom promised to those who love God (2:5). Though "kingdom" here is strongly eschatologically freighted, as its rewards remain in the future, it is also a present reality in the person of the crucified and resurrected Christ. As the King, Christ provides the real substance to the Kingdom. In Himself and His atoning death He actualized what appeared above His cross: "Jesus of Nazareth, the King of the Jews." The Kingdom is so much Christ Himself that if the Kingdom and Christ are not in every respect identical, they are at least coterminous. The royal law is really the law of the King, i.e., Jesus, which He has set down for those who are joined to His kingdom.[2]

The command to love is taken directly from Jesus, though not quoted from the gospels. James' citation is identical to the tradition as it later became inscripturated in the gospels. James, like Matthew, calls these words a law (*nomos*), not in the sense of threat and warning but in the sense of a divine plan.

The entire work of Jesus pulsated with His love for people. This love must reflect itself in the life of the communities that carry His name. Though the command to love is as old as the Pentateuch and permeates the entire Old Testament, it comes to its fullest expression in Jesus, who as the King sets down this principle as basic for all in His kingdom. At the time James was writing, the early Christian communities in Palestine were acquainted with the Kingdom parables of Jesus. James' use of the words "kingdom" and "royal" presuppose this knowledge. The full impact of James' allusions, especially his understanding of "royal," would soon be lost on the communities outside of Palestine. This is one of the reasons his epistle and its message became more obscure to the church and he was falsely seen as Paul's antagonist.

Adultery as Apostasy and Implications of Murder (2:10-11)

With its threats against a breaking of even one commandment this section seems out of place, as there are no previous injunctions against explicit immorality. The Gentile churches and not those chiefly Jewish were known for this kind of behavior. James in his letter from the Jerusalem Council explicitly requests the Gentiles to refrain from fornication (Acts 15:29), and Paul faces this problem in his churches in the western empire. Among Jewish Christians such explicit immorality was unusual. Here James is not warning them about breaking the Decalog, as the word "law" (*nomos*) is used most commonly of the entire written revelation. James sees these sins not merely as unacceptable immoral behavior but as treacherous, treasonous acts against Christ, who embodied God's revelation in Himself, set forth in His preaching for those whom God had attached to His kingdom. In Jesus' preaching ethical behavior is never isolated from who He was and what He did.

Though an offense against one point of the Law is against Scripture in its entirety, James in citing the prohibitions against adultery and murder does not mention them as coming from Scripture—though of course they do—but as coming from the One who spoke these prohibitions. James is not quoting the Scriptures as much as he is referring to Jesus, who in the Sermon on the Mount set forth these commandments with expositions (Matt. 5:21-32). In the Sermon they are also the first two on which Jesus gives an extended exposition and the *only* two commandments He quotes directly from the Decalog (Ex. 20:13-14). Whatever the specific offenses addressed by James were, the offenders' real sin is not only against a written law but against Christ, who put forth the Sermon on the Mount as the descriptive constitution for His kingdom. Herein lies the real enormity of their offense.

While the Sermon prohibitions against adultery and murder follow the Septuagint's future indicative with the negative *ou*, "You will not commit adultery and murder," James substitutes the subjunctive with the negative *mē*, "You will not begin committing adultery and murder." These sins are not even to enter the Christians' thinking. With these slight grammatical changes, James combines into one prohibition the original, longer discourses of the Sermon forbidding the evil intentions as well as the acts (Matt. 5:21-30).

Both commandments reappear as the first two in Jesus's reply to the rich young man, with Matthew (19:18) repeating the future indicative of the Sermon and Mark (10:19) and Luke (18:20) following James with the subjunctive. The last two evangelists by using James' form are like him in addressing a strong homiletical prohibition to their readers that sins in thought are also forbidden. Sinai's commandments take on new force in the church, since the original divine Lawgiver has appeared in the person of Jesus, the God-Man, to reinforce them.

It could be that the readers were guilty of adultery in their hearts (Matt. 5:28), but there is no suggestion that James is addressing such internal immorality. Throughout his epistle he addresses the problem of the Christians' outward behavior, which is contradicting the theological principles of their religion. The outward behavior reflected an internal problem, but it is the external problem which is addressed, not the internal one. That outward problem for James' readers is murder, *not* adultery. Consider the passage carefully: "If you do not commit adultery but do kill, you have become a transgressor of the law" (2:11). They were guilty of adultery not directly, but by their implication in murder. But were these early Christians really guilty of actual murder? And why charge them with adultery? James is addressing a specific and not a general problem.

These first Christians were so taken up in impressing the rich that they not only despised the poor in their worship services (2:1-7) but neglected to provide them with even the most elementary needs (2:14-17). On the other hand the rich, whom the early Christians were trying to impress, were responsible for the miseries of the poor (5:1-6). The failure of these early Christians to recognize the elemental needs of the poor for food and clothing and their alliance with the rich made them coconspirators in the misery and possibly even the starvation of the poor. Luther, who had little enthusiasm for James, saw with him that failure to help the neighbor in his bodily needs was breaking the commandment forbidding murder. The rich Jews to whom the Christians were catering were also responsible for the martyrdom of Stephen and for the persecution of other Christians in Palestine and Syria. This was hardly a subtle form of murder![3]

James not only lays a charge of murder against these Christians but one of adultery also. This approach is reminiscent of the homiletical method of Jesus in addressing His enemies. Those who demand a sign are labeled adulterous by Jesus (Matt. 12:39; 16:4). Jesus gets his enemies to admit that they are the sons of murderers and are thus murderers themselves (Matt. 23:31). In neither case had they committed the actual crime. The similarity between Jesus and James in their approaches is striking. With James we are at the first layer of the oral tradition of Jesus' preaching in the early church. After Paul this type of preaching does not seem to have been used. Still the problem remains of why adultery is charged by both Jesus and James. Just as there is no suggestion of outward adultery in the congregations addressed by James, so the request for a sign hardly seems in itself an adulterous action.

Adultery is so associated with idolatry in the Old Testament that the terms become synonymous. Pagan religions in the ancient world, especially those involving a fertility cult, required adulterous practices.[4] The Jews engaged in these with the Moabites (Num. 25:1-3), and Paul makes this connection between idolatry and adultery explicit (1 Cor. 10:7-8). After the Babylonian Captivity the Jews committed themselves to a strict monotheism with a strict outward morality. This morality did not prevent Jesus from lodging the charge of adultery against His enemies. The charge was one of idolatry and apostasy. In failing to recognize Him as the Messiah they were disqualifying themselves as Abraham's sons and excluding themselves from the final manifestation of the Kingdom (Matt. 8:11-12; cf. Matt. 3:9). In the Fourth Gospel the Jews understand that Jesus has called them children of fornication (John 8:41).

The early Christians addressed by James were placing themselves under the same condemnation which Jesus had leveled against His enemies not many years earlier. In some cases they may have been the very same people, as some opposed to Jesus associated themselves with the church after Pentecost (Acts 2:36; 3:15; 4:10). The sin of the early Christians was not necessarily verbal apostasy; more likely their discriminating behavior to the poor was seen as a form of apostasy. Their lives were direct contradictions not only to the message of Christ but to His life.

The Triumph of the Gospel (2:12-13)

Though the condemnation of James is severe, it is not to be the last word. Law for the Christian insofar as he is unbelieving and apart from Christ is severe condemnation. Insofar as he is a believer and in Christ, the Law is fulfilled and thus the Law means not only possibility and reality, but freedom. Here lies the theological genius of James. The law which threatens condemnation is transformed into a law which holds no threat for the Christian. "So speak and so act as those who are to be judged under the law of liberty" (2:12).

Here again is what later would be called the third use of the Law, i.e., the Law as a guide for Christian life. This guide should not be understood as sterile regulations but as a law granting freedom since Christ has removed its judgments. James is addressing Christian behavior in regard to both acting and speaking. Speaking refers primarily to authorized preaching in the congregation.[5] James has as much concern for adherence to proper doctrine as to proper behavior. Preaching and behavior must reflect the view that Christ's atonement embraces all men, the poor as well as the rich. At so many points in understanding James there is the temptation to slip into a moralistic interpretation, so that only a set of rules for speaking and acting is left which could suit any system of morality, Christian or non-Christian. But such tempting interpretations must be resisted in their crass moralizing, as they offend the fiber of this epistle.

James puts the speaking and acting of Christians within the eschatological dimension. Their behavior is not to conform merely to a written law given in the Old Testament, but to the revelation given in Christ and manifested further on the Last Day. The judgment on that day will not be a delineation of multiple offenses against the Decalog, but it will be based on reaction to God's revelatory deed in Christ. In Him the Law was given and fulfilled. The unbeliever rejecting the Law's fulfillment in Christ will find himself in a position far worse than he who has known only the Law as moral requirement.

For the believer this fulfilled law grants freedom because Christ has removed its threats. In Christ the Law's absolute negative has been absorbed. The Christian as a Christian sees only the Law's positive expression of what his life really has become in Christ. Since the Law's negative prohibitions have been negated by their absorption into Christ, the sin against the law now fulfilled in Christ is the failure to show the mercy that God in Christ has shown. Those who know themselves rescued by Christ from the judgment of the Decalog but still fail to show mercy will face a more severe judgment, because they have never comprehended God's mercy in Christ. "Judgment is without mercy to one who has shown no mercy" (2:13).

James here again is reflecting on a theme found in the Sermon on the Mount (in the Lord's Prayer) and repeated in the parable of the unforgiving servant (Matt. 18:23-35). The petition in the Lord's Prayer, "And forgive us our debts, as we also have forgiven our debtors," immediately receives an exposition by Jesus: "For if you forgive men their trespasses, your heavenly Father also will forgive you; but if you do not forgive men their trespasses, neither will your Father forgive your trespasses" (Matt. 6:12, 14-15). The thought here is identical to that of James. The offender in both cases is not charged with the breaking of still another commandment in the Law, but in failing to forgive others he shows that God's forgiveness has not permeated his own life. James' verdict, "For judgment is without mercy to one who has shown no mercy," finds its parallel at the conclusion to the parable of the unjust servant: "And should not you have had mercy on your fellow servant, as I had mercy on you?" (Matt. 18:33). This parable is also an exposition of what forgiveness means in the Lord's Prayer. As in the Sermon on the Mount, Jesus at the end of this parable threatens God's final wrath upon the unforgiving (vv. 34-35). James, unlike Jesus' exposition on forgiveness, concludes his section with an evangelical ray of hope, "yet mercy triumphs over judgment."

This sentence with its promise of grace, characteristic of the entire epistle, is strongly eschatological. Christians live their lives knowing that on the Last Day they will not face the Law's judgment. This assures them of freedom now. For some their lack of forgiving spirit will not let them face that day unscathed.

But what is meant by James' phrase "yet mercy triumphs over judgment"? The suggestion that God is more merciful than judgmental, true as it may be, does not seem totally appropriate here. There is no reason to think that James is saying something explicit about God's nature. Dogmatically God is hardly dualistic, as if His mercy and justice contended with each other. God's nature is not divided. The word "yet" in the RSV is not really suggested by anything in the Greek. It would be better to translate the phrase "mercy is triumphing over the judgment." James expects to see in these congregations mercy and not condemnation. This mercy by which one Christian forgives another makes Judgment Day for the forgiving Christian a past event. In the Fourth Gospel, judgment (John 3:18; 5:24) and death (John 11:25-26) are past for the Christian. For James the Christians are already beginning to live in that new dimension where their acts of mercy exempt them from God's judgment and its dread. Christians following God do not hold others accountable for sins against them. Then the petition in the Lord's Prayer for forgiveness among Christians is actualized.

X/The New Testament's First Great Discussion on Justification (2:14-26)

14 What does it profit, my brethren, if a man says he has faith but has not works? Can his faith save him? If a brother or sister is ill-clad and in lack of daily food, and one of you says to them, "Go in peace, be warmed and filled," without giving them the things needed for the body, what does it profit? So faith by itself, if it has no works, is dead.

18 But someone will say, "You have faith and I have works." Show me your faith apart from your works, and I by my works will show you my faith. You believe that God is one; you do well. Even the demons believe—and shudder. Do you want to be shown, you shallow man, that faith apart from works is barren? Was not Abraham our father justified by works, when he offered his son Isaac upon the altar? You see that faith was active along with his works, and faith was completed by works, and the scripture was fulfilled which says, "Abraham believed God, and it was reckoned to him as righteousness"; and he was called the friend of God. You see that a man is justified by works and not by faith alone. And in the same way was not also Rahab the harlot justified by works when she received the messengers and sent them out another way? For as the body apart from the spirit is dead, so faith apart from works is dead.

Faith and Works Seen from the Day of Judgment (2:14-17)

If James' argument about forgiveness was previously too abstract for his audience, it becomes quite clear here. Christians within the congregation are poorly clothed to the point of being naked and so hungry that they do not have enough food for a day's nourishment. Though the judgment of the Last Day is carried out on the basis of whether Christians have alleviated hunger, thirst, and nakedness among their co-believers (Matt. 25:35-36, 42-43), for his basic argument James does not use Matthew's abstraction of seeing Christ in the needy. Both in the judgment scene in Matthew and here in James, the needs of deprived Christians are the same. They are without the elemental needs of human existence. But now James directly indicts the offenders for their lack of concern for the poor and promises them condemnation, even though their religion in all other respects may conform itself to the proper norms. At this point James anticipates Paul in his discussion of faith and works.

The lack of charity seems to exist among the clergy, for whom the letter is chiefly intended. James specifically addresses this section to "my brethren," but goes on to speak of the needy brother and sister in the congregation. Would it not have been more appropriate for James to have addressed the congregation as "my brothers and sisters," if he intended to address the entire congregation here? If "brothers" embraces all in the congregation regardless of sex, then he should have referred only to the poorly clad brother without mentioning the sister. The clergy would have more easily been tempted to consider their absorption in church doctrine, ritual, and general organization as legitimate excuses for noninvolvement in charity. Somehow the man who says he has faith but does not have works could easily be one recognized as an authority in matters of the faith.

The question, "Can his faith save him?" is rhetorical and suggests no as the only answer. The ineffectiveness of faith at first glance seems at odds with Jesus, who says to the woman with the issue of blood that her faith has saved her (Matt. 9:22). This apparent contradiction about faith is resolved when James explains that the faith of the one who by lack of works shows no mercy is no faith at all: "So faith, by itself, if it has no works, is dead." Dead faith, that is, a faith without works, is no faith. It cannot save. The contradiction is resolved.

James assesses faith without works from an eschatological perspective. A faith without works will not stand the test on the Day of Judgment. The word "save" (*sōsai*) is in the future tense and does not speak directly to Paul's concern of whether he is justified now. James, like Jesus, views man and his relationship to God from the perspective of the Last Day. In a sense there is a realized eschatology. The Kingdom's coming involves not only death and resurrection but judgment. This makes the call to repentance in the preaching of John the Baptist so urgent (Matt. 3:7-10). The perspective of James is not so much present faith as final salvation, that is, whether the Christian will be acceptable to God on the Last Day. This helps in understanding the scene of the Last Judgment in Matthew 25, a perspective introduced as early as the Sermon on the Mount, where Jesus refuses salvation to the workers of iniquity (Matt. 7:21-23). This eschatological dimension so characteristic of James and so prominent in the New Testament era, beginning with John the Baptist (Matt. 3:7), is the development of a prophetic theme of the Old Testament. Found in the Psalms (98:9), the world judgment becomes prominent in the preaching of the later prophets (Hag. 2:6; Mal. 4:1).

The Peace Ritual in the Liturgy (2:16)

The comparison of faith and works to the body and breath, made by James in v. 26, is also basic for understanding v. 17, "So faith by itself, if it has no works, is dead." The use of the word "dead" suggests the corpse imagery. A dead faith has all the organic parts of a living faith but has no movement and does not do anything. It is just there. The vital force is

First Discussion on Justification (2:14-26) 89

missing. Such a faith can even be lively in worship as it is acquainted with the ritual but dead in works. It recognizes the needs of poor Christians but is incapable of responding to them.

The phrase "Go in peace," spoken to the destitute, could very well have been a formal part of the Christian synagogue worship.[1] The original Hebrew *shalom* may have been used. "Peace" was the greeting of the risen Jesus to His disciples (Luke 24:36) and became a standard greeting in the New Testament epistles (e.g., Rom. 1:7). The greeting of peace suggested that God through the atonement had adopted a posture of contentment, that is, peace, with the world (Luke 2:14). The kiss of peace suggested that Christians were content and forgiving with each other. The peace ritual was connected with the celebration of the Lord's Supper in the early church. Before its celebration all grievances had to be adjusted. The greeting, "Go in peace," suggests that the clergy understood the theological implications of the atonement but did not comprehend what this meant in their behavior to others, especially the poor. James' citing of the greeting of peace could be taken over directly from the specific ritual for the Lord's Supper, as this sacrament was more often and more widely celebrated then than now (Acts 2:42). Also in Corinth the division between the rich and the poor became a scandal in their celebration of the Lord's Supper (1 Cor. 11:20-22).

It should be noted that James does have some liturgical awareness, as the seating of the rich and poor in the synagogue worship service is a question of rubrics (2:1-4) and the next section makes reference to the creedal formula that God is one (2:19), a basic ingredient of the synagogue liturgy.

This chapter's last verses contain the theological conclusion to the very practical problem of Christians' failing to realize what God's atonement should mean in their attitude to others. Deference to the rich and the criminal ignoring of the poor contradicted God's generous attitude to all men in Christ. This paragraph also contains the section at which Luther took offense as he understood James as holding to a doctrine of justification of works in almost direct opposition to Paul's justification by grace.

Faith and Works (2:18)

The commentators have no agreement as to whom James is referring to as the speaker in the phrase, "But someone will say, 'You have faith and I have works'" (2:18). Who is the objector?[2] If these words are addressed to James, they do not fit, as James holds that his faith is seen in his works. Regardless of who is raising the objection, James concludes that salvation as eschatologically rewarded by Christ the Judge is by faith which manifests itself in works. The works that James calls for are identical with those which Christ finds in the justified on Judgment Day (Matt 25:35-40).

James can hardly be seen as putting faith in a position lower than works, since he is intent on demonstrating that his faith is indeed alive. James wants to talk about faith, not works! "Show me your faith apart from your works, and I by my works will show you my faith" (v. 18). Faith is the substance, and works are the characteristics of that substance. Let it be repeated: This is an exposition on faith, not works. James is not here speaking to the question of the Christian's own self-conscious awareness of faith so that he can convince himself of his acceptability before God now. Rather he is addressing the question of the Christian's faith and its acceptability from the perspective of the Last Day. His present behavior will provide faith's evidence for the Last Day and thus be determinative. James is making the standards of Judgment Day applicable to present behavior. The Christian performs his works, fully convinced that the line between today and the final day has been erased. Eschatology, Christ's judgment, has become present reality in the Christian life.

Throughout this section James seems to be using liturgical language for theological purposes. As he made use of the peace formula of the Lord's Supper, he makes use of the creed for his discussion on the nature of true faith.

Again to the Liturgy (2:19)

The phrase "You believe that God is one" is easily recognizable as being taken over from Deut. 6:4, the *Shema*, the basic creed for the Old Testament believer, maintained in early Christian worship. "Hear, O Israel: The Lord our God is one Lord" was used in an abbreviated form outside of Palestine (cf. 1-Cor. 8:6) and was carried over into the creeds of the early church. It survives in the Nicene Creed, which begins: "I believe in *one* God." Clearly James is referring to the recitation of this ancient Old Testament creed within the regular worship of the Christian synagogue.[3] There is no suggestion that James is taking exception to this traditional expression of Jewish orthodoxy which was completely accepted in the Christian community, as he commends the one making the confession (cf. Mark 12:28-30). The difficulty rests not in the confession itself but in the failure of that confession to come to proper expression within the Christian life.

What Christians were doing was hardly different from the devils who were intellectually aware of who God was, but shuddered at what God had in store for them.[4] Again James introduces the eschatological element in that those with an unproductive confession will have to account for their vain religion. As in other matters, James in handling the subject of demons supposes that his audience is so theologically well-versed that he never engages in the theological details. If the tradition later placed in the gospels was known to James' readers, then those accounts in which demons recognized what Jesus could do and who He was were also known to them (Mark 1:23-24; 5:1-13). An audience who knew that demons were not ignorant that Jesus was God's Son would not have difficulty comprehending that these same demons were informed about the unity of God.

Abraham and Rahab:
An Unlikely Combination of Examples of Justification

To clinch his argument that faith without works is useless, vain, and dead, James cites the examples of Abraham's offering Isaac as a sacrifice at the command of God and of Rahab's sheltering spies sent out by Joshua before the Hebrew invasion of Canaan. Both Abraham and Rahab are said to be justified by (*ex*), i.e., 'out of' their works (2:21, 24-25). There is no reason to take James' understanding of justification as any other than a forensic justification. The imagery is that of the divine courtroom. Rather than seeing James as a reaction against a radical Pauline concept of justification by grace without works but through faith, Paul may in fact be dependent on James. Consider Paul's use of Gen. 15:6. Rom. 4:3 is identical to James 2:23 in its citation of Gen. 15:6: "Abraham believed God, and it was reckoned to him as righteousness."

Abraham's Faith and Sacrifice (2:20-22)

James handles the case of Abraham at slightly greater length. The original justification of Abraham in his being called by God and his acceptance of that call (Gen. 12:1-4) is manifested to all when he so submits himself to God that he is willing to sacrifice his son (Gen. 22). James wants his audience to see Abraham's entire life, and not simply one deed, as a manifestation of his faith. Abraham's faith meant a life of obedience. God was putting Abraham's faith to the test between the time when he was first called and his offering up of his son Isaac, a period of some 30 years. The Abraham story in Genesis then quickly comes to a close with the death of Sarah (ch. 23), obtaining a bride for Isaac (ch. 24), and his remarriage and death (25:1-11). James' use of Abraham, who waited long for the fulfillment, fits perfectly the opening theme of the epistle to remain faithful under suffering even when it appears that God has deserted the church. At this point James alludes to Christ's sacrificial death.

On Abraham's sacrifice of Isaac it has been observed that "Jews implore the mercy of God by the sacrifice of Abraham, as Christians by the sacrifice of Christ." The word used for altar (*thusiastērion*) is the same as that used for Jewish ritual sacrifice and for the altar associated with Christ, the sacrificial Lamb, in the Book of Revelation (14:18). In the Sermon on the Mount Jesus speaks of reconciliation with the brother before offering the gift at the altar (Matt. 5:23-24). Atonement is not a developed theme in James, but the use of the word "altar" suggests a common awareness of it. The altar existed in the Jewish cult to proclaim the need for atonement before reconciliation. In the case of Abraham it was not he but God who provided the lamb for the sacrifice (Gen. 22:13-14). The altar was at the center of Jewish worship, and James' use of the word would by itself suggest atonement and sacrifice.

V. 22, "You see that faith was active along with his works, and faith was completed by his works," answers James' own questions on faith and works. Here James is using faith in the Pauline sense of trust in God and not simply knowledge of the truth. In v. 19 the faith of devils is simply knowledge of the revealed truth. Abraham's faith, "active along with his works," was his faith that God would restore Isaac back to life, if the sacrifice had been completed. This is precisely the argument of Heb. 11:17-19. The argument about faith being seen in works is the major theme of that entire chapter, whose central character is Abraham. It is hard to avoid the conclusion of a direct dependence here on James.[5]

James is so theologically precise that he avoids saying that works follow faith in favor of "faith was active along with his works." Works follow faith in a logical but not temporal sense. As soon as faith is conceived, it has no other choice but to express itself in activity. Even before faith can contemplate itself, it is busy in carrying out God's will. Though such a view may be easily recognized as Luther's, it has earlier roots in James.

The RSV translation "faith was completed by works" can be misleading because it may suggest that faith is in some way defective. For James faith contemplated by itself is inadequate. Rather, by works faith is brought to the goal for which it was intended. Works in the Christian life are a natural and unforced maturing of faith.[6]

Abraham's sacrifice of Isaac is viewed as the fulfillment of Gen. 15:6: "[Abraham] believed the Lord; and He reckoned it to him as righteousness." James' claim that "the Scripture was fulfilled" could raise a question, since the Scriptures would only come into existence some centuries after Abraham. Superficially it would mean that they were written after they were fulfilled. For James Scripture is of such high authority that it becomes personified as God's living voice. Paul follows the same procedure in Gal. 3:8: "And the Scripture, foreseeing that God would justify the Gentiles by faith, preached the Gospel beforehand to Abraham." So similar is Paul to James that it seems certain that Paul is here using James. Gen. 15:6 is a Mosaic editorial notation, written centuries later, that Abraham's faith was considered as righteousness before God. Now James observes that in Abraham's willingness to sacrifice Isaac God was vindicated in having justified him. Abraham was justified before the sacrifice took place, but the sacrifice proved it.[7]

There is no explicit Scripture which refers to the occasion when Abraham was called God's friend, though Abraham's close association with God is beyond dispute. The Septuagint in handling Gen. 18:17, "Shall I hide from Abraham what I am about to do?" calls Abraham "God's child," and Philo in citing this calls him "God's friend." Jehoshaphat calls him "God's friend" (2 Chron. 20:7). In the New Testament John the Baptist calls himself "the friend of the bridegroom" (John 3:29). James will later warn against being a friend of the world and an enemy of God (4:4).

Abraham's high status of being considered God's friend can be only understood in the light of what has been considered for so long as the Pauline doctrine of justification by faith. Abraham so totally relies on God that God can only respond to Abraham with the same type of intimate relationship. Luther understood faith as total trust in God. To be sure, God cannot have faith, but God can and does respond to the believer by confiding in him what He intends to do. Jesus speaks of revealing divine secrets to the disciples (Matt. 13:11), and Paul speaks of "a secret and hidden wisdom of God" (1 Cor. 2:7). Jesus' calling His disciples brothers (Matt. 28:10) resembles God's calling Abraham a friend. Faith means that God shares an intimate relationship with the believer.

"You see that a man is justified by works and not by faith alone" (v. 24) again is a reference to the eschatological justification, as James places the works of Abraham before the congregation as the evidence for his being considered justified by God. From the perspective of the Last Day, God will demonstrate Abraham as justified to all, holding up his willingness to sacrifice Isaac as the evidence.[8]

James Introduces Gen. 15:6 into the Justification Discussion (2:23-24)

James, as the first New Testament writer, introduced the use of Gen. 15:6 into the early church discussion on justification. James, writing to a situation of cold callousness, showed how justification by faith fleshed itself out in the life of Abraham. Paul, writing to a situation where works were preached as necessary for earning salvation, saw justification as complete in the moment of faith (Gal. 3:6). If James were teaching a doctrine of justification by works, especially as an antidote to an antinomian perversion of Paul's theology of grace, he would have destroyed his own argument in quoting Gen. 15:6, which ascribes justification to faith and makes no mention of works. Clearly he was not so ignorant either of theological argument or of the Old Testament. James' quotation of Gen. 15:6 proves the exact opposite of his often- alleged doctrine of a justification by works.[9] It is preposterous that a writer as careful and so literally gifted as James would have chosen an Old Testament passage proving the exact opposite of what he was attempting to demonstrate.

James' phrase, literally "justification out of works," uses the preposition "out of, from" (*ek, ex*) and not "through" (*dia*) as Paul uses with faith. While Paul speaks to the question of the personal inward appropriation of righteousness through faith, James addresses the question of how the righteous are identifiable in the world. For Paul the question is: How do I know that I am justified? For James the question is: How does the world know I am justified? Abraham was accepted as righteous before God through faith (Paul), but he was recognized as righteous to the world and to the succession of believers for all time through his willing obedience to sacrifice his son Isaac at God's command (James). Paul and James are speaking to the same forensic reality in which the believer appears before God as the Judge. The believer through faith accepts Christ's righteousness as his own and is viewed by God as righteous (Paul). By works the Christian vindicates God's verdict of righteousness on him by demonstrating to the world the correctness of that verdict (James).

It is no coincidence that James later mentions Job as an example of patience (5:11 KJV). In the Book of Job, God's verdict of righteousness on him is vindicated because Job persists in his faith and does not renounce God. The heavenly courtroom is the scene where Satan challenges God concerning Job's righteousness (Job 1:6-12; 2:1-6). Job is considered righteous by God before the testing, but God's righteous verdict on Job is only later vindicated to Satan in particular by his persistence.[10]

The examples of Abraham and Rahab are striking in contrast. Abraham is the central figure in the Book of Genesis, and Rahab a passing footnote in the conquest of Canaan. Though Abraham can be called our father in faith by non-Jewish Christians, within the context of a letter that breathes the air of the Christian synagogue Abraham must be father both in blood and faith. The argument would lose some of its force if Abraham were held up only as the father in faith. What would make a convincing impression on these Jewish Christians was their failure to act like their common and most admired progenitor (cf. John 8:39-40).

The Superior Faith of Rahab (2:25)

The inclusion of Rahab as an example of works by James would be less problematical if the congregation addressed were facing the crisis of Gentile Christians in their services. But there is no evidence for this. Outside of the reference to Rahab there is no hint that James is at all concerned about Gentiles entering the congregations. The inclusion of Gentiles in the church was later a major problem for Christian Jews, but it does not seem one at this time. Matthew in writing the genealogy of Jesus included her with Ruth, though women are usually not included in Jewish genealogies. In Matthew's gospel Rahab and Ruth are included because as Gentiles they are examples of those who believe the message which was intended for the Jews and not for them. They are prototypes of the Canaanite woman who believed in Jesus, even though He explicitly stated that His ministry did not embrace her (Matt. 15:22-28). Rahab is the ancestress of David and part of the Messianic line leading to Jesus. Matthew's message is that Gentiles have always had a place in God's plan of salvation.

Abraham is an example of works because he follows God's explicit command in his willingness to sacrifice Isaac. By contrast Rahab is given no explicit command. She carries out God's will without command. She is in fact a better example than Abraham in demonstrating that faith must express itself in works, as she acts in response to no specific directive. Since she believes that God has chosen Israel as His own nation, she decides on her own initiative to do everything in her power to protect the representatives of God's nation. For this reason she provides a haven for the Hebrew spies and helps them escape back to their own lines (Joshua 2). The early Jewish Christians are really without excuse, because they had been given explicit directives for helping the poor in the preaching of Jesus as it was handed down to them. Even without such explicit directives, they should have drawn the theological conclusion and recognized the poor as sharing a special close relationship with Jesus. Rahab, the Gentile harlot, had drawn a theological conclusion to which they had been totally blind. They had the direct revelation. She did not![11]

The Imagery of the Body and Breath (Not Body and Soul) (2:26)

"For as the body apart from the spirit is dead, so faith apart from works is dead" seems strange if, as Mayor notes, "the visible part of man should be

First Discussion on Justification (2:14-26)

compared to the invisible principle of faith, and the invisible spirit compared to works which are the outward fruits of faith."[12] But is James comparing faith to the human body and works to a human soul? No! James here is not using the analogy of body and soul as constituting the essence of man, but the analogy of the body and the breath, which comes from the lungs. James' approach throughout has been concrete and less philosophically abstract. He describes how something works and less its nature. If James here by the Greek *pneuma* is referring to the spirit or soul, that part of man by which he resembles God, endures death, and is invisible, such an argument would be useless, as the soul or spirit cannot serve as proof or evidence, simply because the soul cannot easily be empirically demonstrated. Such an argument would be very uncharacteristic of James. Throughout he has been referring to the proof of faith by works. Why would he now compare visible works to the invisible soul? A theologically sophisticated man simply would not make such a blatant blunder!

James here is referring to the not-so-uncommon problem of determining whether a body is really dead. One way to determine this is placing a mirror by the nostrils to see if a mist forms on the glass. Without the moisture from the breath on the glass, the body can be assumed dead, a corpse. It is as if James were saying that a body without a pulse is dead. A faith without works has all the right appearances but, like a corpse without breath, it has no functions and hence is pronounced dead. Breath proves life, but does not cause it. Similarly works prove faith, but do not cause it.

James the Apostle of Faith:
The Second Defense and Summation

It simply will not do to understand James' view of faith as only intellectual knowledge which must express itself in works before it begins to resemble the Pauline understanding of faith. Such a truncated view of faith in James comes from trying to see that James has only one meaning for the words for faith (*pistis*) and believing (*pisteuein*). In the opening pericopes (1:2-4 and 1:5-8) faith can only have the traditionally Pauline understanding of total reliance upon God to accomplish for the Christian the promises made to him in the Gospel. James' encouragement to pray in faith (v. 6) can in no way refer to mere intellectual knowledge. Here it means *fiducia*, total trust in God.[13]

The encouragement to hold the faith of Jesus Christ, our Lord of glory (2:1), offers the grammatical possibility of several interpretations, all of which may be acceptable. It can mean an encouragement either to believe in Jesus Christ as the Lord of glory or to maintain the faith, the doctrinal substance, *corpus doctrinae,* the *fides quae*, which Jesus, who is our Lord of glory, gave. This interpretation seems more comfortable here since there follow instructions on how Christians are to show impartiality, Christ's virtue shown in His atonement. This, however, does not exhaust the meaning, since this is the faith which was not only handed over to the church by Jesus, *fides quae*, but to which Jesus Himself steadfastly held. Christians are to believe what Jesus believed and *in the way* in which He believed it. The *fides quae*, the doctrine, and the *fides qua*, trust in God, are marvelously joined in James.

James' great discussion on faith follows in the same chapter, 2:14-26. Here James shows wide diversity in utilizing this word. Three times James will refer to faith as either dead or barren (vv. 17, 20, 26). In these references James understands faith in its ordinary usage as a living reality, otherwise the adjectives "dead" or "barren" would be redundant descriptions. James is saying that everything which has the appearance of faith is not really the *true* faith at all. In no way can it be shown that for James the primary meaning of faith here is mere intellectual knowledge. Since faith is a vital reality for James, negative adjectives are necessary to describe unbelief posing as belief.

Where James does deprecate the saving value of a dead faith—which is no faith at all—he never attributes any salvific quality to works. This belongs to faith alone. Saving faith is present and identifiable where works are being performed. Faith which exists autonomously, without works, is not even worthy to be considered faith at all. James' reference to the faith of demons is not the controlling reference for his understanding of faith. The devils have a faith without works pleasing to God, and they can only be considered as God's enemies with no faith, i.e., a dead faith. Intellectual knowledge about God without trust in Him to carry out what He wants is not worthy of even being called faith. The case of Abraham is informative, because his believing in God constituted his entire life's story. His faith was not a momentary flash but his life's guiding principle. It required him to obey God in all things to the point of sacrificing everything he had, including his son.

The memory of James is defamed if he is considered an apostle of works. He deserves, along with Paul and even before him, the title "the apostle of faith." James was the first to call attention to the theological freight in Gen. 15:6: "[Abraham] believed the Lord; and he reckoned it to him as righteousness." Later it was Paul in writing Romans and Galatians who developed that thought in the church. Romans 4 and Gal. 3:6-9 show a certain dependence for style, argument, and example on James 2:21-24.

XI/Again to the Pastoral Task (3:1-18)

1 *Let not many of you become teachers, my brethren, for you know that we who teach shall be judged with greater strictness. For we all make many mistakes, and if anyone makes no mistakes in what he says he is a perfect man, able to bridle the whole body also. If we put bits into the mouths of horses that they may obey us, we guide their whole bodies. Look at the ships also; though they are so great and are driven by strong winds, they are guided by a very small rudder wherever the will of the pilot directs. So the tongue is a little member and boasts of great things. How great a forest is set ablaze by a small fire!*

6 *And the tongue is a fire. The tongue is an unrighteous world among our members, staining the whole body, setting on fire the cycle of nature, and set on fire by hell. For every kind of beast and bird, of reptile and sea creature, can be tamed and has been tamed by humankind, but no human being can tame the tongue—a restless evil, full of deadly poison. With it we bless the Lord and Father, and with it we curse men, who are made in the likeness of God. From the same mouth come blessing and cursing. My brethren, this ought not to be so. Does a spring pour forth from the same opening fresh water and brackish? Can a fig tree, my brethren, yield olives, or a grapevine figs? No more can salt water yield fresh.*

13 *Who is wise and understanding among you? By his good life let him show his works in the meekness of wisdom. But if you have bitter jealousy and selfish ambition in your hearts, do not boast and be false to the truth. This wisdom is not such as comes down from above, but is earthly, unspiritual, devilish. For where jealousy and selfish ambition exist, there will be disorder and every vile practice. But the wisdom from above is first pure, then peaceable, gentle, open to reason, full of mercy and good fruits, without uncertainty or insincerity. And the harvest of righteousness is sown in peace by those who make peace.*

Preaching and Doctrine (3:1-12)

The third chapter has practical advice for those who are entrusted with the church's preaching tasks. As previously mentioned, James has the marks of of a pastoral epistle, even though as with other New Testament pastoral epistles most of the general principles are applicable to the entire Christian congregation. Chapter 3 addresses the issue of how sermons are to be delivered and what should constitute their content.

"Let not many [of you] become teachers (*didaskaloi*), my brethren, for you know that we who teach shall be judged with greater strictness" (3:1) puts the pastoral office within the context of the eschatological judgment of the Last Day. Though the letter is addressed to "the twelve tribes in the Dispersion," here as in several other places (1:2, 19; 2:1) James speaks to the addressees as "my brethren." It is not necessary to understand 3:1 as a general address to the congregation whose members were considering themselves for the pastoral office. The phrase "of you" in "let not many *of you* become teachers" is added in translations but is not in the original. It should be taken as an admonition to those who are already holding the pastoral office to exercise the teaching function of explaining doctrine with great care or to leave it to others.

Though Jesus' chief purpose in His incarnation was giving His life as a ransom, He functioned among the people and the disciples as preacher and teacher. He was the only Revealer of the divine (Matt. 7:28-29). Jesus also understood that officially recognized teachers would have the obligation of perpetuating what He did after He was gone (Matt. 28:20) and that those holding the office would have a higher degree of accountability before God at the judgment. James' warning concerning the seriousness in which teaching was to be exercised reflects Jesus' warning in the Sermon on the Mount: "Whoever then relaxes one of the least of these commandments and teaches (*didachē*) men so, shall be called least in the kingdom of heaven" (Matt. 5:19).[1]

The warning in the Sermon about correct teaching comes immediately after the promise of Jesus to maintain the prophetic written revelation in its totality. The divine Word, with alphabetical precision, as it was given, shall remain in place even on the Day of Judgment and can be tampered with by the appointed teachers only at the eschatological risk of receiving the least favorable verdict at that time. James' rendition seems to be dependent on the same oral tradition that would later be inscripturated into the Sermon, as he also makes reference to clergy receiving the greater judgment (*meizon krima*) (3:1).

The outline of the early church's organization as it is reflected in Acts (12:17, 13:1, and 15, especially vv. 6, 7, 22, and 23) can also be seen in James' admonition to clergy in 3:1. The address to the clergy is not only demonstrated by calling them brothers but by James' self-inclusion in their group.[2] Instead of reading "for *you* know," read "for *we* know that we who teach shall receive the greater judgment." In the early church the apostles were soon joined by others who held the pastoral office with them. Together the apostles and pastors held the doctrinal responsibility.

In Antioch Paul's place of authority was based more on his holding the pastoral office and not his apostolic office, as he is there listed simply as

Again to the Pastoral Task (3:1-18)

belonging to the clergy in the local church. They were called "prophets and teachers," terms reflecting their preaching and doctrinal responsibilities (Acts 13:1). A fledgling apostle would only cause disharmony by calling attention among other pastors to the full dimensions of his apostolic office. Paul would not want to add to the early resentment against him because of his persecuting the church. James, a man of more prominence than Paul at this time, admonishes the clergy as a fellow pastor and not an apostle, an office which was certainly his.

In Jerusalem the clergy are called "the apostles and the elders" (Acts 15:6) and in Antioch "prophets and teachers" (Acts 13:1). In Eph. 4:11 Paul calls this same type of group "pastors and teachers." The selected terms referring to the clergy seem to be determined by the function the writer is emphasizing. They are called "prophets" if the kerygmatic or preaching function is stressed. "Teachers" puts the stress on their function of maintaining the doctrinal heritage as it was given them by Jesus through the apostolic tradition. James, like Jesus, gives a severe eschatological warning to those who have the teaching or doctrinal obligations of the clerical office. If derelict, their offense is tantamount to tampering with the divinely given Word itself and making the revelation of no value.

James' admonitions concerning the proper use of the tongue has its specific target in the clergy,[3] but the general arguments are by extension, of course, applicable to all Christians. The reference to the perfect man who is able to refrain from sinning or from making mistakes when he speaks follows James' warning about too quickly assuming the task of explaining Christian doctrine. He is not speaking about absolute sinlessness or even proposing it as a possibility. In the first part of this very verse James rules out any possibility that Christians can avoid sin in their lives, but it is possible for them to avoid making mistakes in their official speaking as preachers. The preacher who properly conveys the divine message is called "a perfect man." Several problems are presented here. What are meant by sinning, making mistakes, and a perfect man? Since all make mistakes, a perfect man cannot be one who overcomes sin in his life. In the light of 3:1 with its special warning for teachers, a perfect (*teleios*) man would be one who conforms his teachings as pastor to the words of Jesus. Perfection here describes not so much the moral quality of the person, but rather the understanding of God's mind, from which perspective he refrains from bringing down curses upon those redeemed by God (3:10). He not only understands God's loving attitude to men, but is able to express it in his preaching and teaching. He resembles the wise man in the Sermon on the Mount who builds his house on a sure foundation (Matt. 7:24-25).

The First Letter of John presents the same type of dilemma about sinless perfection by saying Christians deceive themselves if they claim no sin (1:8) and then seemingly contradicts that by saying that the one who commits sin is of the devil (3:8). Both James and John are agreed in seeing the helplessness of the Christian in overcoming the sinfulness of his nature, which still remains after conversion. The sin which John sees as coming from the devil is a deliberate conspiratorial attitude which despises God and His will.

James considers himself a person who has known the will of God and who has offended against it, since he finds in himself forces which he cannot at all times control.[4]

The analogy of the rudder has even more interesting possibilities. In 2 Peter 2:17 the false teachers are compared to directionless winds, unlike the holy writers, who are directed (*pheromenoi*) by the Holy Spirit (*pneumatos hagiou* 1:21). Heb. 13:9 gives a warning about being "led away (*parapheresthe*) by diverse and strange teachings." Paul in Eph. 4:14 also uses nautical language in describing the haplessness of Christians confronted by false doctrines. "So that we may no longer be children, tossed to and fro and carried about by every wind of doctrine (*peripheromenoi panti anemō tēs didaskalias*)."

With the analogy of the tossed wave James in 1:6 was speaking of the doctrinal directionlessness of Christian pastors, as he is again doing with the ship's rudder in 3:4. The pastors' first obligation is to keep their evil natures so under control that they do not abruptly express themselves, and their second is setting a straight course which does not succumb to every change of doctrine they encounter. With these illustrations of the bridle and the rudder James is offering a positive directive for use of the tongue. Slipping into doctrinal mistakes can be avoided in the same way. Bo Reicke sees James' image of the ship as a reference to the church, with the rudder as the pastor.[5] If this is so, then the tongue ruining the body refers to the pastor's influence in the church.

After describing the force of the tongue (3:3-5a), James indicts the evil of the tongue and the great damage it can inflict on others (3:5b-12). When let loose, it can have the destructive power of a forest fire. The tongue, which can control people, cannot itself be controlled. It is difficult to avoid seeing here the power of the pastoral office and the great evil brought by false preaching.

In spite of sin, man can still exercise the dominion given him by God over the animal creation. "For every kind of beast and bird, of reptile and sea creature, can be tamed ... by humankind" (3:7) is a direct reflection of God's decision to make man lord over creation. "Let us make man in our image, after our likeness; and let them have dominion over the fish of the sea, and over the birds of the air, and over the cattle, and over all the earth, and over every creeping thing that creeps upon the earth" (Gen. 1:26). The tongue is the one thing over which man is incapable of exercising dominion. In fact, just the opposite is true. The tongue exercises dominion over the speaker and, left unchecked, eventually brings him and his listeners to damnation.

James views the tongue as a fire and as that member of the body, that is, the church, which can bring it to the destruction of hell. In Matthew fire is understood as hell's punishment for unbelievers. This is true of the preaching of John the Baptist (3:10-12) and then later of Jesus' preaching in the Sermon on the Mount (5:22) and the Kingdom parables (13:40, 42). James sees the tongue as both the source of fire and a fire set and controlled by hell. The tongue is hell's instrument in time. Understanding of fire as judgment is common to John the Baptist, Jesus, and James. James' understanding of the tongue as part of the body which, left unchecked, can destroy the body is similar to Jesus' warning of the Christian to rid himself of an offending eye or hand if its continued sin results in the damnation of the total body (Matt. 5:29-30).

The surface meaning of plucking out eyes and amputating limbs could be resolved if Jesus is referring to the church as a body. The unchecked sin of one member, especially the pastor, can soon destroy the whole body. In both James and the Sermon on the Mount the unchecked sin of one part of the body results in the damnation of the total body. James does not follow Jesus in suggesting radical surgery for the offending member of the body, as James calls for productive and remedial restitution and not destruction of the tongue. For Jesus the important part is the eye, whose failure to understand divine things darkens the entire body, that is, the church. For James it is the tongue. Both eye and tongue could refer to the pastoral office. The eye comprehends the truth and the tongue preaches it. Comprehending the truth and preaching it constitute the proper functioning of the office.

By referring to the tongue's blessing of the Lord and Father, James is showing the discrepancy between the formal liturgy of the Christian synagogue worship conducted by these pastors and the cursings normally coming out of their mouths (3:9).[6] A theological discrepancy is caused because men in their creation as God's image resemble Him but fail to see the image in others. The early church clergy were guilty of this. As in the reference to controlling all creatures, James with the image of God in man again is commenting on Gen. 1:26-27. Again the theme is repeated that a Christian cannot have one attitude to God and another to God's human creatures.

Perhaps James is here referring to ordinary banal cursing. But there could be an allusion to the type of preaching going on in the congregation, in which some people were led to the impression that they were unworthy of God's salvation. These preachers may have taken to themselves the eschatological prerogatives of Christ in sentencing the damned (Matt. 25:41). Within the same church service, the same preaching praised God and then uttered sharp condemnatory messages on the congregation. This explains that "from the same mouth come blessing and cursing" (3:10).

James, like John the Baptist and like Jesus in the Sermon on the Mount, finds a person's essential nature necessarily reflected in what that person does. If those who come to John are truly repentant, they must produce the works of repentance (Matt. 3:8). A man's action cannot contradict what he really is. Grapevines can produce figs as little as fig trees can produce grapes (cf. James 3:12). James' argument here is only an adjustment of Jesus' argument in the Sermon on the Mount: "You will know them by their fruits. Are grapes gathered from thorns, or figs from thistles?" (Matt. 7:16). Perhaps James is reconstructing a saying of Jesus; here might be another example of an original saying of Jesus which was not retained in the Gospel accounts.

Why James makes no mention of thorns or thistles, as they are both non-productive, is a problem. Both fig trees and grapevines are productive. Thorns and thistles are not. Where James and Jesus preach a message of condemnation in similar terms, James is more likely to be the more lenient in expression. The reason for this is that Jesus is the eschatological Judge appearing in time. James is not. The saying in the Sermon on the Mount is placed within a setting of eschatological condemnation which threatens destruction to every non-fruit-bearing tree (Matt. 7:16-20). James does not add this threat here, but the use of the agricultural and horticultural imagery carries with it the implication that the plant or tree not performing its assigned and expected function must face removal and burning.[7] Could it be that James by adjusting the imagery is indicting Christians not for unbelief but for assuming positions in the church not assigned them?

For the illustration of finding both pure and salty water at the same spring or well (3:11-12) James does not seem to be directly dependent on any other Biblical writer. Just as a tree cannot produce two kinds of fruit, so a spring or well must be consistent in what it produces. But why the illustration of the pure and salty water? The impossibility of the interchangeability of grapes and figs seems less drastic than Jesus' use of grapes and thorns and figs and thistles. In the case of the water, one type is acceptable and the other definitely not. In John's gospel "water" refers to the preaching of the Gospel, Baptism, and Jesus as living water (John 4:10-15). It certainly cannot be absolutely shown that James is making such a Christological allusion, but the illustration in some way might be reflecting Jesus' calling Himself "living water." This could mean that the preacher cannot declare Christ and then deliver a message that destroys this salvation. James is sufficiently creative to take the imagery of Christ as the water and to develop the imagery of condemnatory preaching as foul water.

An Addendum to a Most Difficult Section

Peter Davids is tantalized by Reicke's suggestion that the boat refers to the church, the rudder to the pastor's influence, and the tongue to the preaching function, but he remains finally unconvinced himself.[8] For Davids vv. 3-5a contain material difficult to analyze. Structural form, textual difficulties, and unusual vocabulary with many *hapax legomena* all compound the difficulty. The entire section (3:1-12) makes references to body, horses, bits, mouths, ships, winds, rudder, pilot, tongue, fire, forest, different types of water, fig tree, olives, and grapevine in quick succession. The imagery is quite graphic in the ear of the listener but less capable of detailed grammatical analysis. The listener hearing the message read would have no difficulty following it, but scholars remain unagreed how this all fits together.

Davids gives a clue to solving the problem when he notes that in the same section James is not using the word "tongue" in the same way. Thus in the reference in vv. 2-5a "tongue" is used in a positive way, as a directing force, but beginning in v. 5b it is used in a negative way, as a source of evil. James is

Again to the Pastoral Task (3:1-18) 103

a master in using the same words in different but not totally unrelated ways in the same section.

Davids concedes that Reicke's suggestion that the boat and body imagery refers to the church is attractive since 3:1 mentions teachers and the boat was an early popular image for the church. The boat imagery is taken from Matt. 8:23, and the body imagery was popularized by Paul. The first problem comes in identifying the imagery of putting bits into horses' mouths. This is not a metaphor but only an illustration of how the control of the mouth guarantees the control of the entire body. Thus 3:1 with its eschatological warning about teachers assuming too quickly the role of explaining Christian doctrine is followed by v. 2 with its statement that teachers do make mistakes in preaching but can control the body, i.e., the church, through Gospel preaching. V. 3 illustrates that the church can be as easily controlled by the pastor as a horse can be controlled by the bit in its mouth. In v. 2 body (*sōma*) refers to the church, and in v. 3 it refers to the actual body of the horse. V. 4 with its reference to the ship is not an illustration like the bit in the horse's mouth, but an extended metaphor or parable. This would be one example of a New Testament parable not taught by Jesus. James is asking his readers to consider the churches or congregations as large boats which safely pass through storms under the guidance of a skilled navigator, i.e., a pastor, who exercises the preaching office with careful precision. The adverse winds or storms are doctrinal problems which threaten to shipwreck the congregations. The pastor can steer through them, threatening as they are. V. 5a switches the imagery by referring to the teacher in his preaching office, no longer as the pilot who controls the rudder, but as the tongue. The tongue is small like the rudder and when properly controlled can be beneficial in its preaching, which guides the church.

In v. 5b the tongue is no longer thought of in a metaphorical sense to refer to the preacher, but as an actual part of the body as it engages in preaching. The RSV by not putting a paragraph division between 5a and 5b, as some Greek texts do, makes it appear that the tongue in vv. 3-5a is used in a negative sense. V. 5b, with its reference to the force of a fire, begins a new section. It does not conclude the previous one. In this section James is, however, referring specifically to the tongues of preachers, though a general reference could be drawn. Specifically James is referring to the heavily laden Law sermons—fire suggests hell—which are constantly condemning their congregations. These Law sermons stand in clear contradiction to the church's liturgy, where the Gospel centering in God the Father and the Lord Jesus is proclaimed, perhaps a reference to the early creed of the church (v. 9).

To demonstrate the impossibility of the situation, James uses the illustrations of fig trees producing olives or grapevines yielding figs and one spring gushing sweet and foul water at the same time. These things simply do not happen. Where the Law is confused with the Gospel, the result is not half of each, but rather condemning Law. This is evident from 12b, "No more can salt water yield fresh." Sweet water coming from a salt spring will automatically be contaminated as salty. Even the Gospel coming from a preacher who usually condemns the congregation with the Law will sound not as Gospel but as Law. James' sharp warning against using the pastoral office as an opportunity for condemning the congregation is followed by explanations of how the Gospel should be preached.

Preachers Standing in Christ's Stead (3:13-18)

This pericope with its pointed jabs at the wise and knowledgeable would most fittingly describe the clergy who had become boastful of their own abilities and envious of the talents of their colleagues. James' admonition for a proper use of wisdom and knowledge is not unlike Paul's enumeration of the gifts of the Holy Spirit: "To each is given the manifestation of the Spirit for the common good. To one is given through the Spirit the utterance of wisdom, and to another the utterance of knowledge according to the same Spirit" (1 Cor. 12:7-8).

There are indications that in both pericopes Paul and James are addressing the problem of a clergy caught up in their own self-esteem because of their erudition. James does not deprecate their mental and intellectual gifts but directs them to a fuller understanding of what God's wisdom really involves.

True wisdom (*sophia*), used three times here by James, is the central theme of this section.[9] That James is addressing individuals who professionally were involved in the church's doctrinal task is suggested by several things. First, in 3:1 James addresses specifically the particular class of teachers of whom he was one. Second, in addition to singling out some as wise, he also refers to them as understanding or knowledgeable (*epistēmōn*). Mayor, commenting on this word used only here in the New Testament, remarks that it is "used in classical Greek for a skilled or scientific person as opposed to one who has no special knowledge or training."[10] The reference thus could hardly fit the laity, even those with slightly-above-average knowledge. Rather the evidence points to a group of men who had received their knowledge of Christianity in a precise, detailed manner, over a longer period of time, not unlike the way Jesus communicated His teaching to His disciples. The recipients of this epistle had probably been instructed by James and the other apostles in Jerusalem, as the Corinthian clergy had been instructed by Paul. In both cases their theological knowledge had become a source of boastful pride.

James' challenge to these clergy to show from their good behavior (*deixatō ek tēs kalēs anastrophēs*) their works in the meekness of wisdom is similar to the challenge he puts upon himself in 2:18: "I by my works will show (*deixō ek tōn ergōn*) you my faith." Again, James is addressing the central problem of this epistle, that their outward behavior or works were contradicting what they publicly professed. The quality of meekness does not refer to a hypocritical show of humbleness but to the Christological, self-effacing humility which does not call attention to itself.

James, however, is not so superficial as to understand behavior and works as autonomous activities without any internal moral implications.

Quite to the contrary! Their ill behavior is a direct result of a nature which is opposed to God. James is no Pelagian! In discussing acceptable and unacceptable behavior among the clergy, James in this section resembles Paul's division of works as either fleshly or spiritual: "Now the works of the flesh are plain: immorality, impurity, licentiousness, idolatry, sorcery, enmity, strife, jealousy, anger, selfishness, dissension, party spirit, envy, drunkenness, carousing, and the like.... But the fruit of the Spirit is love, joy, peace, patience, kindness, goodness, faithfulness, gentleness, self-control ..." (Gal. 5:19-23).

Both James and Paul agree in seeing jealousy (*zēlos*) and envy (*eritheia*) as unacceptable qualities and peace as a virtue. James parallels Jesus in Matt. 18:35 in seeing the heart as the source of all evils, whereas Paul resembles the Johannine picture of Jesus, placing the source of evil in the flesh (John 3:6). Matthew is not so unlike John, in that he also knows of the flesh as that part of human existence which is most receptive to Satan's working (26:41; cf. also 16:17).

Good works are attributed by James to the wisdom from above and by Paul to the Holy Spirit. The dualism between the works of God and those of Satan is a theme common to James, the synoptic gospels, Paul, and John. James' readers are combatting no simple problem of mere ethical behavior, but one which afflicts their inborn, yes, inherited natures. All sorts of evil practices arise from "bitter jealousy" and "selfish ambition" within their hearts (vv. 14, 16). James' indictment of their hearts as the real source of their problems carries more than a faint resemblance to these words of Jesus: "For out of the heart come evil thoughts, murder, adultery, fornication, theft, false witness, slander" (Matt. 15:19). The evil perpetrated by his readers is called "earthly, unspiritual, devilish (*epigeios, psuchikē, daimoniōdēs*)," a triad which is clearly the equivalent of Luther's "the world, the flesh, and the devil." Recognizing this similarity makes Luther's distaste for James all the more astonishing.

"Earthly" is used by Jesus in His discussion with Nicodemus concerning human illustrations to make divine truth more understandable. Such illustrations should be comprehended by everyone since they are not the divine truths themselves but vehicles for them (John 3:12). For these the assistance of the Spirit is not needed. Paul uses the term "earthly" to describe the thought processes of those whose god is their belly and who are destined to eternal destruction (Phil. 3:19). "Earthly," which corresponds with Luther's "world," refers to those who have no living awareness of God and so let their thoughts and behavior be governed only by what is observable in the world. Materialistic might cover Luther's "world" and James' "earthly."

"Unspiritual," sometimes rendered in English as "fleshly,"speaks of the condition of a man in his preoccupation with this world. In 1 Cor. 2:13-14 Paul distinguishes between the spiritual person and the fleshly or unspiritual one. While the former comprehends the things of God, the latter does not. The word for unspiritual or fleshly (*psuchikos*) is derived from the word for soul (*psuchē*). The incorporeal part of man which survives death is called either spirit (*pneuma*) (1 Peter 3:18) or soul (*psuchē*) (Rev. 6:9). Though both words describe the incorporeal part of man, "spirit" is used as man contemplates God and "soul" as he contemplates the world he lives in. The unspiritual or fleshly (*psuchikos*) man has directed all the concerns of his soul to his existence in this world.[11] For Luther this internal obsession with this life is called "the flesh."

"Devilish" is last in the triad and is self-explanatory. People who do not share the divine perspective of life are under the control of Satan, but this influence is not direct but exercised through an evil angel, i.e., a demon. James' use of *daimoniōdēs* indicates his awareness of this same type of distinction between Satan and his evil angels. Luther remarked that Satan is omnipresent not in his nature but through the demons.[12] Even though justification can and must be seen in behavior, such empirical evidences for justification flow from faith. In his treatment of evil James adopts the same perspective. The evil, which is seen, has its real source in the heart which is preoccupied with the world and under Satan's control. Just as certain works reflect faith, other works reflect an unbelief obsessed with the world, centered in self, and under Satan's control.

All such evil behavior contradicts the wisdom which "comes down from above" (3:15). A secular definition for wisdom would be inappropriate here. It will not do to understand wisdom as that virtue which simply describes the way the Christian life should be lived. Wisdom (*sophia*) refers to the comprehension of the Gospel, made possible by the Holy Spirit, especially as it sets forth Christ in the humility of His atonement. Matthew uses it of the preaching of Jesus (13:54). Jesus by comparing Himself with Solomon implies that He has the higher wisdom (Matt. 12:42). While its cognate, wise, may be used in a derogatory way of those who have their own wisdom (Matt. 11:25), it is used in a positive way of the apostles themselves (Matt. 23:34).

In Matt. 11:19 Jesus speaks the almost cryptic phrase: "Yet wisdom is justified by her children (*kai edikaiōthē hē sophia apo tōn teknōn autēs*)." Christ's reception of sinners verifies, that is, outwardly justifies, His message of God's love for them. God's reception of sinners can be seen in that Christ has table fellowship with them. Jesus' use of the verb "justify" as the visible verification of an invisible truth is no different from its use in James. Jesus' message is verified (justified) in His actions, and for James the faith of Christians is verified (justified) in their actions.

Wisdom involves not only the acknowledgment of the Gospel of Christ as true, but also the expression of that Gospel in the Christian life. It is not enough to be intellectually capable, as James' readers claimed to be; the works of wisdom must be expressed in works of meekness (*prautēs*), a Christological attribute (Matt. 5:5; 11:29; 21:5; cf. also James 1:21 above). Wisdom in Christian life must be expressed in the meekness or humility in which Christ gave it.

Like the good and perfect gift (1:17), James twice describes wisdom as coming down from above (*anōthen*), the term used in the Fourth Gospel to express Christ's coming down from heaven to participate in the human

Again to the Pastoral Task (3:1-18) 107

condition through the incarnation (John 3:31). This phrase in John, "He who comes down from above (*ho anōthen erchomenos*)," so closely resembles James' phrase, "This wisdom... comes down from above (*hē sophia anōthen katerchomenē*)" (3:15), that it seems impossible not to conclude that John is in some way dependent on it. James anticipates and influences the incarnational language of John.

With several adjectives James describes the character of "the wisdom from above." This wisdom is " pure ... peaceable, gentle, open to reason, full of mercy and good fruits, without uncertainty or insincerity." First of all the wisdom is "pure (*hagnē*)," i.e., without flaw or divided purpose. Some recent commentators see a clear Christological reference to Jesus as a model of purity.[13] Similar is the beatitude, "Blessed are the pure (*katharoi*) in heart (Matt. 5:8)." "Peaceable (*eirēnikē*)" means more than outward serenity, but refers to that content attitude which the Christian necessarily has, because he has begun to share in God's content attitude toward the entire world. He knows how to forgive all, because God has forgiven all. "Gentle (*epieikēs*)" suggests a person who does not live insisting upon his rights, but who acts considerately to those from whom he could justly exact a price or a punishment. It is one of Paul's qualifications for a bishop (1 Tim. 3:3), a virtue to be present in all Christians (Titus 3:2). "Open to reason (*eupeithēs*)," used only here in the New Testament, means willingness to let the opinions of others have sway in your thinking. The phrase "full of mercy and good fruits" only repeats an underlying theme of this entire epistle, that Christians should express the divine mercy God has extended to them in their dealings with others. Wisdom, finally, has the qualities of singlemindedness and lack of pretentiousness.

These characteristics of wisdom are not unlike the Beatitudes in that while they describe the goal of what the Christian life eventually must be, they describe the present reality of what that life is already now in Christ. In Christ the future made certain by God's demand and promise becomes present reality.

Finally, the phrase "And the harvest of righteousness is sown in peace by those who make peace" connects the doctrine of the atonement to the preaching office by using allusions from Jesus' parable of the sower (Matt. 13:3-9) and the Seventh Beatitude, "Blessed are the peacemakers, for they shall be called sons of God" (Matt. 5:9). It seems especially pertinent for the clergy.

The similarity of James' phrase to the Seventh Beatitude is unmistakable. Matthew's "peacemakers (*eirēnopoioi*)" is so strikingly close to James' "those who make peace (*poiousin eirēnēn*)" that, if one is not dependent on the other, they at least must draw upon a common tradition. This beatitude promises that the peacemakers shall be called "sons of God (*huioi theou*)." The singular form, the Son of God, is reserved in Matthew and in the remainder of the New Testament to Jesus. Matthew uses the designation only eight times of Jesus and clearly as a reference to His deity. For Matthew it would seem that the use of the plural "sons of God" could only be applied to Christians in a limited or secondary sense. Even if the plural is used in the Beatitudes, it still would be best to understand this beatitude first as a reference to Jesus, who because of His work of atonement receives from His Father the recognition that He is the Son of God. By His atonement Jesus becomes the Peacemaker and is acknowledged by God as His true Son. Compare Rom. 1:4, where through the resurrection God declares Jesus as His Son. As in the Seventh Beatitude, James refers to the makers of peace in the plural; however, James combines the idea of peacemaker with sowing, an activity accomplished by Jesus alone in the parables of the sower and the tares and the wheat (Matt. 13:37) but involving others by implication (Matt. 9:38). James is clearly referring to a peacemaking activity carried out by many, and not just by one, though the image of Jesus as the Sower remains in this passage. It may even be reflected in 1 Cor. 3:5-7, where Paul plants and Apollos waters but God gives the growth.

The phrase "the fruit (or harvest) of righteousness (*karpos tēs dikaiosunēs*)" is important here. In Matt. 3:15 Jesus describes His baptism, i.e., His submission to the Father's will for Him, as fulfilling all righteousness. It seems improbable that James' "fruit of righteousness" is a reference to what Christians do.[14] Rather it is a reference to the manifestation of the divine righteousness in Christ's atonement. The effect or product of God's righteousness is Christ's death. This message, that is, the Gospel, is sown or distributed. Though in the parable of the sower the reference to the sower is explicitly to Christ and only implicitly to those who preach, in James the use of the plural can only mean all those who are involved in the preaching tasks. They are called makers of peace because only through their message can the peace brought about by the atonement have personal effect among people. Those who preach participate with Christ, who first preached the atonement.

Their message is not only about peace, but it must be preached in such a way that the style of preaching does not destroy this content. A heavy preachment of judgment and condemnation with an attitude of condescension towards their congregations was having a disastrous effect on their comprehension of the atonement. Only an attitude which accepted all human beings was proper for preaching the Gospel as the declaration of peace. These harvesters of peace are an answer to the prayer of Jesus that the Lord of the harvest would send workers into the harvest (Matt. 9:37-38; cf. 1 Cor. 3:9).

XII/Exhortations Against Worldliness (4:1-17)

***1** What causes wars, and what causes fightings among you? Is it not your passions that are at war in your members? You desire and do not have; so you kill. And you covet and cannot obtain; so you fight and wage war. You do not have, because you do not ask. You ask and do not receive, because you ask wrongly, to spend it on your passions. Unfaithful creatures! Do you not know that friendship with the world is enmity with God? Therefore whoever wishes to be a friend of the world makes himself an enemy of God. Or do you suppose it is in vain that the scripture says, "He yearns jealously over the spirit which He has made to dwell in us"? But He gives more grace; therefore it says, "God opposes the proud, but gives grace to the humble." Submit yourselves therefore to God. Resist the devil and he will flee from you. Draw near to God and He will draw near to you. Cleanse your hands, you sinners, and purify your hearts, you men of double mind. Be wretched and mourn and weep. Let your laughter be turned to mourning and your joy to dejection. Humble yourselves before the Lord and He will exalt you.*

***11** Do not speak evil against one another, brethren. He that speaks evil against a brother or judges his brother, speaks evil against the Law and judges the Law. But if you judge the Law, you are not a doer of the Law but a judge. There is one Lawgiver and Judge, He who is able to save and to destroy. But who are you that you judge your neighbor?*

***13** Come now, you who say, "Today or tomorrow we will go into such and such a town and spend a year there and trade and get gain"; whereas you do not know about tomorrow. What is your life? For you are a mist that appears for a little time and then vanishes. Instead you ought to say, "If the Lord wills, we shall live and we shall do this or that." As it is, you boast in your arrogance. All such boasting is evil. Whoever knows what is right to do and fails to do it, for him it is sin.*

The Church Against Itself (4:1-4)

This section is so severe with its condemnation of the readers as warmongers that it would almost seem that James is addressing unbelievers. This is, however, not the case. Commentators have debated whether the early Christians were so incensed at one another that they were actually bringing physical harm against one another to the point of death.[1] "You desire and do not have; so you kill" (4:2). The charge of murder against Christians is so dreadful that a figurative interpretation is almost demanded.

James here is similar to Jesus, who charged His enemies with murder and adultery. Adultery is understood as apostasy from the true religion to engage in idolatrous practices, a matter previously discussed. Murder is enlarged by John (1 John 3:15) to include hatred, but is used by Jesus as meaning not just hatred but actual murder (cf. Matt. 23:29-36). The Jews who had become Christians had come from a milieu where persecution of religious enemies to the point of death was acceptable and in a sense required. By the time this epistle was written Jesus, Stephen, James the son of Zebedee, and perhaps others had been put to death by the Jews.

F. F. Bruce discusses the possibility that Paul's capture in Jerusalem may have resulted from a conspiracy between the Jews and the Jewish Christians.[2] Paul was probably charged with breaking Jewish ritual law, which some of the Christian Jews were still observing. In a situation so fluid that Christian Jews were worshiping not only in their own synagogues but in the regular synagogues, the Christian leaders could easily have conspired with their Jewish counterparts to plot the death of their colleagues. The church particularly at this time was not isolated from the synagogue. A commerce of ideas had flowed back and forth between Jesus and the leaders opposed to Him.

The other question is whether religious fratricide among spiritual brothers was a reality among Christians who were suffering under a common persecution. Jesus' words "and a man's foes will be those of his own household" (Matt. 10:36), written after James, may have reflected this same attitude of fratricide in the church. Under pressure betrayal is more common, not less. The situation in the early church was not one of anarchy so that attendance at a church service was a life-threatening experience. These murders were so subtle as to be carried out by the proper religious and legally constituted authorities. Peter addresses the Jerusalem populace as those who crucified Jesus. Though they did not physically harm Jesus directly, they were judged responsible for His crucifixion (Acts 2:36; 4:10). The early Christian Jews were probably beginning to experience ostracism from their own Jewish community and thus were probably suffering financially and, worse, socially. A situation of conspiracy put one Christian against another.

James' condemnation of their prayers, "You do not have, because you do not ask. You ask and do not receive, because you ask wrongly, to spend it on your passions" (4:2-3), is an adaptation from the Sermon on the Mount, "Ask, and it will be given you" (Matt. 7:7). Such a condemnation corresponds with James' concern over their liturgical life. In their prayers they did not present their real concerns brought on by the persecution but had let their prayers vent their evil emotions, and so these had now come under demonic control.

They were double-minded, lacking total allegiance to God, and thus their prayers came from evil motives.

James calls them adulteresses, rendered by the RSV as "unfaithful creatures." This catches the real problem as one of unbelief. Calling them adulteresses indicated their unfaithfulness in their relationship to Jesus.[3] Only an audience with a thoroughly Jewish heritage and acquainted with Jesus' preaching could appreciate the charge of adultery without further explanation. Just as Israel was joined to God in a bond stronger than marriage, so the church was the bride pledged to Christ the Bridegroom. Jesus taught this in the parables of the marriage feast (Matt. 22:1-14) and the ten virgins (Matt. 25:1-13). James knew the church as Christ's bride.

The impossibility of friendship with both the world and God seems a reflection of Jesus' saying in the Sermon on the Mount: "No one can serve two masters; for either he will hate the one and love the other, or he will be devoted to the one and despise the other. You cannot serve God and mammon" (Matt. 6:24). Where James speaks of "friendship," Jesus speaks of servitude. James substitutes "world" for Jesus' "mammon." Whereas the Sermon stresses the compelling servitude in the relationship between the person and the object of his devotion, James puts the emphasis on the willing and, yes even enjoyable, alliance between the sinner and the world.[4] Friendship with the world has turned the recipients of James' letter into God's enemies.

Correcting the Situation (4:5-10)

In vv. 5-10 James adopts a more positive approach to this problem of double allegiance. V. 5 presents two real problems in interpretation. The first is that there is no clear indication which Old Testament passage James is specifically quoting. Rather than sift among the multiple but all less than totally satisfactory choices, it might be better to see him as calling upon the full weight of Old Testament revelation for his argument. The second problem is determining the exact referent for the word "spirit" in the passage: "He yearns jealously over the spirit which He has made to dwell in us" (4:5). The RSV by putting spirit in lower case understands it as a reference to the noncorporeal part of man, which God desires for Himself. A reference to the Holy Spirit seems preferable not only because it is grammatically adequate but also because it fits the context. The translation would then be: "The Spirit which He made to dwell in us yearns enviously." One commentator aptly remarks that the Spirit who dwells in Christians "can brook no rival for our affection."[5] The double-minded person who tries to serve two masters by attempting the impossible feat of being friends with both God and the world puts the Holy Spirit in an intolerable position. The Spirit's concern for the Christian is nullified by the Christian's unacceptable commitment to unholy living.

"The Spirit which He made to dwell within us yearns enviously" is not that far from Paul's understanding of the Spirit's indwelling, praying, and interceding (Rom. 8:9-11, 26-27). Paul's "inward groaning" (Rom. 8:23) might be developed from James' "envious yearning."

The word for "dwell" (*katōkisen*) suggests taking up permanent residence. Should this refer to a man's spirit or soul, James would border on a Platonic view of man in which the spirit as an almost foreign guest takes up residence in the body for the duration of life.[6] James here is not making an anthropological statement about man's constitution consisting of body and soul, but a theological statement about the Holy Spirit. The Greek word *pneuma* here is used of the Holy Spirit, who does not belong to man by nature but through Baptism and faith becomes permanently committed to the believer. In a nontheological sense "dwell" is used of Jesus living in Nazareth (Matt. 2:23), a place of His permanent residence. James' point is that the Holy Spirit does have a permanent residence in Christians, but willful alliance with the world and Satan can eventually cause the Spirit to leave.

With the promise of more divine grace James adds a note of triumph to the Christian who is demonically afflicted. This promise of ultimate victory resembles John's assurance that if our hearts condemn us God is greater than our hearts (1 John 3:20). James supports this with a quotation from Prov. 3:34, "God opposes the proud, but gives grace to the humble," a verse which also appears in 1 Peter 5:5. This further supports that 1 Peter makes use of James.

Peter may have been dependent on James for more than the use of this passage. If James is written to Christians in exile from Jerusalem because the Christian synagogues were persecuted, it would not be improbable that Peter, addressing persecuted Christians in Asia Minor, would borrow some of James' themes. Peter sees his audience dispersed in the *diaspora* (1 Peter 1:1), and he directs a specific section of his letter to the clergy (5:1-4). James' word for "submit" (*hupotagēte* 4:7) is also a favorite word with Peter. Where James sees submission to God as the solution for sin, Peter sees submission to others as the proper posture for Christians to adopt in their social relationships: 1 Peter 2:13, human institutions; 18, masters; 3:1, 5, husbands; 5:5, clergy. The audience addressed in both epistles is suffering persecution, and humility is offered as the solution to their problems. If in discussing humility and submission Peter is dependent on James for his terminology and the use of Prov. 3:34, James in turn is reflecting Jesus' own admonition to humility.

In vv. 7-9, James repeats themes he has introduced previously in his epistle. Submission to God and resistance to the devil are the remedies for getting rid of him and his influence in the Christian's life. The actual presence of Satan in the Christian's life suggests more strongly that the Spirit in 4:5 is the Holy Spirit. The struggle within the Christian is cosmic in that the Christian's own spirit or soul does not contend alone against Satan, but the Holy Spirit fights for him.

Behind James' instruction to resist Satan and to rely on God is the account of Jesus' temptation by Satan (Matt. 4:1-11). James is careful to use the word "devil" here and not "demon" as he previously had done. Matthew specifically identifies the tempter as the devil. In His temptation Jesus submitted Himself to God's will (Matt. 4:7), and after Jesus' victorious resistance Satan left (Matt. 4:11). James by this reference holds up the tempted Jesus as the model for Christians satanically afflicted. It is a reminder to them that Jesus suffered under the same temptations.[7] For James, as for Hebrews, Jesus is the Pioneer of faith, having suffered all persecutions now being endured by Christians (Heb. 12:2).

Drawing near to God reflects several sections in the Old Testament. One commentator sees it as a reference to the actions of the priests as they engage in offering sacrifices to God. The cleansing of the hearts and hands means a total catharsis of sin from the thoughts and actions. Again James calls them double-minded men, whose allegiance is divided between God and Satan. Though the Spirit dwells in them, for their evil deeds they are rightfully called sinners.

James calls them as sinners to repentance. "Be wretched and mourn and weep. Let your laughter be turned into mourning and your joy to dejection." Paul in 2 Cor. 7:10 calls this godly sorrow necessary if damnation is to be avoided. Nevertheless James addresses his readers as sinners, and for this reason the same word of condemnation can be addressed to them that is addressed to unbelievers. A Christian insofar as he is a sinner and unbeliever still must hear a word of condemnation no different than that spoken to those who have totally rejected Christ. The goal is godly repentance (2 Cor. 7:9-10). Though the word of condemnation is preached with finality, it is but a prelude to God's restoration of the believer. James' call to repentance resembles one of the woes in Luke: "Woe to you that laugh now, for you shall mourn and weep (6:25)."

Following James' condemnation of his readers is a specific Christology, offering a solution to the dilemma of sin that threatens them with damnation. "Humble yourselves before the Lord and He will exalt you (*tapeinōthēte enōpion kuriou, kai hupsōsei humas*)" reflects these words of Jesus: "He who is greatest among you shall be your servant; whoever exalts himself will be humbled, and whoever humbles himself will be exalted" (Matt. 23:11-12). These words carry with them a specific Christology. Here is a clear case of a general reference most appropriately used of Christ, though later it is applicable to all Christians. As Christ humbled Himself to be exalted by God, so Christians sharing in His humility will also be exalted in Him. The same literary method is used in the Beatitudes and is traceable in James. The same words for "humbled" and "exalted" are used in James and Matthew, and thus a dependence in some sense or a common source for them seems probable. In Matt. 23:11-12 Jesus is referring to Himself, as He is also in Matt. 20:26. He is both servant and slave, and in that capacity He offers up His life in death as the atonement (Matt. 20:26-28). Paul in his great hymn to Christ uses the same terminology in describing Christ's humiliating Himself and His subsequent exaltation by God (Phil. 2:8-10).[8]

The concept of humiliation is introduced into this pericope by quoting Prov. 3:34, where the Greek word for humble in the Septuagint is *tapeinos*, a term Jesus applied to Himself in a very special way in Matt. 11:29: "Take My yoke upon you, and learn from Me; for I am gentle and *lowly* in heart." Humility for its own sake is for James no virtue; it has value only as the believer shares in Christ's humiliation, which is reliance on God.[9] This means release from sin and Satan.

In Phil. 2:5-11 Paul preserves the great hymn to Christ which may have originated in the Jerusalem church, headed by James. This hymn blends the great themes of Christ's humility and exaltation by God into the Christian life. James has done no less than Paul with "Humble yourselves before the Lord and He will exalt you."

Both Paul and James seem to develop their themes from Jesus' words in Matthew 20 and 23. Paul may have been influenced by James in developing his discussion of Christ's humility as well as other central themes such as justification by faith. Paul makes a point of having seen James, the Lord's brother, in Jerusalem (Gal. 1:19), and he counted him as a reliable witness of the resurrection (1 Cor. 15:7). In the twofold division of witnesses to the resurrection, Paul places James at the head of the second list and himself at the bottom (1 Cor. 15:7-8). All of this points to Paul's reliance on James in some sense.

Putting Judgment in Its Proper Place (4:11-12)

James places evil words spoken against other Christians within the eschatological context derived from the Sermon on the Mount: "Judge not, that you be not judged. For with the judgment you pronounce you will be judged" (Matt. 7:1-2). Speaking evil against the brother is seen by James as an offense against the Law and the Lawgiver. James here is probably speaking of the commandment to love one's neighbor, which along with love to God comprises all of God's demands on mankind. The person who hates his brother and speaks evil of him has in effect judged the Law as inadequate and established himself as the Giver of the Law. This can be nothing other than blasphemy, since the offender is functioning in God's place as the Lawgiver. The final question in this section, "But who are you that you judge your neighbor?" makes it obvious that James is referring to Jesus' command to love one's neighbor.

The phrase "There is one Lawgiver and Judge, He who is able to save and to destroy" is generally seen as a reference to God.[10] Since in this section James is making clear allusions to the words of Jesus, it is natural to assume that the "Lawgiver and Judge . . . who is able to save and destroy" is specifically Jesus Himself. Jesus is Lawgiver since in Him God authoritatively gives the new law, i.e., the new revelation of salvation in the Gospel. It is inadequate to understand Law here as Decalog, God's prohibitions. He is the Lawgiver, and all His words constitute the Law, i.e., the *torah*, the divine revelation.

Here James seems to be thinking of Jesus, specifically in His giving of the Sermon on the Mount. Such a conclusion would be natural simply because of the numerous parallels between James and the Sermon. In Matt. 5:19 Jesus identifies His words as the new divine law when He puts an eschatological threat on those who dare to break it. James places an equally damaging threat on those who tamper with the law of love. They find themselves in the unenviable position of sitting in judgment on the Judge Himself. The view that Jesus is the Lawgiver is reinforced by the following reference to the Judge. In the New Testament Jesus as Christ has been given divine authority to judge.

In Matthew Jesus sees Himself as God's appointed Judge at the world's end (25:31-46). He is the One who "separates the sheep from the goats" (v. 32) and passes sentence (vv. 34, 41). The judgment is based on whether love was extended to those who were in distress, the same problem James' readers have. As mentioned, understanding the Judge as Christ is preferable to understanding Him as God. In the Old Testament the Son of Man comes to carry out God's judgment (Dan. 7:13-14). Jesus sees Himself as the Son of Man, to whom judgment has been given. Paul in speaking of the appearing of "the righteous Judge" is clearly referring to Christ (2 Tim. 4:8). James' reference in 5:9 to "the Judge . . . standing at the doors" is also to Jesus. Characteristic for the New Testament is understanding Jesus and not the Father as Judge.[11] In the Fourth Gospel Jesus says that "the Father . . . has given all judgment to the Son" (John 5:22).

James' reference to the Judge "who is able to save and to destroy (*ho dunamenos sōsai kai apolesai*)" so closely resembles Jesus' admonition about fearing "Him who can destroy both soul and body in hell (*ton dunamenon kai psuchēn kai sōma apolesai en geennē*)" (Matt. 10:28), that it is difficult not to see common origin for both phrases. In James the thrust is slightly more evangelical, as the words of Jesus are pure threat. In both cases the fate of the individual on Judgment Day should determine his behavior now. In Matthew the threat is to arouse fear of God rather than of the enemies of the Gospel. In James the words of threat and promise are directed to believers who refuse to show consideration for the neighbor.

The First Ending: A Gentle Rebuke (4:13-17)

Vv. 13-17 constitute one of the milder rebukes in the epistle. The section is directed to those in the congregation, not necessarily the pastors, whose behavior was not as flagrantly repulsive as that of those who were conspiring with the enemies of the church against their fellow Christians. They were living their lives according to ordinary patterns of life and were not fully aware of its transitory nature. James reminds them that their lives are under divine control and could come to an end at any time. This is not the first time James has introduced the theme of life's transitory nature, as in 1:10-11 he compared the rich man to withering grass and flowers. Here the comparison is more pointed, as man's nature has no more lasting substance than a wisp of air.

James here zeroes in on the mercantile interests of these Christians. Matthew has a close parallel in Jesus' remarks about the Flood's coming in the days of Noah. Those people, too, were consumed with ordinary things, marrying and giving in marriage, and were not aware of the eschatological doom awaiting them in the impending Flood. The greater eschatological doom shall come in the judgment of Jesus (Matt. 24:37-39). "If the Lord wills, we shall live and we shall do this or that" (James 4:15) places the entire Christian life under the will of Jesus. Here it is easiest to assume that the Lord (*ho kurios*) is a reference to Jesus, as this title is most appropriately applied to Him throughout the entire New Testament. James should not be seen as an exception.

"If the Lord wills" is more than a recognition of divine control over all of life; it is a confession that Jesus can appear at any time as God's appointed Judge and terminate the ordinary course of time.[12] The boasting condemned by James is that supreme confidence that a human being can direct his future affairs without fear of divine intervention. "All such boasting is evil (*ponēra*)" (4:16). "Evil" here has the same intent as it does in the Lord's Prayer (Matt. 6:13), an attitude inspired by the devil. Boasting about what a man is able to accomplish in the future is not only silly, because no man is totally in control of his destiny, but worse, the boasting man puts himself in the place of God the Creator. This is, of course, an affront against the First Commandment in not letting God have that honor which can only rightly belong to Him. This is the most satanic of all sins. For this reason James sees boasting about the future as evil from Satan. It is the opposite of faith which relies totally on God.

"Whoever knows what is right to do and fails to do it, for him it is sin" (v. 17) might appear to be out of flow with the general context of this pericope. It definitely does not fit into the next pericope (5:1-6), one not directed to Christians and undoubtedly the most severe in the epistle. Others here attribute a rather shallow concept of sin to James, as morality involves merely outward acts of good or the omission of such acts. One recent commentator claims that "unlike Paul, James is silent on man's moral depravity." Leveling a charge tantamount to Pelagianism against James hardly does him justice.[13] For James sin infects man's entire nature. Evolving from innate desires, it expresses itself in the most hideous of acts.

This statement about failing to do right could by itself stand as a theme for the entire epistle, as a goodly portion of the readers in giving attention to the rich had neglected the poor (2:15-17). It is obviously directed to Christians who knew the divine will for positive action in certain situations but who failed to undertake the appropriate action. This sentence summarizes the malady which called for the writing of the epistle. It thus concludes the major body of the epistle, which is a treatise directed to the problem of the contradiction between Christian life and their professed faith. Those who are only buying and selling in carrying out their ordinary life's pursuits and thus neglecting the needs of the poor are guilty of sin as much as those who are actively persecuting some Christians. Sin is not only an explicit offense against the Decalog, it is also the failure to provide needed assistance.

The sentence "Whoever knows what is right to do and fails to do it, for him it is sin" in its thought content is not unlike the condemning words of Jesus: "Truly, I say to you, as you did it not to one of the least of these, you did it not to Me" (Matt. 25:45). Some have thought it could be a logion of Jesus unrecorded in the gospels. The sin of omission in not offering assistance puts such an offender in a condition of unbelief. Faith without works is, of course, James' central message. It can only be speculated whether James knew the parable of the good Samaritan, as that account certainly develops the same theme of failure to help the distressed.

This sentence concludes and summarizes the major portion of the epistle, since Chapter 5 begins with a tirade against the rich, who seem to be outside of the congregation (5:1-6).[14]

XIII/Addenda (5:1-20)

1 *Come now, you rich, weep and howl for the miseries that are coming upon you. Your riches have rotted and your garments are moth-eaten. Your gold and silver have rusted, and their rust will be evidence against you and will eat your flesh like fire. You have laid up treasure for the last days. Behold, the wages of the laborers who mowed your fields, which you kept back by fraud, cry out; and the cries of the harvesters have reached the ears of the Lord of hosts. You have lived on the earth in luxury and in pleasure; you have fattened your hearts in a day of slaughter. You have condemned, you have killed the righteous man; he does not resist you.*

7 *Be patient, therefore, brethren, until the coming of the Lord. Behold, the farmer waits for the precious fruit of the earth, being patient over it until it receives the early and the late rain. You also be patient. Establish your hearts, for the coming of the Lord is at hand. Do not grumble, brethren, against one another, that you may not be judged; behold, the Judge is standing at the doors. As an example of suffering and patience, brethren, take the prophets who spoke in the name of the Lord. Behold, we call those happy who were steadfast. You have heard of the steadfastness of Job, and you have seen the purpose of the Lord, how the Lord is compassionate and merciful.*

12 *But above all, my brethren, do not swear, either by heaven or by earth or with any other oath, but let your yes be yes and your no be no, that you may not fall under condemnation.*

13 *Is anyone among you suffering? Let him pray. Is any cheerful? Let him sing praise. Is any among you sick? Let him call for the elders of the church, and let them pray over him, anointing him with oil in the name of the Lord; and the prayer of faith will save the sick man, and the Lord will raise him up; and if he has committed sins, he will be forgiven. Therefore confess your sins to one another, and pray for one another, that you may be healed. The prayer of a righteous man has great power in its effects. Elijah was a man of like nature with ourselves and he prayed fervently that it might not rain, and for three years and six months it did not rain on the earth. Then he prayed again and the heaven gave rain, and the earth brought forth its fruit.*

***19** My brethren, if anyone among you wanders from the truth and someone brings him back, let him know that whoever brings back a sinner from the error of his way will save his soul from death and will cover a multitude of sins.*

The final chapter consists of self-contained sections of advice without the sharp and theologically developed criticism of the first four chapters. This is not unlike some of the epistles of Paul, where the final sections contain random thoughts not woven into the central themes. Romans 16 and 1 Corinthians 16 have such scattered thoughts which Paul seems to have appended to these letters after he developed his major arguments. James, Chapter 5, also contains such scattered thoughts that might be appropriate at a letter's end. They are, however, in keeping with the general message of the epistle that the contradiction between faith and behavior is intolerable.

A Condemnation of Unbelievers (5:1-6)

This section is not directed to the congregations or their pastors, but to a group outside of the congregations which was having a negative but persuasive influence on them. The device of addressing persons not present in the group is called apostrophe, a rhetorical device common in the ancient world. This is the last of five times in the epistle in which James makes reference to the rich. Of the five this is the most severe, with permanent condemnation leaving no possibility of escaping the day of slaughter (5:5).

James is not here leveling a blanket condemnation against rich people for their wealth. From 1:10 it is obvious that the rich had a legitimate part in the congregation, with the proviso that they adopt an attitude of impoverishment over against God. Every previous word of rebuke in the epistle was followed by a solution. Here there is none. The hypothesis that the rich outside of the congregation are being singled out for their exploitation of the poor is less than completely satisfactory. The New Testament writers never really show any interest in economic or political excesses and abuses unless they have a direct relevance within the church.

Luke in the parable of Lazarus and the rich man (16:19-31) is most pointed in attacking economic evils, but the real problem with the rich man is less his wealth and more the lack of willingness to share it in assisting the needy. All three synoptic gospels contain the pericope of the rich young man (Matt. 19:16-30; Mark 10:17-31; Luke 18:18-30); but since with God all things are possible, even the rich can be saved. Matthew's explicit inclusion of Joseph of Arimathea as the rich man who buries Jesus (27:57) is a demonstration that the rich can belong to the Kingdom. Wealthy people are not being condemned simply for their wealth. Another avenue must be found.

In Matthew the poor become synonymous with those for whom the Gospel is intended. Matthew's "poor in spirit" (5:3) becomes simply Luke's "poor" (6:20). The poor are the ones to whom the Gospel is preached (Matt. 11:5) and the rich can enter the kingdom of God only when they sell their possessions and give to the poor (Matt. 19:21). Christ accomplishes salvation for mankind by exchanging His wealth for the condition of impoverishment (2 Cor. 8:9). The term "poor" becomes another synonym for "Christians," as they share with Christ in His poverty.

The term "rich" here in James is understood as those people who resist the call of the Gospel, since answering that call means financial inconvenience for them.[1] The rich young man is representative of all those who face this dilemma. Like the rich fool, they are not rich towards God. The rich addressed by James in 5:1 are those who have heard the call to repentance and have understood its demands, but have rejected this call precisely because of those demands. Devotion to their wealth has prevented their acceptance of the Gospel. In retaining their wealth they are having a foretaste of the condemnation they cannot escape: "Come now, you rich, weep and howl for the miseries that are coming upon you (5:1)."

James has a colorful description of their plight:

> Your riches have rotted and your garments are moth-eaten. Your gold and silver have rusted, and their rust will be evidence against you and will eat your flesh like fire. You have laid up treasure for the last days (5:2-3).

This appears to be an adaptation of the words of Jesus later placed in the Sermon on the Mount:

> Do not lay up for yourselves treasures on earth, where moth and rust consume and where thieves break in and steal, but lay up for yourselves treasures in heaven, where neither moth nor rust consumes and where thieves do not break in and steal. For where your treasure is, there will your heart be also (Matt. 6:19-21).

In the Sermon on the Mount the words appear as a warning to Christians against involving themselves in the pursuit of material wealth and pleasures as the ultimate goals in life. Laying up treasures in heaven refers to concern for other people by bringing them into a proper relationship with Christ's work. These people are the enduring treasures. In addressing his audience with his own adaptation of the Sermon, James presupposes that his readers and the accused who are absent are acquainted with this section of the Sermon. They knew it through tradition or, not so impossibly, directly from Jesus Himself.

The warning of the Sermon is transformed by James into an eschatological verdict. The rich have not paid heed to Jesus' words and have concentrated their pursuits on the elegance of their attire and their collecting of gold and silver.[2] These have become their real treasures. The treasures that escaped theft (Matt. 6:20) are in their deteriorated condition being used as evidence for the condemnation on the Day of Judgment (James 5:3). The word for "evidence" (*marturion*) refers to what is brought before a judge to convict the accused. "The miseries that are coming" refers to penalties given on the Day of Judgment, as the word "coming," especially in connection with the last days, is decisively eschatological throughout the New Testament.[3] James' picture of the final doom as fire (5:3) is reminiscent of the preaching of

John the Baptist, who threatens fire to those who are unproductive in good works (Matt. 3:12).

Luther in his explanation of the First Commandment in the Large Catechism saw man as either worshiping the true God or creating idols for his own devotion. In the Sermon Jesus sees men placing treasures either in heaven or on earth. James' sentence, "You have laid up treasure for the last days" is for those who have chosen the latter option of forgetting heaven and thinking only of earth. Here James has written a sequel to the Sermon on the Mount. Without some minimal awareness of the Sermon, much of James' message is lost.

James' statement about the underpaid laborers, "Behold, the wages of the laborers who mowed your fields, which you kept back by fraud, cry out; and the cries of the harvesters have reached the ears of the Lord of hosts" (5:4), is generally taken as a specific protest against social and financial injustice by rich and often absentee landlords. The Mosaic code has specific injunctions prohibiting theft from laborers by keeping back their fairly earned wages (Deut. 24:14-15). The question arises why James is concerned solely with deceptive farming practices. Why is he concerned with field workers and not with those engaged in working in vineyards, herding, fishing, crafts, or trading? Are landlord farmers the only employers guilty of defrauding their employees? Such social concern does not fit and is more appropriate in the 20th century than the first.

It might be more appropriate to suggest that James is condemning the rich who during their connection with Christians in their synagogues did not contribute to the support of the clergy. They were miserly in spirit and in their contributions. That this is a church problem would be supported by Jesus' use of agricultural terminology in the parables to describe God, salvation, and even the clergy. The reference to Jesus as the farmer (5:7) would lend further support to the view that James does not have specific agricultural concerns.

The similarity of James here to 1 Tim. 5:18 and Matt. 9:37 is striking. James 5:4, "the wages of the laborers (*ho misthos tōn ergatōn*)," bears a marked similarity to 1 Tim. 5:18 "The laborer deserves his wages (*axios ho ergatēs tou misthou autou*)," a section in which Paul is addressing the necessity of paying the clergy a salary. The section in James is also similar to Matt. 9:37, "The harvest is plentiful, but the laborers are few (*ho therismos polus, hoi de ergatai oligoi*)," a pericope speaking of the need for proclaimers of the Gospel and the establishment of what would later be called the pastoral office. The early church expressed God's work in the Gospel with agricultural terms to such an extent that these terms were used without any further theological explanation. The parables of the sower and of the tares and the wheat with the final harvest (Matt. 13:3-8, 24-30) operate with this understanding. The participation of others with Jesus, especially the apostles, in this work of harvesting, that is, preaching, is assured by Him! "The harvest is plentiful, but the laborers are few; pray therefore the Lord of the harvest to send out laborers into His harvest" (Matt. 9:37-38). In 1 Tim. 5:18 Paul uses the term "laborers" of those who along with the apostles hold the pastoral office. Within the context of the epistle itself, the synoptic gospels, and the New Testament in general, it seems best to understand the defrauded field workers as preachers of the Gospel.

The problem of poverty in the congregations seems to have caused some members and especially the clergy to cater to the rich during the worship services in a most conspicuous way. The rich did not provide for the poor and, worse, were dragging members of the congregation into court, probably ecclesiastical ones. They did little, if anything, to provide for the support of the clergy, a problem later faced by Paul (2 Cor. 11:9; Acts 18:3).

The agricultural imagery of Jesus, in which He compared His work of converting, sanctifying, and judgment to planting, growing, and harvesting, was taken over by Paul to explain his work as a preacher of the Gospel in relation to other preachers and to God:

> I planted, Apollos watered, but God gave the growth. So neither he who plants nor he who waters is anything, but only God who gives the growth. He who plants and he who waters are equal, and each shall receive his wages (*misthon*) according to his labor. For we are God's fellow workers (*sunergoi*); you are God's field (*geōrgion*), God's building (1 Cor. 3:6-9).

Paul's use of the agricultural imagery is more detailed, but James is addressing an audience for whom the agricultural terminology did not need the theological explanation. James' readers were well acquainted and comprehended the original agricultural terminology of Jesus and without further explanation knew what James was talking about.[4] Vv. 7 and 8 will make further use of this terminology.

James' phrase, "Lord of hosts," taken from Isaiah 6, is used of Jesus as God's appointed Judge on the Last Day, as the title "Lord" (*kurios*) is the most appropriate for addressing Jesus in judgment (Matt. 7:21; 25:37). He may also refer to Himself as the Lord of the harvest to whom prayers are to be addressed requesting workers in that harvest (Matt. 9:38). What they have kept for themselves from those who justly earned it was only unnecessary luxury. They were fattening themselves as cattle for butchering on Judgment Day, when they would be slaughtered as God's enemies (5:5).

The sentence, "You have condemned, you have killed the righteous man; he does not resist you" has been taken by some ancient church fathers and some contemporary commentators as a reference to Christ's crucifixion, though most commentators tend to distance themselves from this Christological interpretation. Preferred often is understanding "the righteous man" in a generic sense. This would allow for James to be included. It seems best to take this as a specific reference to Jesus primarily and to persecuted Christians secondarily. James' Christology involves the church suffering at the hands of God's enemies.

Throughout this epistle there is an underlying Christology with references to Christ's humility and exaltation. In the eschatological references James is careful to identify Jesus as the Lord. In this final chapter James will continue to refer to Jesus (5:4, 7, 8, 9, 10, 11, 15). It would fit the context for

James here to make another Christological reference to Christ in the statement about killing the righteous man. At least nine New Testament references are made to Jesus as the Righteous One (*ho dikaios*).[5] Significant among these is Stephen's defense (Acts 7:52) addressed to the same audience for whom James' words are intended:

> Which of the prophets did not your fathers persecute (*ediōxan*)? And they killed those who announced beforehand the coming of the Righteous One (*tou dikaiou*), whom you now have betrayed and murdered (*phoneis*).

The audience whom James addressed were accustomed to hearing Jesus referred to as the Righteous One.[6]

Their flight from Jerusalem as a result of persecution was the occasion for this epistle and came shortly after Stephen's martyrdom. This martyrdom was the part of the persecutions which they were now facing somewhat unsuccessfully. James here uses the past tense of the aorist. James' terminology is forensic and suggests an act of legal prosecution and execution. This certainly fits Christ's trial and execution, instigated by the Jews. The rich whom James is addressing could have been the same people spoken to by Peter and Stephen in the addresses recorded in Acts.

"He does not resist you" (5:6) is present tense and suggests to some that "the righteous man" is generic, referring to suffering Christians in general. The phrase "the Righteous One" is appropriately reserved for God and His Messiah. The Lord of hosts is the Righteous One. The problem of the present tense used in describing the nonresistance of the Righteous One may be resolved by seeing the continued suffering of the Messiah in His people. Actions against Christians are directed against Christ also, since Christ and His church are organically joined. This theme has become axiomatic to James. "He does not resist you" would be similar in meaning to Jesus' words to Paul: "I am Jesus, whom you are persecuting (*diōkeis*)" (Acts 9:5). Though Jesus is glorified, He indicts Paul for persecuting Him, though Paul had not known or persecuted the earthly Jesus. Even if a generic sense is seen as fitting, it must nevertheless have some Christological overtones. The context and the wording still favor understanding this as a reference to Christ. The RSV is slightly inconsistent in translating *ho dikaios* in upper case as "the Righteous One" in Acts 3:14 and in lower case as "the righteous man" in James 5:6. Nothing would be more damaging for the rich who persecuted these congregations than to have received the indictment leveled against those responsible for Jesus' crucifixion. The "rich" can only be understood as Christ's enemies. The friend of the world is the enemy of God (4:4) and the murderer of Christ (5:6).

A Few Final Suggestions

In the final sections (5:7-20) James brings his epistle to a close by addressing the issues of patience among pastors (vv. 7-11), a more careful use of God's name, even when the intentions may seem pious (v. 12), personal religious problems (vv. 13-18), and then lastly handling the problem of doctrinally erring pastors (vv. 19-20). This entire final section has all the marks of having been written by a supervising pastor or bishop offering specific suggestions and advice for pastors who are not only removed by distance from their supervisors for the first time, but whose situation has been compounded by their first taste of persecution.

Patience and the Parousia (5:7-11)

The section on patience (vv. 7-11) is strongly eschatological. In both vv. 7 and 8, James urges patience in direct connection with the return of Jesus:

> Be patient (*makrothumēsate*), therefore, brethren, until the coming of the Lord (*tēs parousias tou kuriou*). Behold, the farmer (*geōrgos*) waits for the precious (*timion*) fruit of the earth, being patient over it until it receives the early and the late rain. You also be patient (*makrothumēsate*). Establish your hearts, for the coming of the Lord (*hē parousia tou kuriou*) is at hand (*ēggiken*).

Parousia is used regularly in the New Testament for the visible return of Jesus on the Last Day (Matt. 24:3, 27, 37, 39) and is often transliterated into English without translation. Among the gospels only Matthew uses the term, but it is used prominently in Paul's letters to the Thessalonians, a congregation particularly beset by problems on this matter (1 Thess. 2:19; 3:13; 4:15; 5:23; 2 Thess. 2:1, 8, 9) which was a prominent issue in the early church. Whereas Jesus refers to the *parousia* of the Son of Man, His own self-designation for His own Messianic work, James is careful to speak of Jesus as "Lord" (*kurios*), the proper title of address to Jesus as the eschatological Judge (Matt. 25:37), and not as "Son of Man." The final appearance of Jesus as Judge is put forth as the overarching reality in the life of the suffering congregation.

For two reasons James urges patience on these pastors (vv. 7 and 8). In the first instance, patience is urged because Jesus is still applying the benefits of His atonement on earth through the preaching of the Gospel, and a premature return would disrupt this work. In the second place, patience is soon to be rewarded by Christ's imminent return.

In v. 7 Christian patience is modeled after that of a farmer waiting for his crop to mature for the harvest. Patience in the New Testament is not only a virtue required of Christians, as James indicates here, but it is also a virtue of God, who hesitates to express His anger in judgment to allow time for unbelievers to repent. This is clearly the case in 1 Peter 3:20, where "God's patience waited in the days of Noah" before the destruction of the world by water. Such divine patience or waiting should not be interpreted to mean that God is really only looking for an opportunity to express His wrath at the right time, but rather it is an expression of His love to give a time for repentance. This is clearly the intention of James, who sees the farmer's patience as absolutely necessary for bringing in the fullest-possible harvest.

As mentioned, the agricultural imagery of this section (v. 7) and the previous section (v. 4) is strongly reminiscent of the parables of the sower and of the tares and the wheat. The farmer who waits for the precious fruit of the earth is Jesus Himself. Jesus is sower, farmer, and harvester. This is not to deny that Jesus uses His church to accomplish sowing and cultivating and His angels to do the harvesting; nevertheless, all this remains His work. Here He is called the farmer because He is cultivating His crop for the fullest harvest possible. The word "farmer" describes His present activity in preserving His church. The Fourth Gospel uses the vine imagery for the same purpose (John 15:1-11). For John, the Father is the farmer (*geōrgos*), translated in English as "vinedresser." The pastors addressed by James are co-workers with Jesus and must share in His patience. The same kind of imagery is used in 1 Cor. 3:6-9, where Paul sees himself and his associates as co-workers with God, planting and cultivating God's crop. In the parable of the sower, fruit or harvest (*karpos*) is used of Christians among whom the Gospel has been successful. In the parable of the vineyard (Matt. 21:33-41) the workers not producing what is expected are removed and replaced by others. That parable refers to the Jews with their failure to carry out the responsibility given them by God. James uses the same imagery of Christian pastors who also have their responsibility over the harvest entrusted to them by Jesus. Lack of patience among pastors is ultimately destructive of what God is now accomplishing in the world through the Gospel.

"The early and the late rain" refers to the rains which come in Palestine just after the sowing, causing the seed to germinate, and before the final harvest, causing the plants to produce the most abundant crops possible. The early rains come in late fall, and the late rains in early spring. In referring to the rains James is speaking no more of agriculture than Paul is with his reference to watering what has been planted. James with the agricultural imagery used in Jesus' parables is referring to God's providing the Gospel for the church. In 1:21 James has already referred to the implanting of God's Word "which is able to save ... souls." James envisions God's entire work toward the world, from the coming of Jesus to His final appearance, as embraced between the early and the late rains, the planting of fruit by the Word and its continued maintenance. This fruit or harvest is made possible by the atonement.

The harvest is described as precious (*timion*), a term closely associated with the atonement.[7] Paul speaks of Christians as precious stones (1 Cor. 3:12). Precious means something which has been purchased for a price or which has great value. The harvest which the farmer, i.e., Jesus, wants to preserve has value because He has purchased it for a great price. There is something precious about it worth preserving. The thought cannot be that the farmer, Jesus, will sell the harvest in order to procure a profit for Himself; but rather God procured the harvest for Himself at a great cost. Its value lies in the investment that Jesus has made. Peter speaks about Christians being purchased by the precious or highly valued (*timion*) blood of Christ (1 Peter 1:19). Jesus provided Himself as the price for the harvest.

The similarity between the precious harvest in James 5:7 and the parable of the pearl of great price (*polutimon*) in Matt. 13:46 cannot pass unnoticed.

Besides the obvious similarity between the value of the harvest and the value of the pearl, God or Jesus is the One who is interested in having each for Himself. As the merchant goes to great expense to obtain the pearl for himself, so the farmer has almost limitless patience in assuring that he reaps the fullest benefits of his harvest. Matthew 13 contains the agricultural parables, i.e., the sower and the wheat and the tares (vv. 3-30) along with the pearl of great price (vv. 45-46). In speaking of the precious harvest, James, who is as bound to preserving the words of Jesus as he is personally creative in handling those words, combines into one thought the agricultural parables with the parable of the pearl of great price. Before and at the end of this chapter with the parables, Matthew refers to James (12:46 and 13:55). No mention of James is made in connection with any other discourses of this evangelist. This may be Matthew's signal that James, leading pastor of the Jerusalem church at this gospel's writing, had firsthand knowledge of these parables. Matthew may even have been aware that James had incorporated the terminology of these parables into his epistle.

In John 15:1 Jesus' Father is called the farmer (*geōrgos*) or vinedresser, as the RSV has it. James might be using parabolic language, but he is not using an example, parable, or analogy. Rather the language of the parables has become theological. Though this is obvious in John, there is a hesitancy to recognize that James, closely dependent on Jesus, used this technique earlier. If farmer is used of the Father in John, it is used of Jesus in James.

The command to strengthen the heart (v. 8) is a plea for Christians not to desert the faith. Standing firm in Christianity, especially in the midst of the temptations associated with persecution, becomes more tolerable when Christians realize that the delay in the *parousia*, God's coming in judgment, is for the purpose of a greater salvation. It is not an opportunity to store up more wrath.

The phrase "the coming of the Lord is at hand (*ēggiken*)" closely resembles the announcements of John the Baptist and Jesus, "Repent, for the kingdom of heaven [literally "the heavens"] is at hand (*ēggiken*)" (Matt. 3:2; 4:17), a phrase in which Matthew summarizes the preaching content of the Baptist and of Jesus. James' phrase reflects a situation in the church advanced from that of John the Baptist and Jesus. Their original message focused on Christ's death for sins, His resurrection, and His judgment of the world—all as future events, all comprising one divine activity among men. With death and resurrection accomplished, James focuses on the *parousia*, the return of Christ in judgment. James' readers were in the same position of waiting for Christ's return as Jesus' hearers were as they waited for His crucifixion and resurrection, those acts in which the kingdom of the heavens appeared. The early church was caught up with the lively hope of the imminent return of Jesus. James' forthright announcement that the coming of the Lord is at hand places this epistle at the threshold of the New Testament era. On this point it resembles First Thessalonians and is a further argument for a very early dating.

James does not let go of understanding eschatology as the primary motivation in Christian life. Not only should they avoid speaking against one another (4:11), but their less than fully articulated grumblings against each other are unacceptable. This groaning and moaning really consisted of statements of judgment against one another. They were putting themselves in the place of God, the Judge, to whom alone the right of passing judgment belongs. Now He is about ready to exercise this prerogative Himself: "Do not grumble, brethren, against one another, that you may not be judged; behold, the Judge is standing at the doors" (5:9).

Such a warning could only be fully appreciated by those who both heard and understood Jesus' saying in the Sermon on the Mount: "Judge not, that you be not judged. For with the judgment you pronounce you will be judged" (Matt. 7:1-2). The person who passes judgment against another Christian has not felt the full impact of the atonement in his life. James' warning against judging is the converse of the Lord's Prayer, "And forgive us our trespasses as we forgive those who trespass against us," a theme developed first right after the prayer (Matt. 6:14-15) and further in the parable of the unforgiving steward (Matt. 18:23-35).

"Behold, the Judge is standing at the doors" reflects Jesus' use of the word "doors" in connection with His final coming: "So also, when you see all these things, you know that He [the Son of Man] is near (*eggus*), at the very gates (*thurais*)" (Matt. 24:33). The RSV translation of the same Greek word in Matthew as "gates" and in James as "doors" makes it difficult to see from the English translation that James is developing a saying of Jesus used in connection with the lesson from the fig tree (Matt. 24:32). The idea of Jesus standing at the gates or doors means that He is now ready to enter into the world to exercise judgment. The imminent return of Jesus is a motivation not only for patience but also for refraining from exercising the judgment which belongs to Him alone. Behind the idea of Jesus' standing at the gates is Ps. 24:7-10, the traditional psalm for the Advent season, where the King of glory, the Lord of hosts, waits for the proper time to enter.

The examples of the suffering prophets are offered as further inducement for patience under persecution:

> As an example of suffering (*kakopatheias*) and patience (*makrothumias*), brethren, take the prophets who spoke in the name of the Lord. Behold, we call those happy (*makarizomen*) who were steadfast. You have heard of the steadfastness of Job, and you have seen the purpose (*to telos*) of the Lord, how the Lord is compassionate and merciful (*polusplagchnos estin ho kurios kai oiktirmōn*) (vv. 10-11).

Further evidence that James' primary audience is clergymen comes from his urging them to follow the example of the prophets. They like the prophets were afflicted by a melancholia (*kakopatheia*), a type of internal agony which Luther identified as *Anfechtung*. Note also that James in this section (vv. 7-11) addresses his readers as "brethren" and in the next section as "my brethren" (v. 12), i.e., men associated with him in the pastoral and supervisory care of the congregations. The one quality singled out about the prophets is that they, like James' readers, "spoke in the name of the Lord (*elalēsan en tō onomati kuriou*)" (5:10).

It is doubtful whether this phrase can be pushed to the point that it should be understood as a reference to the uniquely inspired quality of the Old Testament. The New Testament references to such inspiration are more precise, attributing a more direct speaking activity to God or the Holy Spirit. But the phrase must mean more than a general type of religious speaking of which all Christians are capable. The parallel made by James between his readers and the prophets must be meaningful. It is not simply a random comparison. His readers must have preached Christ as had the prophets who for this suffered persecution.

It is not improbable that "prophets" here, as in Acts 13:1, refers to pastors or elders who now have been martyred and not to Old Testament religious authorities. This view would be supported by the resemblance of the next verse (11a), "Behold, we call those happy (*makarizomen*) who were steadfast," to the more familiar passage from the Book of Revelation (14:13): "And I heard a voice from heaven saying, 'Write this: Blessed (*makarioi*) are the dead who die in the Lord henceforth.' 'Blessed indeed,' says the Spirit, 'that they may rest from their labors, for their deeds follow them!'"

The James reference could be translated into this paraphrase, "Behold, we bless those who did not succumb during the persecution," and could be taken along with the parallel from Revelation as a reference to early Christian pastors martyred for their faith. Similar to Hebrews 11, it might refer to both Old and New Testament martyrs. It is agreed by most that the Book of Revelation came from a period of great persecution by the Roman Empire. James also came from a period of intense persecution, though it was limited to Palestine. References in both James and Revelation seem to be liturgical. As in the current liturgical formula which refers to "all the company of heaven," the Christian dead were seen as alive in Christ and part of the one fellowship of the church. The earliest church did not have to wait long to build its list of martyrs.

James finds that his readers (i.e., the pastors of the congregations in the Diaspora) and the prophets both spoke officially in God's stead, even though the pastors were not directly inspired. As pastors they were authorized to speak in God's stead. Their message and their office in preaching was not essentially different from that of the prophets. This is suggested by James' use of *laleo*, which when used without modifiers refers to official speaking in the congregation in distinction from casual speaking among Christians. A modifying phrase, "in the name of the Lord," confirms the idea that James is speaking about preaching. James by using the word "Lord" identifies Jesus as the authorizing agent. The one who is standing at the doors ready to come in judgment is the one who also authorized the Old Testament prophets to speak. This same message was now entrusted to these early pastors and was bringing about the same type of hardship as that endured by the prophets. The Jewish persecution of the early church and its similarity to the persecution of the prophets may have been behind Matthew's inclusion of

Jesus' saying: "Therefore I send you prophets and wise men and scribes, some of whom you will kill and crucify, and some you will scourge in your synagogues, and persecute from town to town" (23:34).

For "patience" (KJV, v. 11) James does not use *makrothumia*, the divine quality of waiting for the performance of the plan of salvation, but *hupomonē*, persistence in spite of unfavorable environment. Job is held up as an example for several reasons: the length of his suffering, his complaining, and the relief which God finally brought him. Their severe affliction should not be interpreted as a sign of disfavor, but to the contrary, their affliction, even if it brought them to the brink of despair, was a sign they were the successors to the prophets in proclaiming the message of salvation and that God would bring them relief. Some commentators have noticed the absence of Jesus as an example of suffering. It would be inappropriate to mention Jesus as an example, since He, unlike Job and Elijah, did not complain.[8]

If Luther along with others failed to see the Gospel as central in James, it may have been because he was not aware that James, with the early church, commonly called Jesus "Lord." For James "the Lord is compassionate and merciful," terms carrying the message of divine assistance in human distress. The Greek word for "compassionate," *polusplagchnos*, means the internal churning of the organs at the sight of suffering. In the Benedictus God is said to be full of such visceral mercy (Luke 1:78). Jesus looking at the shepherdless crowd is said to be "moved with compassion (*esplagchnisthē*)" (Matt. 9:36 KJV) and out of such mercy establishes the pastoral office in conjunction with His apostles (Matt. 10:1). In the parable of the unforgiving steward such mercy is the quality of the lord who forgives the unpayable debt (Matt. 18:27). And it is the attitude of the good Samaritan who aids the stricken traveler (Luke 10:33). The Greek word for "merciful," *oiktirmos*, suggests that mercy which is moved to tears. Luther's statement, "But this James does nothing more than drive to the Law and its works" hardly fits the data.

For Christians in their tribulations James does not present Jesus as a divine detached, punishing Judge, but Jesus whose very essence is so touched by the suffering of His church that He is willing and ready to relieve it. "You have seen the purpose of the Lord" points to what God was accomplishing with Job. The Book of Job ends with the optimistic note that God relieved him out of his sufferings. His trials were transitory. Job does not face eternal despair. There might have been still one more reason for choosing Job as an example. Both Job and the addressees of James' epistle are beset by Satan to the point of doubting God's plan. They, like Job, will be rewarded at the end of their trials.

Careful Use of the Divine Name (5:12)

James' warning on taking oaths, "But above all, my brethren, do not swear, either by heaven or by earth or with any other oath, but let your yes be yes and your no be no, that you may not fall under condemnation" (5:12), is similar to the Sermon on the Mount. It is an abbreviated variation of the following section from the Sermon:

> Again you have heard that it was said to the men of old, "You shall not swear falsely, but shall perform to the Lord what you have sworn." But I say to you, Do not swear at all, either by heaven, for it is the throne of God, or by the earth, for it is His footstool, or by Jerusalem, for it is the city of the great King. And do not swear by your head, for you cannot make one hair white or black. Let what you say be simply "Yes" or "No"; anything more than this comes from evil [or "the evil one"] (Matt. 5:33-37).

The problem is determining what kind of situation existed in which Christians were finding oaths necessary or helpful. Vulgar profanity using God's name as an oath may have been less of a problem than calling upon God as a witness to a promise to carry out an anticipated action. The one making such an oath called the judgment of God upon himself if he failed to carry out what he had sworn to do. Jesus did not make this kind of oath before Caiaphas, but rather He made an oath concerning the truth. Jesus willingly put Himself under oath in His self-confession that He was "the Christ, the Son of God" (Matt. 26:63-64). This was an oath concerning the truth, not a performance oath with the promise to carry out a future action. It is hardly plausible that Matthew would put Jesus in a position of contradicting Himself on an issue against which He spoke so forcefully (Matt. 5:33-37; 23:16-22).

James' readers were making their future plans and asking God's judgment on themselves if they failed to accomplish them. Here the circumstances would be similar to those of the Sermon. In the Sermon Jesus finds the taking of oaths concerning future actions to be inspired by Satan (*ek tou ponērou*), because such an oath asserts man's free control of the future and denies God's continuing role as Creator. James warns of the eschatological danger. Calling upon God as the Judge over future matters which no man can control is dangerous. This section on oaths concerning the future seems to be related to 4:13-16, where plans are made without any awareness that God ultimately controls all things.

Personal Problems (5:13-18)

Next, James offers some specific remedies for those afflicted with depression, euphoria, and illness:

> Is anyone of you suffering (*kakopathei*)? Let him pray. Is any cheerful (*euthumei*)? Let him sing praise. Is any among you sick? Let him call for the elders of the church (*tous presbuterous tēs ekklēsias*), and let them pray over him, anointing him with oil in the name of the Lord (5:13-14).

This section attracts attention because of his reference to the healing of the physically sick. Less attention is given to the problems of depression and euphoria. The depression brought by the persecution had been the real source of problems of backbiting, grumbling, and apostasy. Rather than condemning this depressed spirit, James suggests that such affliction can be relieved by prayer. Martin Luther was sorely afflicted in his spirit and called these spiritual afflictions *Anfechtungen,* a German word carried over into English theological language to express that sore depression in which the Christian finds himself deprived of a gracious God and His salvation. This suffering was caused by real persecution, but it affected the spirit and the emotions. In prayer the Christian is drawn closer to the God who he believes has rejected him.

James also has a word for those who were enduring the persecution with some success: "Is any cheerful? Let him sing praise (*psalletō*)." This advice is the same given by Paul to the charismatics in Corinth. There some Christians had limited their faith to their emotions so that their minds or intellects had become dead. Paul's solution was to pray and sing (*psalō*) with the mind and emotions (1 Cor. 14:15). There is no suggestion that the Palestinian congregations and their pastors knew of any charismatic problem as faced by Paul in Corinth; nevertheless, the emotions are an essential part of a human being, especially of the Christian. The religious use of the emotions is not equivalent to faith, but the emotions affect faith and cannot be disregarded. The depressed Christian finds his release in prayer, and the euphoric Christian in singing. In the early church such singing expressed itself in psalms which, as for Jesus, remained its hymn book.

The problem of physical illness, unlike emotional problems, requires the attention of the church elders (*tous presbuterous tēs ekklēsias*). Such a phrase indicates a highly developed form of church government at a very early period. James here does not use "synagogue," which is more the equivalent of a local congregation, but "church," which may also refer to a wider body of Christians, as in Acts 9:31. It cannot be determined when the church adopted the term "elder," but it appears very early. On his return to Ephesus, Paul calls the elders together, and James at the Council of Jerusalem supervises the elders gathered as a group. Elders were simply pastors and were probably a carryover from the synagogues, from which the early Christians naturally patterned their congregations. The office had nothing to do with their age. One congregation may have had several pastors, or several congregations together may have been supervised by a group of clergymen together.

As the clergy are called (*proskalesasthō*) to the bed of the sick person, a more formal and solemn meeting is intended. Such a solemn gathering is intended by Matthew when Jesus commissioned His disciples (10:1) and when the child is called into their midst (18:2). James has in mind something more than a casual visit. The ill is so sick he cannot leave his bed, and the clergy are called as a group and not as individuals.

The saving efficacy is attached to the prayer rather than to the oil, as James says "and the prayer of faith will save the sick man, and the Lord will raise (*egerei*) him up" (5:15).

There is no solid agreement over the meaning of the phrase "anointing him with oil in the name of the Lord," an action which accompanies the prayer of the clergy. In the Roman Catholic Church this passage was traditionally, but now less frequently, cited to support the doctrine of extreme unction, a sacrament provided as a salvific benefit in the afterlife for those who are on the verge of dying. It became for them a necessary sacrament.[9] An opposite point of view sees in the application of the oil only a medicinal purpose, without religious significance. Some see the pouring of oil as symbolic of God's healing power or the presence of the Holy Spirit. Such views are not necessarily foreign to James, as he does have a doctrine of the Spirit's indwelling (4:5) and the next verse speaks of the Lord's raising up the ill person. As this pouring of oil takes place in the name of the Lord, it may be viewed as an activity of Jesus, the exalted Lord, in the congregation. Since Jesus is the One who is primarily acting in His church, it is in this sense a sacramental act, a continuation of His earthly ministry of healing.

James continues this section on prayer with a discussion of its power, vv. 15-18:

> And the prayer of faith (*pisteōs*) will save the sick man, and the Lord will raise (*egerei*) him up; and if he has committed sins, he will be forgiven. Therefore confess your sins to one another, and pray for one another, that you may be healed. The prayer of a righteous man (*dikaiou*) has great power in its effects. Elijah was a man of like nature (*homoiopathēs*) with ourselves and he prayed fervently that it might not rain, and for three years and six months it did not rain on the earth. Then he prayed again and the heaven gave rain, and the earth brought forth its fruit.

James continues to develop thoughts for which he has already laid the groundwork. His phrase "the prayer of faith will save the sick" resembles the words of Jesus to the woman with the issue of blood, "Your faith has made you well" [or "saved you"]" (Matt. 9:22). There is no major theological problem in ascribing salvation to either faith or the prayer of faith. "Faith" here in James is used in a way not essentially different from that of Paul and Jesus. The faith acceptable to God places its trust solely in Him. This "prayer of faith" is offered in the full anticipation that God will answer it and grant its request. Her "prayer of faith" saved the woman with the issue of blood because her faith was directed to Jesus with the complete confidence that He would grant her request. Since faith places all its reliance on Jesus, such faith is always in a state of prayer. Faith is always at prayer.

It is of no value to debate whether for James the saving quality resides in faith and its prayer or in God or Jesus. Though James speaks of the prayer of faith saving the sick, he immediately adds that the Lord, i.e., Jesus, will raise him up. James is also careful not to say that the prayer of faith justifies, but rather that it saves. Faith justifies, but such justifying faith always exists in a condition of prayer, through which faith's deepest desires are made known to God.

"The prayer of faith will save the sick man, and the Lord will raise him up" sounds like an absolute promise to heal the sick.[10] Yet, though the apostles heal on different occasions, it would be difficult to demonstrate that healing miracles were common experiences among the early Christian congregations. Strikingly, the words for saving and raising up are both future, actions which will happen. Salvation in its completeness lies in the future, to be completed by God at His own choosing. So here James is not speaking to the question of justification but to the issue of whether the sick person can be assured of salvation. The present sickness should not be interpreted by the afflicted as a sign of God's disfavor on the Last Day. There is no suggestion that his sickness is a result of his sin. The word for "raise" (*egeirō*) in raising the sick person is frequently used in the New Testament of the resurrection and is used by Paul of the general resurrection (1 Cor. 15:29, 32). Rather than being a promise for immediate healing, it can be understood as a promise that Jesus will grant the sick one the resurrection. James has been eschatological throughout his epistle. In the crisis of a sickness that might bring death, the sick person is to focus on the final salvation and resurrection wrought by Christ. Without cause some suggest that illness is the result of a specific sin and that the sick person should examine himself for secret sin.

Also forgiveness of sins is spoken of in the future tense: "And if he has committed sins, he will be forgiven (*aphethēsetai*)." Certainly James is not speaking to the question of whether the justified person is now forgiven by God. Rather he is speaking of the Last Day, when God will find the righteous to be innocent of all sins. The same futuristic idea is present in the Lord's Prayer, in which the petitioner asks God to forgive sins (Matt. 6:12). Jesus provides His own explanation that the Father *will* forgive (*aphēsei*) their sins to those who forgive others (Matt. 5:14-15). The Father's forgiveness is the eschatological forgiveness of the Last Day.

There is no necessary connection between sins and sickness; however, without an eschatological understanding of this section that could easily be the meaning, as some have suggested.[11] The present distress in no way indicates God's final disposition to the sick person. Just the opposite is so. Regardless of the fatality of his sickness, he still has the promise of the resurrection.

The admonition to pray and confess sins seems to apply to the entire Christian life and not merely to one life-threatening moment: "Therefore confess your sins to one another, and pray for one another, that you may be healed (*iathēte*)" (5:16). The Greek word for "confess" (*exomologeō*), is used of those who confessing their sins come to John the Baptist (Matt. 3:6) in order to avoid the final display of God's wrath. The prayer offered for others asks for God's forgiveness after the confession. It matters little whether the sins confessed are against God or against others, especially fellow Christians. Essential for James is that the offense of disregarding the poor expresses contempt for Christ. The problem for these Christians lies in recognizing that God is offended by disregarding others. The promise of healing coming after a confession of sins is best understood as a reference to the forgiveness wrought through Christ's atonement.

While some might want to see healing as the response to physical sickness,[12] in 1 Peter 2:24 healing is the response to sin as spiritual sickness: "He Himself bore our sins *(harmartias)* in His body on the tree, that we might die to sin and live in righteousness. By His wounds you have been healed *(iathēte)*." Healing for James is the immediate release from the distress of sin and not the final deliverance. James here is not so much concerned with eschatological salvation as he is with removing those internal feelings of distress which were disturbing the church members.

The absence of the definite article before "righteous" in the sentence "The prayer of a righteous man has great power in its effects" (v. 16) points not to Christ but to those who have given evidence of their righteousness in their attitude, a matter previously discussed by James (2:18-26). The RSV translation that the prayer "has great power in its effects," as it must in translation, glosses over the grammatical ambiguity of whether *energoumenē* is a participle in the passive or the middle voice. The passive voice would say that a righteous man's prayer, engendered by God, is very effective. The middle sense, preferred by the RSV, would see the prayer springing from the man's own initiative. Arguments for both understandings are grammatically possible. In order to remain within James' own theological perspective, it might be best to stay with the passive understanding that sees the prayer engendered by God and not by the person praying. James sees justification as passive (2:24). Though he has a high attitude toward prayer, he still states that Jesus is the One who raises up the sick (5:15). Thus the sentence could be paraphrased: "The prayer engendered by God in the man whom He has justified is extremely effective."

The effectiveness of such a prayer is seen in Elijah, whose prayers actually affected the weather cycle between drought and rain. Striking is that Elijah is called "a man of like nature *(homoiopathēs),*" that is, a man who faced the same dilemma as James' readers. The selection of Elijah as an example might further suggest that James' readers are primarily early church pastors. Elijah, considered the greatest of preachers, was, like the pastors in the Diaspora, confronted with persecution and afflicted with a sense of personal failure to the point of finding his own ministry useless. An Elijah complex is such a near-constant feeling of persecution. The external persecution of the early Christians was also the cause of their emotional and spiritual distresses. Elijah is held up as an example not of despair but of one whose despair was relieved by God's answering his prayers.

Correcting a Doctrinal Problem (5:19-20)

The last verses in the epistle, vv. 19-20, address the problem of handling doctrinal aberrations.

> My brethren, if anyone among you wanders *(planēthē)* from the truth *(alētheias)* and someone brings him back, let him know that whoever brings back a sinner from the error of his way *(ek planēs hodou)* will save *(sōsei)* his soul from death and will cover a multitude of sins.

James shows a concern for the necessity of true doctrine not in punishing the erring teacher by exclusion but in restoring him. The Greek work *planaō* is used of erring teachers (2 Peter 2:15). It means wandering. It is the root word for planets, bodies in the heavens (unlike the more predictable stars) whose course appeared irregular to the ancients. The erring Christian was one who forsook the message delivered by Christ. Teachers err (Matt. 24:4-5), and believers are led astray (1 Peter 2:25). "Truth" refers to the entire revealed body of Christian doctrine as a pattern for living, a thought adopted from the Old Testament and Judaism. The sinner has forsaken Christian truth for an erring way (*hodos*). The erring way is opposed to "the Way," a term used as a synonym for Christianity (Acts 9:2). In the very earliest period of the church it would be most natural to see erring ways thus.

Returning the erring teacher is said to cover a multitude of sins. James is in no way suggesting that the act of returning an erring brother to the truth is an atoning or sacrificial act, but rather his returning to the truth will have the effect of preserving his congregation, i.e., those who listen to his preaching, in the truth. The soul of the erring preacher and those who listen to him will hear the message of forgiveness preached and will be saved.[13] It is with this evangelistic note that James ends what is probably the first New Testament writing.

XIV/Epilog: At the Dawn of the New Testament

With few exceptions the books of the New Testament fall into recognizable categories as either gospels or epistles. Other books, such as Acts, Hebrews, and Revelation, whose style or content are unique, defy classification with other writings. James belongs with these. Its form is that of an epistle, but its language resembles a gospel. As no other epistle, it breathes the air of the gospels, but without providing easily recognizable direct sayings of Jesus or recording His deeds.

Here James resembles Paul, who makes general reference to Christ's life in the standardized creedal formulas of birth, death, burial, resurrection, ascension, session, and return. Unlike Paul, he reworks Jesus' preaching material, most notably the Sermon on the Mount and the parables, to address his audience. While resemblance to the synoptic gospels is easily recognized, James uses such characteristic Johannine words as "truth," "way," "love," and "coming down." James and Paul are the only two New Testament writers to offer an abstract doctrinal discussion on the nature of justification. Both use Gen. 15:6 as the core of this discussion and cite Abraham as an example. Both James and the writer of Hebrews use Abraham as an example of faith in the same way and make mention of Rahab. It is hard to escape the impression that Paul and the writer of Hebrews are amplifying material found in James. First Peter follows James in addressing Christians suffering persecution and using the word "Dispersion" to describe them. Mark and Luke seem dependent on James for their renditions of the commandments prohibiting murder and adultery. Characteristic Johannine words are also prefigured in James. By making these references to James, nearly all the later New Testament writers may have been recognizing this epistle as authoritative in the church at the time they wrote.

Early 20th-century New Testament scholars, most prominently Albert Schweitzer, began recognizing Jesus as an eschatological preacher. Regardless of the extremes that some positions went to, a new dimension to Jesus and the gospels was opened. With this newly discovered perspective James appears as an eschatological preacher whose message at many points resembles John the Baptist and Jesus. The coming kingdom with its crucifixion and resurrection in the preaching of the Baptist and Jesus is transformed by James into Christ's final coming in judgment and is preached with the same urgency as was the original message.

James' uniqueness also rests in putting gospel material in a more highly developed Greek style. Still the charge made particularly in the 19th century against Paul that he had changed the religion of Jesus could not ever be effectively leveled at James. If the charge against the gospels stands, that they are merely collections of Jesus' sayings and deeds, then James must be understood as offering another collection. But if the gospels are seen as serious theological documents, then James can be taken in the same light.

James stood at the dawn of the New Testament, before Paul began standardizing theological vocabulary through the influence of his epistles and before the sayings of Jesus were collected into the gospels. He was the first to give written expression to a message which up to that time had been shared only by word of mouth. As with many pioneers his role was forgotten, and when revived, it was misunderstood. Paul, the apostle to the Gentiles, had so changed the face of the church and theology that the Jewish milieu in which the Gospel first came and the church first lived was soon relegated to history. The prominence of Paul was furthered by Luke, a Gentile, in writing Acts. Though passing reference is made to James, the center of attention shifts quickly from Peter to Paul. Even in the apostolic era and into the postapostolic age the position of James became more unenviable when he was made patron by those insisting on the retention of certain Jewish customs. His descendency in the church was in direct proportion to Paul's ascendency. It was almost a cause-and-effect situation.

During his lifetime James remained as a symbol of the church's unity in the midst of its controversies as no other apostle did. He guided the church through persecution and supervised it as it left Jerusalem. As a rallying point for the dispersed Christians, he conducted the first church council at Jerusalem. He was the first to write an epistle, one that was directed to persecuted Christians. James stood between Jesus and Paul at the dawn of the New Testament, but the dawn lasts for only a short time. His epistle is a window to what that dawn looked like.

XV/Luther, the Lutherans, and James: An Attempt at a Defense

Luther

Since Luther's Preface to James appeared in 1522 and again in the year of his death, 1546, it can hardly be argued that his negative assessment of James was limited to simply one period of his life. It cannot be blamed on reforming adolescence or the stagnant orthodoxy of old age. In his Preface he raised two basic arguments against James: It was contrary to Paul's doctrine of justification by faith without works and made no mention of Christ's saving works. (This book was in some way intended to answer these objections.) For Luther a book without justification and Christ could not be the work of an apostle, as the apostles were chosen to preach Christ.[1] Luther reversed the logic here and said that if Judas, Annas, Pilate, or Herod preached Christ, such preaching would be apostolic. A critical analysis of Luther's concept of apostolicity should not be drawn from this, as it seems that he is speaking to the question of the Word of God's validity as converting Gospel. The Gospel, regardless of the speaker, is God's Word and effective. It is an anti-Donatistic statement. In his Preface Luther hedged a little on the nonapostolicity of James by conceding that the author had made use of other apostolic writings. But what he gave with one hand he took back with the other by saying that he was disorganized and not qualified for the task. Luther's use of James in a very favorable way in the Large Catechism raises the question of whether his followers took his negative criticism of James more seriously than he did. Later Luther tended to rely more on historically verified authorship and less on content in making his verdicts about the Biblical books.[2]

When he came to writing the Large Catechism, only seven years after the Preface, Luther twice cites James in an authoritative way as Scripture. In discussing sins of slander in his exposition of the Eighth Commandment, he used James 3:5 with its description of the tongue as the most destructive member of the body.[3] This presents no problem as Luther said in his Preface that this James "does nothing more than drive to the law." Quite inconsistent with this, however, is his use of James 1:6-7 in connection with the closing paragraph of his exposition of the Lord's Prayer. He says that people who doubt that God will hear their prayers "have their eye not on God's promise but on their own works and worthiness, so that they despise God and accuse him of lying. Therefore they receive nothing, as St. James says, 'If anyone prays, let him ask in faith . . .'"[4] It is hard to escape the conclusion that Luther understands James as requiring a faith that puts its trust totally in God without in any way relying on one's own merits or worthiness. The question that remains unanswered is whether he was aware of his own apparent inconsistency. It perhaps did not bother him much. In fact Luther then says that James condemns those people who pray relying on themselves. Here Luther's assessment of James as an apostle of faith is essentially no different than what has been offered on these pages.

It is difficult to say why Luther permitted the Preface to be republished in 1546. He simply may not have checked it that carefully. On the other hand, he may have been so infuriated by the use his Roman Catholic opponents were making of James 2:24 in the discussion of justification that he simply let his first words stand.

Throughout his life Luther was committed to the *semper virgo* doctrine, developed by St. Jerome, that Mary had no marital relations with Joseph. This made it impossible for Luther to recognize that in addition to the two Jameses, one the son of Zebedee and the other the son of Alphaeus, who were counted among the original 12 disciples, there was another James, the uterine brother of Jesus. Luther's inability to acknowledge that Jesus had a uterine brother made it difficult for him to designate a specific historical apostolic figure as the author. In spite of this he did have to admit that the Epistle of James copied from other extant apostolic writings and thus was not totally devoid of apostolic thought.

The Lutherans

Luther's most prominent and influential co-worker, Philip Melanchthon, the author of the Augsburg Confession, the chief of the Lutheran Confessions, made use of James in some detail in the Apology of the Augsburg Confession, in the article on justification.[5] The Roman Catholic opponents had in the Confutation of the Augsburg Confession made use of James 2:24, "You see that a man is justified by works and not by faith alone" to support their position that works played a part in the justification of the sinner. Melanchthon's use of James is strikingly modern in its approach. He handles the matter of justification within the context of the entire epistle without concentrating on one passage, isolated out of its context, as later theologians often did, and never once suggests that its chief value is its moral admonitions.

Melanchthon first notes that in speaking of justification by faith and works, James is keeping faith in Christ as central. Without such faith Christ as the Propitiator is excluded. Second, he points out that James is speaking about the works of those who have already been reconciled and justified and therefore this passage cannot be appropriately used to demonstrate that we merit the forgiveness of sins. Third, Melanchthon understands James 1:18 as a reference to regeneration and justification by faith—a most amazingly modern observation! Fourth, the reformer notes that James himself makes the distinction between a living faith and a dead faith, a faith of devils, which consists only in knowledge and not trust. Finally, Melanchthon shows that James teaches that those who are righteous by faith produce works acceptable to God. He does not teach that works merit forgiveness, regenerate hearts, propitiate, and please God without Christ.

Fifty years later the Formula of Concord in the article on righteousness makes reference to Melanchthon's discussion on James and adds the note that James is speaking to the question of how justifying faith can be identified.[6] Good works indicate the presence of a justifying faith.

The Formula of Concord was the last of the Lutheran Confessions, but its chief writer, Martin Chemnitz, was addressing issues in other writings very much in the style of Luther and Melanchthon. In his *Examination of the Council of Trent,* written before the Formula, he addresses himself to the issue raised by the Roman Catholics that James 2:21-24 teaches justification by works. His response here is similar to the treatment of the matter in the Formula: "James, therefore, is speaking of this, that the obedience and good works of Abraham declared and furnished proof that he had truly been justified by faith. For to James 'to be justified' means to be declared righteous through external testimonies."[7]

Neither Luther nor Melanchthon nor Chemnitz made an attempt to understand James as a total or complete theological treatise in itself, but where they cited him, they indicated for the most part a penetrating understanding. While Luther's use of James 3:5 as a prohibition against slander was consistent with his verdict that this epistle is moralistic in tone, he contradicted his stated position by using James 1:6-7 as a description of faith. What he in theory denied to James, he in fact gave him. Luther's use of James in this way disproved his own verdict that "this James does nothing more than drive to the law and to its works." Melanchthon saw in James a developed doctrine of regeneration and justification. Chemnitz came closest to James' understanding of justification by pointing out that works verify that justification has taken place.

On two points they were less clear. They never say explicitly that justifying works were to be understood not in the context of fulfillment of the Decalog but in the context of the sacrificing activities demanded by the Gospel. Abraham in his willingness to sacrifice his son and Rahab in her hiding the Hebrew spies were really making sacrifices of themselves and not merely fulfilling legal commandments to prove that they had faith. They also did not make note of James' eschatological understanding of justification. Not only do good works verify faith in the context of this life, as Chemnitz pointed out, but they are evidence valid before Christ the Judge on the Last Day. The eschatological tenor of the New Testament writings is an observation which has become prominent only in more recent times. What is important is that they did recognize the Epistle of James as Gospel, a recognition which their followers did not always make.

James

The Lutheran attitude towards the Epistle of James has been one of predicament, embarrassment, and confusion. The predicament was caused by Luther's less-than-positive views about the epistle on one side and a hesitancy to adjust the received canon to accommodate him. The embarrassment came from certain statements in the epistle which made it appear, at least superficially, that a justification doctrine different from Paul's was being presented. Another less sensitive doctrine might have been ignored, but not justification. This was at the heart of the Reformation. Confusion came from an attempt to identify an author of the epistle whose credentials would require his writing to be regarded as apostolic.

Historically it was inevitable that James would be overshadowed by the more prolifically literary Paul. The ascendancy of Paul as church theologian was furthered by the Reformation. To make matters worse, James was admired by those who saw Christianity as a religion of morals. Such an abuse of his memory in modern times was only a repetition of what happened to him early in the church's history. The Judaizers who bothered the church in Galatia claimed his support, and the Ebionites, an early Jewish Christian sect, made him their involuntary patron.

James should be read, not from the Pauline perspective but from the perspective of Jesus, especially as He appears in the Sermon on the Mount. The similarity between James and the Sermon has often been recognized by scholars. What is destructive about the parallel is that the Sermon, like James, has been read as chiefly Law, for which Paul provided the corrective antidote of free salvation. This was also Luther's view. In practice Luther handled the matter slightly differently. William R. Farmer explains it this way:[8]

> The Sermon on the Mount is admirably designed to represent Jesus' teaching in a most attractive manner. In reference to the Beatitudes in general and their introductory character, Martin Luther was moved to remark: "That is, indeed, a fine, sweet, friendly beginning of his teaching and sermon. For he does not proceed, like Moses, or a teacher of the law, with commands, threats, and terrors, but in a most friendly manner, with pure attractions and allurements, and pleasant promises."

Jesus must not only be understood as the Content of the Gospel, the One who is preached about, but He is also *the Preacher* of the Gospel. The Sermon, which enjoys, as Farmer says, "pride of place in Matthew,"[9] is also the written form of the first Gospel still preserved for the church. Jesus did not preach the Sermon so that His listeners might find refuge in Paul, but He presented Himself as the Rock who provides safety in the storms.

When the Sermon is understood as Jesus presenting the Gospel about Himself, then James can be understood as also presenting the Gospel about Jesus for the lives of troubled Christians. James is not the moralistic whip against sinners, but the extension of the Gospel's hand into the frantic lives of persecuted Christians who are stumbling and falling under burdens they find oppressive. In a very real way James is extending the invitation of Jesus to the weary to come to Him.

Notes

Preface

1. William R. Farmer, *Jesus and the Gospel* (Philadelphia: Fortress, 1982), p. 236. This author speaks of the martyr's canon in regard to the gospels and the Pauline epistles.
2. Farmer, pp. 227-28. The same writer develops the theme of the Spirit of the Lord speaking directly through Jesus and then through the apostles.
3. Farmer (p. 231) holds that the translation into Greek of the oral teachings of Jesus happened in Jerusalem where James, assumably the Lord's brother, could vouch for expression and then Peter and John could serve as witnesses.

Chapter I: Introduction

1. Martin Luther, "Prefaces to the New Testament", trans. Charles M. Jacobs and ed. E. Theodore Bachman, *Luther's Works*, American Edition, 35 (Philadelphia: Muhlenberg, 1960), 396—97.
2. Martin Dibelius, *James: A Commentary on the Epistle of James*, rev. Heinrich Greeve, trans. Michael A. Williams, Hermeneia—A Critical and Historical Commentary on the Bible. (Philadelphia: Fortress, 1976), p. 3.
3. James 2:24 was cited in the Council of Trent, Chapter X, Canon XXIV, to show that good works contribute to justification.
4. Though Lenski has none of Luther's difficulties concerning the canonicity of James, he comes not much further than Luther in seeing that James "speaks of the moral life which these Jewish Christians should lead in the midst of the unconverted Jews." R. C. H. Lenski, *The Interpretation of the Epistle to the Hebrews and of the Epistle of James* (Lutheran Book Concern, 1937; reprinted Minneapolis: Augsburg, 1961), p. 511. Such an assessment suffers from its failure to recognize that the Jews were highly moral, at least in an external sense.
5. Luther, *Prefaces*, p. 44.
6. Consider the attitude of Luther, at least on one occasion: "Therefore St. Paul's Epistles are more a Gospel than Matthew, Mark, and Luke. For these describe little more than the history of the works and wonder-signs of Christ; but the grace which we have through Christ, none expounds so energetically as St. Paul, especially in the Epistle to the Romans." Cited by Lenski, op. cit., p. 522.
7. J. Armitage Robinson, gen. ed., *Texts and Studies: Contributions to Biblical and Patristic Literature*, Vol. 3: *The Lord's Prayer in the Early Church* by Frederic Henry Chase (Cambridge: University Press, 1891), p. 48:

    > The Epistle of St. James is a mosaic of *logia kyriaka*, among which those "oracles" which have a place in the Synoptists' record of the Sermon on the Mount are especially numerous. Sometimes these references to Christ's teaching are obvious; sometimes they lie beneath the surface; sometimes they have become so assimilated to the context in which they are embedded that they fail to attract attention.... No tabulated statistics can give any idea of the living connexion which, even with our fragmentary knowledge of the Lord's discourses, we feel to exist between the letter of the Disciple and the words of his Master.

8. Two of the more useful commentaries to recognize in James a developed theology are James B. Adamson, *The Epistle of James*, The New International Commentary on the New Testament (Grand Rapids: Eerdmans, 1976), and Peter Davids, *Commentary on James*, New International Greek Testament Commentary (Grand Rapids: Eerdmans, 1982). Davids' commentary, appearing as this manuscript was being prepared for publication, does not receive the attention in the notes and body of this book that it deserves. His is the most exhaustive up-to-date study, with an abundance of references to Biblical and rabbinic sources and critical reviews of other commentaries.
9. Willi Marxsen, *Introduction to the New Testament*, trans. Geoffrey Buswell (Philadelphia: Fortress, 1968), p. 228. He sees in James a feeble attempt to Christianize an originally Jewish writing.
10. "EARLY JEWISH CHRISTIAN theology was 'almost exclusively Christology.' Belief in a theistic God—the one true God, who is both Creator and Redeemer—was axiomatic. What

concerned the earliest Christians, and that which they centred [sic!] their attention upon, was the redemptive activity of God in the person and work of Jesus." Longenecker, p. 25. (The words in single quotes are from O. Cullmann, *The Christology of the New Testament*, 1959, p. 3.)

Chapter II: The Person of James

1. Joseph B. Mayor, *The Epistle of James*, 2nd ed. (Grand Rapids: Baker, 1894; reprinted 1978), pp. i—xlvii. D. Edmond Hiebert, *The Epistle of James: Tests of a Living Faith* (Chicago: Moody Press, 1979), pp. 25-36. Coming to no firm conclusion about authorship is Martin Dibelius: "What can be inferred from the text about the *actual author of James* is next to nothing." *James: A Commentary on the Epistle of James*, rev. Heinrich Greeven, trans. Michael A. Williams. Hermenia—A Critical and Historical Commentary on the Bible (Philadelphia: Fortress, 1976), p. 20.
2. The idea that the Epistle of James reflects the tradition that would later be incorporated in the gospels is suggested by Simon J. Kistemaker: "The Epistle of James is commonly believed to date from the same time as 1 Thessalonians, if not five years earlier. The point is that the writer of this epistle could not rely on any written Gospels because they did not exist at that time. And yet throughout James' epistle, references and allusions—not to speak of verbal similarities—to the canonical Gospels are frequent." *The Gospels in Current Study* (Grand Rapids: Baker, 1972; reprint ed. 1980), 91—92.
3. Matt. 13:55; 27:56. Dibelius (pp. 12, 20) is convinced that the Biblical references to James the brother of the Lord are to Jesus' real brother, but does not identify this James with the epistle's author.
4. The three most common attempts to identify the Biblical figure of James the brother of the Lord are called the Epiphanian, the Helvidian, and Hieronymian views, named after their most prominent proponents. The first, named for Epiphanius, saw James and other siblings of Jesus as Joseph's children by a previous marriage. The second, named for Helvidius, saw them as the uterine brothers and sisters of Jesus, children of Mary and Joseph. The Hieronymian view, the most recent, named for St. Jerome, held that the Lord's brothers were the first cousins of Jesus. Jerome was determined to defend the perpetual virginity of Mary and Joseph. Clearly this position is determined more by theological and less by exegetical considerations and was not known in the earliest sources. Cf. F. F. Bruce, *Commentary on Galatians*, New International Greek Testament Commentary (Grand Rapids: Eerdmans, 1982), p. 99. Luther, like Dibelius later, holds that James is a pseudonym. For Luther the author had taken the name of James the son of Zebedee, and for Dibelius the name of James the uterine brother of Jesus. Those agreeing with Jerome's view of Mary's perpetual virginity, a view also held by Luther, and not agreeing with Luther's view of pseudonymous authorship, see the letter's author as James the son of Alphaeus. This is the most unlikely view of all, as the gospel writers are agreed in constantly identifying him as James the son of Alphaeus, indicating the least important of the three, and never simply James. Mayor has a most detailed presentation of the problem and supports the view that James, the author of the epistle, was really the Lord's brother.
5. F. F. Bruce, *Peter, Stephen, James and John* (Grand Rapids: Eerdmans, 1979), pp. 49—52.
6. Dibelius (p. 66) takes exception to the view that "God" refers to Jesus, but does not offer any reasons for his position. For a discussion of Paul's identifying Jesus as God (*theos*) see Murray J. Harris, "Titus 2:13 and the Deity of Christ," *Pauline Studies*, ed. Donald A. Hagner and Murray J. Harris (Grand Rapids: Eerdmans, 1980), pp. 267—77. Cf. the following observation by Sophie Laws: "The phrase *theou kai kuriou Iesou Christou* could in fact be translated as referring solely to Jesus Christ, described as 'God and Lord,' but that Jesus should be called 'God' unequivocally would be very unusual in the light of the NT practice (Jn xx. 28 is an outstanding exception), and is hardly to be expected of the author with his distinctly limited christological interest." *A Commentary on the Epistle of James*, Harper's New Testament Commentaries (New York: Harper and Row, 1980). Laws' decision is based not on grammatical evidence but on her understanding of the epistle in its entirety. The procedure could be reversed. Should the epistle begin with a reference to Jesus as God, then the interpreter would be more prepared to view other passages as references to Jesus and not to God in general.
7. "It is certainly no longer possible to assert with complete confidence that James of Jerusalem could not have written the good Greek of the epistle, since the wide currency of that language in Palestine is increasingly appreciated. J. N. Sevenster in his monograph on that subject uses the epistle of James as a test-case for his investigation and concludes that it 'must not be deemed impossible' that James the brother of Jesus could have acquired the facility to compose a letter in reasonable literary Greek." Laws, p. 40.

For additional arguments supporting the possibility that both Jesus and James were fluent in Greek see J. A. T. Robinson, *Redating the New Testament*, (Philadelphia: Westminster, 1976), pp. 132—33, where extensive bibliographical data is offered. Robinson makes the point that the "devout Jews from every nation" mentioned in Acts 2 as present for Pentecost had become permanent residents in Jerusalem and that from the beginning they had been in the majority in the church. The Aramaic-speaking Jews, commonly known as Hebrews, were at first a minority, and their growth into the majority in the Jerusalem church was threatening to the Hellenists. Regardless of which group constituted the majority, it does seem evident that the church from the earliest times was Greek-speaking. With his command of the language, James would quickly become the spokesman and be acceptable to both groups. Commenting on the work of J. N. Sevenster, "Do You Know Greek? How Much Greek Could the First Jewish Christians Have Known?" in *Supplements to Novum Testamentum* (Leiden: E. J. Brill, 1968), pp. 3—21, Robinson notes: "His conclusion is that there is in fact no reason why Jesus or the first apostles or James should not have spoken Greek as well as their native Aramaic" (p. 133).

Chapter III: Origin, Setting, Destination and Greeting

1. Hort is right in seeing the epistle's recipients as Jewish Christians before the Pauline period, but his assessment that we know little about them might be worth revising. Fenton John Anthony Hort, *Judaistic Christianity*, ed. J. O. F. Murray (1894; reprint ed., Grand Rapids: Baker, 1980), pp. 147—53).
2. The thought of fleeing from Jerusalem to the mountains for safety has been offered by Willi Marxsen in his explanation for the origin of the Gospel of Mark, *Der Evangelist Markus*, 2nd ed. 1959; Willi Marxsen, *Mark the Evangelist*, trans. Roy A. Harrisville (Nashville: Abingdon, 1969). It could very well be that this first church in Jerusalem thought of the first persecution in terms of Jesus' warning about fleeing to the mountains (Matt. 24:16). In a sense all calamities and persecutions coming on the church, e.g., the destruction of Jerusalem, are part of the eschatological judgment of God, a prominently developed theme in James.

    The similarity between the *diaspora* in James 1:1 and the "scattered" Christians in Acts 8:1, 4 is also noted by John A. T. Robinson, *Redating the New Testament* (Philadelphia: Westminster, 1976), p. 136. This leads Robinson to date the epistle in A.D. 48 (p. 138). The evidence all leans in this direction. A letter coming in A.D. 49 or after would reflect the Gentile controversy handled at the Jerusalem Council. Robinson holds that James was already a prominent leader in the church by A.D. 35 when Paul mentions him in Gal. 1:19. He had assumed the leadership between A.D. 42 and 44 when Peter went into hiding. Robinson's discussion of James (pp. 118-39) is of great value.
3. James' place in history is attested to by Jewish sources including Josephus, who recognized him for his piety and leadership qualities. Cf. F. F. Bruce, *Peter, Stephen, James and John*, (Grand Rapids: Eerdmans, 1979), pp. 110—19.
4. Willi Marxsen recognized that this greeting and the one used in the apostolic letter (Acts 15:23), along with Acts 23:26, are the only examples of the purely Greek preface in the entire New Testament. *Introduction to the New Testament*, trans. Geoffrey Buswell (Philadelphia: Fortress, 1968), p. 227.

Chapter IV: Chiefly a Pastoral Epistle

1. Hans-Joachim Schoeps, *Jewish Christianity*, trans. Douglas R. A. Hare (Philadelphia: Fortress, 1964), p. 18.
2. For a discussion of this entire matter see J. H. Bernard, *The Pastoral Epistles* (1899; Grand Rapids: Baker, reprint 1980).
3. For a discussion of the prominence of James over Peter see F. F. Bruce, *Peter, Stephen, James and John*, (Grand Rapids: Eerdmans, 1979), pp. 90—93.
4. There is a definite sense in which the designation "brothers" applies to those of similar rank or occupation. Striking is Jesus' designation of His disciples as brothers in His address after the resurrection (Matt. 28:10). The intent is that now they are with Him fully authorized to preach the message of salvation (Matt. 28:16-20).
5. In his exegetical study of 5:14, "the elders of the church," Davids discusses the type of church organization prevalent at the time of the epistle's writing. Peter Davids, *Commentary on James* (Grand Rapids: Eerdmans, 1982), p. 192. He favors the view of Günther Bornkamm that the office of elder was absorbed from the synagogue with earlier roots in the Old Testament and was a position adopted early in the church. Davids holds that this church in James was the local congregation, but in places like Rome and Corinth one church embraced more than one congregation. Davids' view is preferable to Hiebert's, who sees the elders as older lay leaders in the congregation. D. Edmond Hiebert, *The Epistle of James* (Chicago: Moody, 1979), p. 319. But since the apostles Peter and John call themselves elders, and these elders constitute a recognizable group throughout Acts, this office is better understood simply as the pastoral office, whose incumbents function together in carrying out their mutual responsibilities.
6. Cf. Hans Lietzmann, *Mass and the Lord's Supper*, trans. Dorothea H. G. Reeve, with an

Introduction and Further Inquiry by Robert D. Richardson (Leiden: E. J. Brill, 1979), pp. 204—08.
7. Joachim Jeremias, *Jerusalem in the Time of Jesus*, trans. F. H. and C. H. Cave (Philadelphia: Fortress, 1975), p. 27. Josephus suggests a much higher number.
8. J. N. Sevenster, "Do You Know Greek? How Much Greek Could the First Jewish Christians Have Known?" in *Supplements to Novum Testamentum* (Leiden: E. J. Brill, 1968), p. 81. Sevenster mentions that while some hold that these Jews were only temporary visitors to Jerusalem, he personally believes that "they were Jews from the diaspora who had resided for a longer period, or even permanently in Jerusalem."
9. Werner Vogler, "Die Bedeutung der urchristlichen Hausgemeinden für die Ausbreitung des Evangeliums," *Theologische Literaturzeitung*, 107 (November 1982), 785—94.
10. J. Julius Scott Jr., "James the Relative of Jesus and the Expectation of an Eschatological Priest," *Journal of Evangelical Theological Society*, 25 (September 1982), pp. 323—33. Scott concludes from the postcanonical literature that James was the actual brother of Jesus, since he was accorded the position of high priest. This happened since as the brother of Jesus he was given the same honor accorded Aaron the brother of Moses. See also his unpublished doctoral dissertation for research into the early church situation. *The Church of Jerusalem, A.D. 30—100: An Investigation of the Growth of Internal Factions and the Extension of Its Influence in the Larger Church* (unpublished dissertation; Manchester, England: University of Manchester, 1969).

Chapter V: Temptation, Persecution, and Faith

1. Cf. F. F. Bruce, *Peter, Stephen, James and John* (Grand Rapids: Eerdmans, 1979), p. 114: "According to Hegesippus, James' ascetic life and strict devotion to prayer and temple-worship earned him the reverence of the Jerusalem populace, who called him James the Just and the 'bulwark of the people.'"
2. Dibelius is seen as one of those who hold James as "a collection of material from impersonal paraenetic tradition, an arranging together of admonitions of general ethical content, according to the manner characteristic of Greek and Jewish proverbial wisdom." Paul Feine and Johannes Behm, *Introduction to the New Testament*, completed, reedited by Werner Georg Kümmel, 14th ed., trans. A. J. Mattill Jr. (Nashville: Abingdon, 1964), p. 286. Cf. Martin Dibelius, *James: A Commentary on the Epistle of James* (Philadelphia: Fortress, 1976), pp. 1—7.
3. Cf. G. W. H. Lampe, *God as Spirit* (Oxford: Clarendon, 1977), p. 163.

Chapter VI: The Pastoral Office, the Lure of the World, and Christ

1. It cannot be determined whether the hymn to Christ in Philippians 2 (as well as in 1 Tim. 3:16) was original with him or adopted from an already extant tradition, even though the latter option seems more probable. The language of humiliation and exaltation, as known from Jesus, could very well have served as the model on which the first Christians constructed their hymnology.
2. Simon J. Kistemaker, *The Gospels in Current Study* (1972; Grand Rapids: Baker, reprinted ed. 1980), p. 36.
3. Luther totally supports a Messianic interpretation of Psalm 1. *First lectures on the Psalms, Luther's Works*, American Edition, Vol. 10, ed. Hilton C. Oswald, trans. Herbert J. A. Bouman (St. Louis: Concordia, 1974), pp. 11—34. He also sees a description of the Christian within the Christological framework.
4. James Adamson cannot himself escape seeing the crown of life as a reward for a type of moral living. *The Epistle of James* (Grand Rapids: Eerdmans, 1976), p. 68.
5. Mayor makes a convincing case that the similarity of these words to 2:5, which in turn resembles the Sermon on the Mount, points to the live possibility that Jesus in His earthly ministry first spoke these words. James does seem to be quoting direct words of Jesus. Joseph B. Mayor, *The Epistle of James* (Grand Rapids: Baker, 1894; reprinted 1978), p. 47.
6. For a discussion of the conception language used here by James see Mayor, pp. 53—54.
7. Mayor, p. 55.
8. *Theological Dictionary of the New Testament*, ed. Gerhard Friedrich and Gerhard Kittel, trans. and ed. Geoffrey W. Bromiley (Grand Rapids: Eerdmans, 1967), Vol. 5, 887 "*pas, hapas*," by Bo Reicke. Though Reicke does not make reference to the James passage, he does note that *pas* as an adjective in the singular without the article means full, supreme, total, and pure. Similar is the "every Scripture" or "all Scripture" (*pasa graphē*) of 2 Tim. 3:16. The Scripture is only one, but its divine character is evident in all of its parts.
9. Richard N. Longenecker, *The Christology of Early Christianity*, (London: SCM, 1970; reprint ed., Grand Rapids: Baker, 1981), pp. 58—61. Longenecker finds that "a further feature of early

Jewish Christianity appears to have been the description of Jesus and the redemption accomplished by Him in terms of the *katabasis* (descent)—*anabasis* (ascent) motif." His argument is built on the understanding that the Christological hymn of Phil. 2:6-11 is originally non-Pauline and that it reflects "the convictions and piety of early Palestinian Christians." The same scheme is found in John 3:13 and 6:62. Longenecker also holds that the first half of the motif underlies the Prologue of John's Gospel, speaking as it does of pre-existence, divinity and incarnation." The same theme is located in the Book of Hebrews with "its presentation of the lowering, obedience, and temptations of the Son in chapter two and five, and in its doctrine of the heavenly priesthood of Jesus in 4:14-10:8." Other New Testament references cited by Longenecker include 1 Peter 3:18-22, Eph. 4:8-10, Rom. 10:5 f., and 1 Tim. 3:16. Longenecker makes no mention of the use of these terms in James and thus does not recognize the possible inclusion of this theme there. His arguments, however, which point to an early Christian, Palestinian, and pre-Pauline origin for these words in relation to this theme, can only indicate that James does know of incarnation and redemption and expresses them in the earliest forms.

10. Mayor, p. 59.
11. None of the commentators consulted see the James 1:17 passage as an incarnation and atonement reference, though some see here a reference to regeneration with the birth imagery. Amazing is that the Formula of Concord, the last of the officially recognized Lutheran Confessions, uses James 1:17 in just this way. Article II on the "Free Will" states that "conversion, faith in Christ, regeneration, renewal, and everything that belongs to its real beginning and completion in no way [is ascribed] to the human powers of the natural free will ... but altogether and alone to the divine operation and the Holy Spirit, as the Apology declares." In support of this position, the Formula states, "In short, every good gift comes from God (James 1:17)." *The Book of Concord*, trans. and ed. Theodore G. Tappert (Philadelphia: Fortress, 1959), p. 526. What is striking is that the Formula understands the passage not as referring to God's creative goodness for the world, but to regeneration as His sole responsibility. The passage is again used in the discussion of the incarnation to demonstrate that not even incarnation affects the deity. Article VIII on "The Person of Christ" states: "Since there is no variation with God (James 1:17), nothing was added to or detracted from the essence and properties of the divine nature in Christ through the incarnation, nor was the divine nature intrisically diminished or augmented thereby." Op. cit., p. 600.

Chapter VII: Guidelines for Pastors

1. Bertril Gärtner, *Didaskalos: The Office, Man and Woman in the New Testament*, trans. John E. Halborg (no publisher, no date), pp. 9—10. The information for the original Swedish publication is more complete: *Ambet, mannen och kvinnan i Nya Testamentet* (Lund, Sweden: Gleerupsk Universitets Bokhandels Förlag, 1958). Bishop Gärtner notes that when *lalein* is used in connection with the church service, it always means to preach in the sense of proclamation, exposition, and teaching. He calls it the *nomen technicum* for preaching.
2. Cf. F. F. Bruce, *Tradition: Old and New* (Grand Rapids: Zondervan, 1970), pp. 58-73.
3. Cf. Hans-Joachim Schoeps, *Jewish Christianity*, trans. Douglas R. A. Hare (Philadelphia: Fortress, 1964).
4. Mayor notes the similarity to the baptismal terminology used in 1 Peter 3:21. Joseph B. Mayor, *The Epistle of James* (Grand Rapids: Baker, 1894; reprinted 1978), p. 64.
5. Adamson favors seeing this reference to the Law as chiefly moral, idealized in the life and death of Jesus. He concludes that the phrase points to Christianity "as a way of life, a standard of conduct... a gift of the Jew to his Gentile fellow Christian." *The Epistle of James* (Grand Rapids: Eerdmans, 1976), p. 34. Hiebert is closer to the meaning of the "perfect law of liberty" when he writes: "This law is final and complete, embodying the full and effective revelation of God in Christ Jesus." D. Edward Hiebert, *The Epistle of James* (Chicago: Moody, 1979), p. 136.
6. Mayor (p. 70) offers the suggestion that the Pauline passage is a comment on James and that the reference to the perfect law of liberty is to the Gospel.
7. Donald Guthrie notes that in the Sermon on the Mount the word for "perfect" (*teleios*) strictly means complete. *New Testament Theology* (Downers Grove, Ill.: InterVarsity, 1981), p. 663. In 3:2 James will use it in a sense similar to that of the Sermon as showing love. When "perfect" is applied to the Law, it should be seen as regarding its *completeness*, rather than its lack of *imperfection*.
8. Hiebert (pp. 136-37) correctly notes that the Law here is called the law of freedom or liberty because of the "well-known Christian freedom from bondage which believers know through faith in Christ (John 8:31-36)" but sees the Law's perfection in its ability to give the "beholder a true and undistorted revelation of himself." While Hiebert seems to understand the perfect law

of liberty as the Gospel, he also seems to see it as condemning law. This would be, of course, a confusion of Law and Gospel.
9. This regretfully could be the suggestion of Hiebert (p. 138): " 'The life of obedience is the element wherein the blessedness is found and consists.' The voluntary doing of God's will is the secret of true happiness."

Chapter VIII: Christ's Poverty and Its Implications

1. This view is favored by Hiebert, *The Epistle of James* (Chicago: Moody, 1979), p. 149 and Adamson, *The Epistle of James* (Grand Rapids: Eerdmans, 1976), p. 103. A slightly different perspective is offered by Sophie Laws, who sees *doxa* as the Septuagint's "regular translation of the Hebrew *kabod* [as] part of the language of theophany denoting the splendour, sometimes actual light, that is both a sign and effect of the presence of God." Laws sees a relationship between the Exodus theophany and the transfiguration of Jesus suggested in this word. Thus all of the New Testament writers, including James, who use *doxa* within its Exodus context, use it of Jesus to express "a revelation of God that was perhaps his final revelation." "So when James calls Jesus *the glory*, he may be seen to reflect his understanding of Jesus as 'theophany,' a manifestation of the presence of God." *A Commentary on the Epistle of James* (New York: Harper, 1980), pp. 95—97.
2. Mayor sees this as objective genitive, i.e., the faith which places its trust in Christ. Joseph B. Mayor, *The Epistle of James* (Grand Rapids: Baker, 1894; reprinted 1978), p. 76. This view is very tempting simply because it would put to rest as totally false that James has any hint of righteousness by works.
3. Mayor, p. 157. Cf. also Simon J. Kistemaker, *The Gospels in Current Study* (Baker, 1972; reprint ed. 1980), p. 83. "The word *ekklesia* is a synonym of *synagogue*; the words are used interchangeably in the Septuagint, and even in the New Testament such an interchange is evident." Kistemaker also notes that with the passing of time synagogue referred to the people of Israel and church to the Christian community. The interchangeability of these words in James would thus point to the earliest period of the church's history. The word "synagogue" was, however, used by early fathers for "church" on occasion.
4. Donald Guthrie has an excellent discussion of the concept of "poor" in the Sermon on the Mount. He notes that for Matthew the First Beatitude has a religious connotation, but for Luke a social one. *New Testament Theology* (Downers Grove, Ill.: Inter Varsity, 1981), p. 900.
5. Guthrie (p. 663) remarks that "No man who considers himself to have attained perfection has a right understanding of perfection." This could easily apply to anyone who thinks he has impoverished himself for Christ.
6. Guthrie (pp. 667 and 224) again remarks that Paul's reference to the impoverishment of Christ is all the more remarkable since he makes only limited reference to actual events in His life. Generosity is urged by Paul because of Christ's generosity in giving up His riches. Guthrie also opines that Paul may have known of the saying that the Son of Man had no place to put His head. We observe that the same might even more definitely be said of James.
7. If Paul was desirous of the approval of the Jerusalem church and its leading pastor, James, it is not unlikely that in his writing he would incorporate a theology and method that was easily recognizable as belonging to James.
8. Guthrie (p. 663) notes that the rewards of the Beatitudes are eschatological. Their similarity with James on this point can again be noted.
9. Adamson, p. 65.
10. Hiebert agrees in seeing this as a reference to Baptism and states that this is the commonly held opinion. D. Edmond Hiebert, *The Epistle of James* (Chicago: Moody, 1979), p. 161.
11. Peter Davids, *Commentary on James*, (Grand Rapids: Eerdmans, 1982), pp. 109-10. Davids relies on W. B. Ward, "The Communal Concern of the Epistle of James," Ph.D. diss., Harvard, 1966.
12. J. Duncan M. Derrett, "Where Two or Three Are Convened in My Name . . ." *The Expository Times*, 91 (Dec. 1979), 83—86.

Chapter IX: Love, Scripture, Apostasy, and the Triumph of the Gospel

1. Concerning James' attitude Guthrie states: "James' mind is clearly saturated with the Old Testament and he treats it as authoritative. He expects its dictates to be obeyed." Donald Guthrie, *New Testament Theology* (Downers Grove, Ill.: Inter Varsity, 1981), p. 975.
2. Hiebert finds that the law is called royal because its command to love is above all others. D. Edmond Hiebert, *The Epistle of James* (Chicago: Moody, 1979), p. 163. Adamson does see this as a reference to Christ's law. James B. Adamson, *The Epistle of James* (Grand Rapids: Eerdmans, 1976), p. 114.
3. F. F. Bruce makes a plausible case for the arrest of Paul in Jerusalem as contrived by such an

unholy alliance. *Peter, Stephen, James and John* (Grand Rapids: Eerdmans, 1979), pp. 103—08.
4. Hiebert (p. 168) notes that James is not lodging a charge of adultery against his readers.
5. Bertril Gartner, *Didaskalos*; see note 1 of ch. VII.

Chapter X: The New Testament's First Great Discussion on Justification

1. Werner Elert, *Eucharist and Church Fellowship in the Early Church*, trans. Norman Nagel (St. Louis, Concordia, 1969), p. 81, writes: "The kiss of peace had its firm place in the liturgy either at the beginning of the Eucharistic section or later, but always after the catechumens were dismissed and before the Communion proper." For a fuller discussion of the matter see Willy Rordoch, "The Lord's Prayer in the Light of Its Liturgical Use in the Early Church," *Studia Liturgica*, 14 (No. 1), 1-20.
2. Hiebert offers several possibilities. D. Edmond Hiebert, *The Epistle of James* (Chicago: Moody, 1979), pp. 182—85.
3. J. N. D. Kelly, *Early Christian Creeds*, 2nd ed. (New York: McKay, 1960), p. 28. For a detailed discussion of the use of the *Shema* see Bruce M. Metzger, gen. ed., *New Testament Tools and Studies*, Vol. 5: *The Earliest Christian Confessions*, by Vernon H. Neufels (Grand Rapids: Eerdmans, 1963), pp. 32—35.
4. "However that may be, the acceptance of so central a tenet of belief cannot be other than approved, and *you do well* is not ironical. The sting in the tail is in what follows: *the demons believe that too, and they shudder*. This passage is often cited to show that James's understanding of faith is of it as mere intellectual assent to a proposition, which even a demon can make. This is greatly to undervalue James's argument. The demons' assent is by no means merely intellectual: in believing that God is one they believe something about Him that evokes a response: that as *one* He is wholly and consistently their enemy, *and they shudder*. The picture of the demons' recognition of God is comparable to that of demons recognizing Jesus in the Markan exorcism traditions (Mk i. 24, iii. 11, v. 7), where the naming should not be seen as merely identification but as a defiant attempt to gain power over the adversary whom they can see has come 'to destroy us' (Mk. i. 24)." Sophie Laws, *A Commentary on the Epistle of James* (San Francisco: Harper, 1980), p. 126.
5. "It is worth noting that there is strong affinity between James' approach to faith and that of Hebrews. In the reference to Abraham's offering up of Isaac in Heb. 11:17ff., it is specifically Abraham's faith in God's power to raise Isaac which is emphasized." Guthrie, p. 599.
6. Adamson (p. 130) makes the valid point that the meaning cannot be that previous to his works Abraham's faith was defective, but that it was already perfect and that "faith was fulfilled, strengthened, and matured by exercise."
7. "Aware of the true nature of justifying faith, James saw that the state of mind that God accepted as righteousness in Genesis 15 must ultimately manifest itself in the unquestioning obedience described in Genesis 22." Hiebert, p. 195.
8. This section is taken by some as the most obviously anti-Pauline. Hiebert (p. 197) rightly stresses that the problem is removed if James is seen as espousing a working faith. "James believes that faith justifies, but not a 'faith' that remains alone and produces no works." Theologically there can be no major quarrel with this, but nevertheless in Pauline justification there is no stress on the activity of faith in the process of justification. The simple solution is understanding that justification here is God's public justification of the sinner before the world.
9. Guthrie sees no contradiction in Paul's and James' concepts of faith. While Paul describes the passive nature of faith, James describes its active side. He also remarks that "James lends no support to the view that man can do anything to earn his salvation. But he gives a salutary reminder that initial faith must have a practical outcome." Donald Guthrie, *New Testament Theology* (Downers Grove, Ill.: Inter Varsity, 1981), p. 599. John A. T. Robinson supports the view that James is not answering Paul in the matter of justification, since Paul never suggested that works were detrimental to salvation. Robinson suggests that Paul is answering the Judaizers who had thought they had a champion in James. *Redating the New Testament* (Philadelphia: Westminster, 1976), pp. 127—28. One further aside: Sophie Laws (p. 46) notes the irony that Luther's famous *sola fide*, faith alone, which became the byword of the Reformation and meant the triumph of Pauline theology, was taken from James 2:24.
10. Adamson offers the illustration of a hospitalized man accused of a traffic offense. "In our opinion, the difference between James and Paul in this matter is not one of fact but of apperception: when in a law court a man accused of a traffic offense 'proves' that he was in bed in a hospital all that week, James would have said the man 'proved his innocence'; Paul would say the man 'tendered proof,' and that what 'saved him' was the court's acceptance thereof." James B. Adamson, *The Epistle of James* (Grand Rapids: Eerdmans, 1976), p. 37. This illustration is valuable in seeing how justification can be ascribed either to the sinner or to God, depending upon perspective.

Notes 149

11. Some have tried to lessen the force of harlot. Cf. Hiebert, p. 198. The specific mention of Rahab as a harlot makes James' argument more forceful. A woman who was a *professional* sinner was still able to see that faith demanded appropriate action.
12. Joseph B. Mayor, *The Epistle of James* (Grand Rapids: Baker, 1894; reprinted 1978), p. 103. Understanding the analogy this way requires understanding faith as the profession of orthodoxy as the body and the principle of love as the soul.
13. Even Luther had to take it this way in his explanation of the Lord's Prayer in his Large Catechism. Cf. Chapter XV for a discussion of this matter.

Chapter XI: Again to the Pastoral Task

1. Mayor has a good summary of the teaching office in the early church. Joseph B. Mayor, *The Epistle of James* (Grand Rapids: Baker, 1894; reprinted 1978), p. 103. Hiebert offers a congregational understanding of this passage. "The term 'teachers,' occurring only here in this epistle, is not to be restricted to officially appointed teachers, but includes all those who arise to instruct their fellow members. This prohibition clearly reflects the democratic nature of the early Christian assemblies. As seen from 1 Corinthians 14:26-34, almost any believer might contribute something to the meeting." D. Edmond Hiebert, *The Epistle of James* (Chicago: Moody, 1979), p. 204. The evidence however, points in just the opposite direction. Later James refers to the elders who on the basis of other New Testament evidence were the same as the teachers. The church, like the synagogue, was not a free for all, but had set rules for leading the service and preaching. James here is speaking about the latter.
2. This is also the opinion of Mayor (p. 104), who for his position also cites 3:9 and 2:18.
3. Hiebert (p. 207) remarks that the Greek word for man, *anēr*, should not mean that only the male should strive for perfection. But if James had intended both genders, *anthrōpos* should have been employed, since it applies to all human beings. James is precise with his language, and the use of *anēr* would fortify the argument that this section is intended for the clergy.
4. Hiebert (p. 207) is right in seeing that James places himself among sinners. Of course this is also characteristic of Paul.
5. Bo Reicke, *The Epistles of James, Peter, and Jude*, The Anchor Bible, ed. W. F. Albright and D. N. Freeman, 37 (Garden City, N.Y.: Doubleday, 1964), 37—38.
6. Adamson sees this as a possible reference to the practice of imprecation, a more formal and ritualistic cursing, but prefers common slandering within the community. He also sees this as evidence that James knows of no doctrine of "total depravity" and that for both Jew and Christian "though impaired the *imago dei* is not totally destroyed." James B. Adamson, *The Epistle of James* (Grand Rapids: Eerdmans, 1976), p. 146. The early Christian liturgies had no imprecations, and an entirely different spirit existed in the Christian synagogues compared with the Jewish ones, especially in regard to forgiveness. Any suggestion that the image of God means that man apart from God can recognize and bless Him borders on Pelagianism. James is Augustinian in his concept of man's corruption and God's act of salvation.
7. Adamson (p. 26) sees for James an almost Pelagian view of sin.
8. *Commentary on James* (Grand Rapids: Eerdmans, 1982), pp. 135—49.
9. Here Adamson (p. 149) suggests a near-Pelagian view of wisdom. While acknowledging that no man except Jesus "can be absolutely innocent of sins, in his nature and behavior, it is the *effort* that distinguishes between those who seek and those who do not seek righteousness." However, James' illustrations of the trees and the springs not only see sin and good works as necessary results of what man is by nature, but also show that any change can be brought about not by effort but by a radical readjustment of that nature.
10. Mayor, p. 125.
11. Hiebert (p. 232) might be going a bit too far in seeing that this "adjective describes that part of man's nonmaterial being that he has in common with the animal world around him." He is on firmer ground in saying: "It refers to the forces and endowments of unregenerate human nature, man as he is in Adam."
12. So also Hiebert says: "There is only one devil, Satan, but there are vast numbers of demons who further Satan's work." Ibid.
13. Both Adamson (p. 154) and Hiebert (p. 234) catch the Christological connection in the Greek word for pure (*hagnē*) from its use in 1 John 3:3 and conclude that Christ is being held up as a model for this virtue. The greater Christological significance lies in the word for wisdom (*sophia*).
14. This view is held by Hiebert (p. 237), who sees righteousness as the fruit which is sown. He admits a problem in that fruit and not seed is sown. We hold that the phrase "fruit of righteousness" suggests that something has already happened and is then distributed. Mayor (p. 128) also sees the same problem as does Hiebert, but also does not resolve it.

Chapter XII: Exhortations Against Worldliness

1. Cf. Joseph B. Mayor, The Epistle of James (Grand Rapids: Baker, 1894; reprinted 1978), pp. 129—31.
2. *Peter, Stephen, James and John* (Grand Rapids: Eerdmans, 1979), pp. 108-10. While Bruce does not attribute evil motives to James and the Jerusalem pastors, he does suggest that Paul's work among the Gentiles was an embarrassment to them, as they saw the Jewish community as their chief evangelistic responsibility.
3. Not only does Hiebert mention that "the nation of Israel was viewed as bound to Jehovah by the marriage tie, and any turning to idols by the Israelites was stamped as spiritual adultery," but he observes that the language also reflects the unfaithfulness of the church to Christ as the Bridegroom. D. Edmond Hiebert, *The Epistle of James* (Chicago: Moody, 1979), p. 250.
4. Adamson handles the relationship between James and the synoptic gospels. In his understanding of the world (*kosmos*) James could have been influential on the Fourth Gospel's dualism, the world opposed to Christ. Cf. John 14:17. James B. Adamson, *The Epistle of James* (Grand Rapids: Eerdmans, 1976), pp. 21—22.
5. See also Mayor, p. 137.
6. Adamson (pp. 172—73) adopts this view in a somewhat modified form, holding that the disputed word refers "to the sinful propensities of the spirit implanted in man" and citing the NEB translation for support: "The spirit which God implanted in man turns to envious desires."
7. Mayor calls attention to 1 Peter 5:8-9 as a parallel. As Peter has begun a specific address to the clergy in 5:1, it may be that the warning about Satan may also be specifically addressed to them. This would be substantiated if "brotherhood" in the 1 Peter passage is understood as a reference to the clergy.
8. For a discussion of Servant theology in the New Testament see Donald Guthrie, *New Testament Theology* (Downers Grove, Ill.: Inter Varsity, 1981), pp. 258—68.
9. Hiebert (p. 265) interprets humility as "a voluntary self-abasement ... [before] their heavenly Master in all His ineffable majesty." Granted, this catches the necessary Christological theme, but it should be applied primarily and chiefly to Christ in His own humiliation of crucifixion, not in His glory.
10. E. g., Hiebert, p. 270, who sees this as evidence for monotheism, i.e., "the unique and sovereign God."
11. One of the three ways and perhaps the most determinative way for using the title "Son of Man" of Jesus is in regard to His eschatological mission, especially judging the world (Guthrie, p. 277). With only one exception, it is used only by Jesus of Himself and only in the gospels. The one who had called Himself the Son of Man is called the Judge by James, as "Son of Man" would have been totally inappropriate if used by another.
12. Hiebert (p. 277) does not recognize any eschatological element in this phrase and sees it as a reference to the Christian's recognition that God is absolute and sovereign. He favorably quotes E. H. Plumptre that this means "God in His Absolute Unity, without any thought of the distinction of the Persons." But the question must be raised whether the Christian can ever think of God apart from the distinction of the three Persons, especially as the Second Person became incarnate in Jesus. As the word "Lord" applies most commonly to Jesus, especially as eschatological Judge, it would not seem fitting to break from that understanding here.
13. Adamson, p. 181.
14. Mayor puts forth this view (p. 147), seeing that this sentence closes a section that began as early as 1:22. Hiebert (pp. 270—80) challenges this on the assumption that then James should have placed the sentence at the end of the epistle. In our view, the major theological portion having come to a conclusion, the final chapter contains scattered thoughts and it would be inappropriate to put the summary after them.

Chapter XIII: Addenda

1. Cf. F. F. Bruce, *Peter, Stephen, James and John* (Grand Rapids: Eerdmans, 1979), p. 103. Bruce remarks that the term "poor" came to refer to the congregation in Jerusalem. Since "poor" took on a specific religious meaning, the term "rich" could also have undergone this same kind of transformation and became virtually synonymous with unbelievers.
2. It should not be overlooked that Peter in answer to a request for alms says he has no silver and gold (Acts 3:6) and in his first epistle speaks about being "ransomed ... not with perishable ... silver or gold, but with the precious blood of Christ" (1:18-19). Gold and silver, besides representing financial wealth, could have meant for the early church any useless attempt at self-atonement, as with Judas (Matt. 27:3-10).
3. Mayor lists the several passages in the New Testament where "the last days" or an equivalent

phrase has definite eschatological reference. Joseph B. Mayor, *The Epistle of James*, 2nd ed. (Grand Rapids: Baker, 1894; reprinted 1978), p. 151.
4. Hiebert notes the similarity between this section in James and the agricultural references in Matthew used by Jesus, but fails to see that by his use of the agricultural terminology James could be speaking of the same subject as is Jesus. D. Edmond Hiebert, *The Epistle of James* (Chicago: Moody, 1979), p. 289.
5. James B. Adamson, *The Epistle of James* (Grand Rapids: Eerdmans, 1976), pp. 294—95.
6. Longenecker has no difficulty in seeing this reference along with its use in Acts 3:14, 7:52, 22:14, 1 Peter 3:18, and 1 John 2:1 as a Christological title. *The Christology of Early Jewish Christianity* (London: SCM, 1970; reprint ed., Grand Rapids: Baker, 1981), pp. 46-48.
7. Mayor (p. 156) briefly remarks: "The preciousness of the fruit justifies waiting." But he makes no remarks about what makes that fruit so precious.
8. Adamson (pp. 190-92) aptly remarks that Jesus is in a class by Himself and thus is not mentioned as an example. Job's virtue was not that he refrained from complaining but that he persisted.
9. According to Adamson (p. 205) the Roman Catholic Church in the Second Vatican Council may have backed away from this view and now identifies it as the anointing of the sick.
10. Hiebert (p. 322) wrestles with the problem of what he calls "James' unconditional language" and calls it "the prayer prompted by the Spirit-wrought conviction that it is the Lord's will to heal the one being prayed for."
11. Hiebert (p. 323) agrees that in certain cases sickness results from personal sin: "Whenever sickness does come, it is desirable for each believer to examine himself before the Lord if the sickness is due to personal sin." But just how does the Christian find this out?
12. This is Hiebert's opinion also (p. 325). If this is a reference to a miraculous cure and not the resurrection, then physical healing is the natural interpretation. Cf. Mayor, p. 170. Mayor (p. 168) also feels that Roman Catholic interpreters refer the raising up to spiritual comfort.
13. Adamson (pp. 202—03) also sees this as a special admonition for the clergy. However, he sees those who are converted as simply members of the congregation.

Chapter XV: Luther, Lutherans, and James: An Attempt at a Defense

1. Luther, "Prefaces to the New Testament," *Luther's Works*, American Edition, Vol. 35 (Philadelphia: Fortress, 1960), pp. 395-97.
2. Karl Gerhard Steck, *Lehre und Kirche bei Luther* (Munich: Chr. Kaiser Verlag, 1963), pp. 50—52.
3. *The Book of Concord*, trans. and ed. Theodore G. Tappert (Philadelphia: Fortress, 1959), p. 404.
4. Ibid., p. 436.
5. Ibid., pp. 141—43.
6. Ibid., p. 547.
7. Martin Chemnitz, *Examination of the Council of Trent*, Part I, trans. Fred Kramer (St. Louis: Concordia 1971), p. 539.
8. *Jesus and the Gospel* (Philadelphia: Fortress, 1982), p. 151.
9. Ibid., p. 155.

Bibliography

Adamson, James B. *The Epistle of James.* The New International Commentary on the New Testament. Grand Rapids, Mich.: Eerdmans, 1976.
Barclay, William. *The Letters of James and Peter.* The Daily Study Bible. 1958. 2nd ed. Philadelphia: Westminster, 1960.
Barr, James. *Holy Scripture: Canon, Authority, Criticism.* Philadelphia: Westminster 1983.
Bennet, W. H. *The General Epistles, James, Peter, John, and Jude.* The Century Bible, A Modern Commentary, edited by H. H. Rowley and Matthew Black. London: Blackwood, Le Bas, n.d.
Bernard, J. H. *The Pastoral Epistles.* Grand Rapids, Mich.: Baker, 1899; reprint ed. 1980.
Blackman, E. C. *The Epistle of James.* Torch Bible Commentaries, edited by John Marsh and Alan Richardson. London: SCM, 1957.
The Book of Concord: The Confessions of the Evangelical Lutheran Church. Translated and edited by Theodore B. Tappert. Philadelphia: Fortress, 1959.
Brochman, Jesper Rasmus. *In Canonicam et Catholicam Jacobi Epistolam Commentarius.* Copenhagen, 1706.
Bruce, F. F. *Commentary on Galatians.* New International Greek Testament Commentary. Grand Rapids, Mich.: Eerdmans, 1982.
———. *Peter, Stephen, James and John.* Grand Rapids, Mich.: Eerdmans, 1979.
———. *Tradition: Old and New.* Grand Rapids, Mich.: Zondervan, 1970.
Calvin, John. *Calvin's New Testament Commentaries.* Translated by A. W. Morrison and edited by David W. and Thomas F. Torrance. Grand Rapids, Mich.: Eerdmans, 1972.
Carr, Arthur. "The General Epistle of St. James." In *Cambridge Greek Testament.* 1896. Reprint. Cambridge: U. Press, 1930.
Carson, T. "The Letter of James." In *A New Testament Commentary.* Edited by G. C. D. Howley. Grand Rapids, Mich.: Zondervan, 1969.
Chemnitz, Martin. *Examination of the Council of Trent*, Part I. Translated by Fred Kramer. St. Louis: Concordia, 1971.
Davids, Peter. *Commentary on James.* New International Greek Testament Commentary. Grand Rapids, Mich.: Eerdmans, 1982.
Derrett, J. Duncan M. "Where Two or Three Are Convened in My Name . . ." *The Expository Times*, 91 (Dec. 1979), 83—86.
Dibelius, Martin. *James: A Commentary on the Epistle of James.* Hermeneia—A Critical and Historical Commentary on the Bible, revised by Heinrich Greeven, translated by Michael A. Williams. Philadelphia: Fortress, 1976.
Easton, Burton Scott, and Poteat, Gordon. "The Epistle of James." In *The Interpreters Bible*, edited by George Arthur Buttrick et al., Vol. 12. New York: Abingdon, 1957.
Elert, Werner. *Eucharist and Church Fellowship in the Early Church.* Translated by Norman Nagel. St. Louis: Concordia, 1969.
Farmer, William R. *Jesus and the Gospel.* Philadelphia: Fortress Press, 1982.
Feine, Paul, and Behm, Johannes. *Introduction to the New Testament.* Translated by A. J. Mattill Jr. and reedited by Werner Georg Kümmel, 14th ed. Nashville: Abingdon, 1964.
Friedrich, Gerhard, and Kittel, Gerhard, eds. *Theological Dictionary of the New Testament.* Translated and edited by Geoffrey W. Bromily. Grand Rapids, Mich.: Eerdmans, 1967.

Bibliography

Gärtner, Bertril. *Didaskalos: The Office, Man and Woman in the New Testament*, n.p., n.d. Translated by John E. Halborg from *Ambet, mannen och kvinnan i Nya Testamentet*. Lund, Sweden: Gleerupsk Universitets Bokhandels Förlag, 1958.

Guthrie, Donald. *New Testament Theology*. Downers Grove, Ill.: Inter Varsity, 1981.

Hamann, Henry P. *Chi Rho Commentary on James, Jude*. Adelaide, Australia: Lutheran Publishing House, 1980.

Harris, Murray J. "Titus 2:13 and the Deity of Christ." *Pauline Studies*, ed. Donald A. Hagner and Murray J. Harris. Grand Rapids, Mich.: Eerdmans, 1980.

Hiebert, D. Edmond. *The Epistle of James: Tests of a Living Faith*. Chicago: Moody, 1979.

Hort, Fenton John Anthony. *Judaistic Christianity*. Edited by J. O. F. Murray, 1894; reprint ed. Grand Rapids, Mich.: Baker, 1980.

Jeremias, Joachim. *Jerusalem in the Time of Jesus*. Translated by F. H. and G. H. Cave. Philadelphia: Fortress, 1975.

Kelly, J. N. D. *Early Christian Creeds*, 2nd edition. New York: McKay, 1960.

Kistemaker, Simon J. *The Gospels in Current Study*. Grand Rapids, Mich.: Baker, 1972; reprint ed. 1980.

Lampe, G. W. H. *God as Spirit*. Oxford: Clarendon, 1977.

Laws, Sophie. *A Commentary on the Epistle of James*. Harper's New Testament Commentaries. New York: Harper and Row, 1980.

Lenski, R. C. H. *The Interpretation of the Epistle to the Hebrews and of the Epistle of James*. Lutheran Book Concern, 1937; reprinted Minneapolis: Augsburg, 1961.

Longenecker, Richard N. *The Christology of Early Jewish Christianity*. London: SCM, 1970; reprint ed. Grand Rapids, Mich.: Baker, 1981.

Luther, Martin. *First Lectures on the Psalms, Luther's Works*, American Edition, Vol. 10, translated by Herbert J. A. Bouman and edited by Hilton C. Oswald. St. Louis: Concordia, 1974. *Prefaces to the New Testament, Luther's Works*, American Edition, Vol. 35, translated by Charles W. Jacobs and edited by E. Theodore Bachman. Philadelphia: Fortress, 1960.

Marxsen, Willi. *Introduction to the New Testament*. Translated by Geoffrey Buswell. Philadelphia: Fortress, 1968.

———. *Mark the Evangelist*. Translated from *Der Evangelist Markus*, 2nd ed. 1959, by Roy A. Harrisville. Nashville: Abingdon, 1969.

Mayor, Joseph B. *The Epistle of James*. 2nd ed. Grand Rapids, Mich.: Baker, 1894. Reprinted 1978.

Neufels, Vernon H. *The Earliest Christian Confessions*. Grand Rapids, Mich.: Eerdmans, 1963.

Reicke, Bo. *The Epistles of James, Peter, and Jude*, The Anchor Bible, ed. W. F. Albright and D. N. Freeman, Vol. 37; Garden City, N. Y.: Doubleday, 1964.

Robinson, J. Armitage, gen. ed. *Texts and Studies: Contributions to Biblical and Patristic Literature*, Vol. 3: *The Lord's Prayer in the Early Church* by Frederic Henry Chase. Cambridge: University Press, 1891.

Robinson, John A. T. *Redating the New Testament*. Philadelphia: Westminster, 1976.

Scaer, David P. *The Apostolic Scriptures*. St. Louis: Concordia, 1971.

———. *What Do You Think of Jesus?* St. Louis: Concordia, 1973.

Schoeps, Hans Joachim. *Jewish Christianity*. Translated by Douglas R. A. Hare. Philadelphia: Fortress, 1964.

Scott, J. Julius Jr. "James the Relative of Jesus and the Expectation of an Eschatological Priest." *Journal of Evangelical Theological Society*, 25 (Sept. 1982).

———. "The Church of Jerusalem, A.D. 30—100: An Investigation of the Growth of Internal Factions and the Extension of Its Influence in the Larger Church." Ph.D. Dissertation, Manchester, England: University of Manchester, 1969.

Sevenster, J. N. "Do You Know Greek? How Much Greek Could the First Jewish Christians Have Known?" *Supplements to Novum Testamentum*. Leiden: E. J. Brill, 1968.

Steck, Karl Gerhard. *Lehre und Kirche bei Luther*. Munich: Chr. Kaiser Verlag, 1963.

Vogler, Werner. "Die Bedeutung der urchristlichen Hausgemeinden für die Ausbreitung des Evangeliums." *Theologische Literaturzeitung*, 107 (Nov. 1982).
Weinrich, William C. *Spirit and Martyrdom*. Washington, D. C.: University Press of America, 1981.

Index

Abraham 28, 75, 83, 89-94, 96, 136, 140
Adultery 72, 79, 81, 82-84, 105, 110-11
Agriculture, agricultural (imagery, terminology) 50, 59, 102, 122, 124-26
Altar 87, 91
Anfechtung 56, 127, 131
Anger 63, 64-66, 105, 124; *see also* Wrath
Antioch 29, 33-34, 37, 63, 77, 98-99
Apology of Augsburg Confession 139-140
Apostasy 44, 56, 84-85, 110, 130
    as adultery 82
Apostle(s), apostolic(ity) 14, 19, 20, 22-23, 24-25, 27, 28-30, 32-36, 37, 42-45, 53, 69, 76, 98-99, 104, 106, 121-22, 129, 132, 138-39
Astronomical 59
Atonement, atoning 26-27, 41, 57-60, 65, 67-68, 85, 89, 91, 95, 106, 107-08, 113, 124-25, 127, 133
Augsburg Confession 139
Augustine, Augustinian 57, 61
Authority 50, 60, 88
    of Apostles (apostolic) 30
    of Christ 59, 61
    of James 25-27, 30, 34
    of pastors 69
    of Scripture 92
Authorship 19, 30-31, 138

Baptism(al), baptized 21, 50, 60-61, 65-66, 77-78, 81, 102, 108, 112
    infant 78
Barnabas 34, 35
Beatitude(s) 51-52, 54, 66, 69, 74, 75, 107-08, 113, 141
Blood of Christ 125
Body 78, 87, 88, 94-95, 100-01, 102-03, 112, 115, 138
    see also Soul
    of Christ 133-34
    of doctrine 134-35
Brother(s), brethren 25, 26, 27, 32, 34-35, 47-48, 63-64, 70, 79 80, 87-88, 92, 98, 110
    of Jesus 23-27, 32, 55
Bruce, F. F. 13, 77, 110
Bultmann, Rudolf 13, 19, 21

Canon, canonical, canonicity 19-21, 141
Catholic(s), Catholicism; *see* Roman Catholic(s), Catholicism
Chemnitz, Martin 140
Christology, Christologically 22, 42, 46, 48-49, 51-52, 54, 58, 60-61, 72, 76, 80, 113-14

Church as court 78-80, 122
Circumcision 22
    party 33
Clergy, clergymen 33-34, 35, 38, 48, 50, 57, 63, 69, 89, 98-99, 101, 103-04, 107, 112, 121, 127, 131 *see also* Pastors
Confession, confess 27, 29, 51, 72-73, 78-79, 80, 90, 133
Confessions, Lutheran 75, 139-140
Confutation of Augsburg Confession 139
Congregation(s), congregational 19, 30, 32-34, 35-37, 37-38, 39, 47, 48-50,63, 68, 69-70, 73-74, 78-80, 81, 83-84, 85, 86, 87-88, 93, 94, 97-98, 101, 103-04, 115, 117, 119, 122, 124, 128, 131-32, 135
Contrition 51
Conversion 34, 55, 64, 65, 71, 78, 99
    of James 24-26, 55
    of Jude 25
    of Paul 25, 34-35, 37, 77
Coram Deo 42
Corpus doctrinae 95
Crown(ing), crown of life, 20, 51-55, 60, 76
Crucifixion 19, 30, 33, 36-37, 48, 52, 54, 76, 82, 122, 123, 126, 136

David 94
    Son of 29
Davids, Peter 78
Death (temporal and eternal) 28, 30, 42-43, 54-55, 57, 60, 61-62, 70, 86, 88-89, 95, 105-06, 110, 133
    of Christ 30, 42, 65, 67, 68, 76, 82, 91, 113-14, 126, 136
Demon(s), demonic 90, 112; *see also* Devil, Satan Devil 99-100, 112-13, 116; *see also* Demon(s), Satan
Diatribes 32
Dibelius, Martin 18, 21
Dispersion, *diaspora* 28-29, 77, 98, 112, 128, 134, 136
Doctrine(s) 20, 27, 33, 35, 37, 42, 45, 50, 57, 60-62, 63-65, 82, 85, 88, 95-96, 97-98, 99, 103, 107, 131-32, 135, 138-40
    of justification 91-93, 141

Ebionism, Ebionites 33, 141
Elijah 129, 132, 134
Eschatology, eschatologically 21, 49, 67, 68-69, 76, 80, 82, 85, 86, 88, 90, 126-27
Evil 55-57, 65, 70, 100, 102, 105, 106, 109-11, 113, 114, 116, 130; *see also* Sin

Exaltation 48-50, 54, 113-14, 122

Faith 19, 20, 21, 26-27, 28, 39-42, 43-45, 47, 49, 51, 54, 56, 60, 65-66, 68, 72-74, 78, 87-96, 104, 105-06, 112-13, 114, 116-17, 119, 126, 131-32, 136, 138-41
Farmer, William R. 141
Father (God) 24, 27, 32, 41-42, 46, 52-54, 59-61, 67, 70, 75, 76, 78, 80, 101, 103, 108, 114-15, 125, 126, 133
Fides qua 96
Fides quae 96
Forgive(ness), forgiving 41-42, 78, 80, 86, 87, 89, 133, 135, 139-40
Form criticism 19, 21-22, 27
Formula of Concord 140, 146
Fourth gospel 27, 59, 61, 84, 86, 106-07, 115, 125; *see also* Gospel(s); John, Gospel of

Galatians 96
Galilee, Sea of 43
Gentile(s), Gentile Christians 20, 22, 25-26, 27, 28-31, 34, 49, 51, 57, 73, 83, 94, 92, 137
Glory 27, 40-41, 53, 55, 62, 72-73, 74, 76-77, 95, 114, 127
Gospel (Good News) 20-22, 29-31, 40, 43, 60-61, 64-65, 66-68, 74, 76, 81, 85-86, 92, 95, 102, 103-04, 106, 115, 120, 121-22, 124-25, 129, 137, 138, 140-41
Gospel(s) (books of Bible) 13, 21-22, 23-24, 27, 30, 39, 43, 45-46, 48, 50, 53, 54, 64, 74, 82, 90, 94, 101, 105, 116, 119, 122, 124, 136-37; *see also names of individual gospels*, Fourth gospel

Hellenistic, Hellenization, Hellenized 27, 29, 57, 69
Holy Spirit 27, 60, 67, 78, 100, 104-06, 111-13, 128, 132
Humiliation 47-49, 54, 70, 75, 76-77, 113
Humility 26, 48-49, 55, 66, 70, 75-76, 104, 106, 112, 113-14, 122

Incarnation, incarnate 58-60, 61, 72, 76-77, 98, 106-07
Isaiah 26, 50
Israel(ites) 28-30, 33, 54, 69, 70, 73, 77, 90, 94, 111

James
    son of Alphaeus 24, 139
    son of Zebedee 24, 29, 36, 53, 110, 139
Jerome 139
Jerusalem 23-24, 25-26, 28-30, 32-38, 40, 43-45, 53, 54, 63, 64, 66, 69-70, 73, 76-78, 99, 104, 110, 112, 113-14, 123, 130, 137
    Council of 25, 29-30, 33-34, 35, 37, 45, 83, 131
Jew(s), Jewish, Jewish Christian(s) 20, 25-26, 27-31, 32-34, 36, 37-38, 40, 42-43, 44, 51, 54, 55, 57-58, 64, 69, 73, 77, 79, 82-83, 84, 90, 91, 94, 110, 125, 128, 137, 141; *see also* Judaism

Job 93, 127-29
    Book of 93, 129
Johannine 53, 59, 76
John
    the Baptist 26, 49-51, 60, 65, 74, 88, 92, 100-01, 120-21, 126, 133, 136
    First Letter of 99
    Gospel of 102, 126
    son of Zebedee 21, 29, 36, 41, 50, 54, 59, 61, 99, 105, 110
Joseph (foster father of Jesus) 23-24, 27, 36, 139
    of Arimathea 119
    brother of Jesus 24
Joy 56
Judaism 26, 33, 44, 51, 64, 73, 135; *see also* Jews
Judaizers, Judaizing 37, 141
Jude 23-25, 59, 69, 72, 75
Judgment Day (final judgment) 87-90, 98, 114-15, 120; *see also* Last Day
Justification, justify(ing) 19-20, 31, 42, 49, 79, 87-88, 89, 91, 92, 93, 106, 114, 132-33, 134, 136, 138-41

King 30, 52, 66, 70, 82, 127, 130
Kingdom 51, 54, 66, 70, 74-76, 82-83, 84, 88, 98, 100, 119-20, 126, 136

Large Catechism 138-39
Last Day 53, 69, 79, 86, 87, 88, 90, 93, 98, 122, 124, 133, 140; *see also* Judgment Day
Law 19-21, 22, 24, 52, 63-65, 66-68, 70, 79, 81-86, 114, 138, 140-41
    of liberty 20, 68, 79, 85
    new 114
    relationship of Gospel to 103-04
    royal 81-82
    third use of 68, 85
Law preaching; *see* Preaching, of Law
Legalism 64
Life 50, 54, 57, 60, 67-68, 79,, 82, 86, 91, 95, 106, 112, 115-16, 124, 133, 140; *see also* Crown of life
    of Abraham 96
    of Christ 85, 98, 113-14, 136
    Christian 39-43, 46, 48, 51-52, 54, 56, 65-66, 67-68, 84-86, 90, 92, 106-07, 112-13, 114, 116, 126-27, 133
    eternal 39-40, 52-55, 57, 68
    Jewish 43, 44
    liturgical 110
    of Luther 138-39
Liturgy(ies) 30, 88-89, 101
Lord's Prayer 41-42, 56, 79-80, 86, 116, 127, 133, 138
Lord's Supper 21, 30, 35-37, 78-80, 89-90
Love (noun and verb) 20, 52, 53-55, 60, 64, 70, 74, 76, 81-82, 105, 106, 111, 114-15, 136
Luke 21, 34, 50, 53, 113, 119, 137
Lutheran(s,ism) 138, 139-41
Luther, Martin 14-15, 17-20, 42, 45, 47, 54, 55, 56, 61, 67, 84, 92, 105-06, 121, 127-29, 131, 138-41

Index

Mark(an) 21, 35, 43, 50
Martyrdom 42-43, 53-54, 84, 123
Mary
   mother of Jesus 23-24, 36, 70, 139
   mother of Mark 35
Matthew, Matthean 21-22, 23, 29, 39, 43, 44, 48-49, 50, 52, 66, 68, 71, 74-76, 77-78, 79-80, 81, 82-83, 87, 94, 100, 105-06, 107-08, 112-13, 114-15, 119, 126-27, 128-29, 130, 131, 141
Meekness 65-66, 69, 104, 106
Melanchthon, Philip 139-40
Messiah, Messianic 26, 34, 36, 50-52, 54, 66, 72, 74-75, 84, 94, 123, 124
Moses 83
Murder 79, 82-84, 105, 110

Name(s) of God, of Jesus 46, 76-78
Noah, Noahic 66, 115

Old Testament 19, 24, 25-26, 29, 40, 50-51, 60, 61, 72, 82, 84, 85, 88, 90, 93, 111, 115, 128-29

Parable(s) 45, 103
   agricultural 126
   of good Samaritan 117, 129
   of Kingdom 100
   of Lazarus and rich man 119
   of pearl of great price 125-26
   of sower 41, 47-48, 68, 107, 121, 125
   of two foundations 66, 68
   of unforgiving servant 86, 127, 129
   of vineyard 125
   of wheat and tares 121
Parousia 124, 126
Pastor(s) 30, 33-34, 38-39, 42, 44, 46, 63-64, 70, 98-101, 103-04, 124, 127-28, 130-31, 134; *see also* Clergy
Pastoral epistle(s) 32, 35, 51, 97-98
   James as 23, 32
Pastoral office 33, 47, 98-99, 100-01, 104, 121-22, 129
Patience 93, 105, 124-26, 127-29
Paul(ine) 19-20, 25, 26, 29, 30, 31, 33-35, 37-38, 40, 42, 44, 45, 48-49, 53, 55, 57-58, 61-62, 63, 67, 72, 74-80, 81-82, 84, 88, 89, 93, 91-95, 96, 98-99, 100, 103-05, 107-08, 110, 111, 113-15, 116, 119, 122-23, 124, 125, 131-33, 136-37, 138, 141
Peace 97, 104-05, 107-08
   greeting or formula of 31, 88-90
Pelagius, Pelagian(ism) 55-56, 116
Pentecost 24-25, 34, 36, 44, 85
Perfect, perfection(ism), perfectionist(s) 20, 40-42, 43, 67-68, 69, 99, 106
Persecution(s) 22, 28-29, 33, 36, 37-40, 42-43, 48, 49, 51-53, 54, 55, 56, 77, 81, 84, 110-11, 112, 123-24, 126, 127-28, 130-31, 136, 141
Peter 197, 23, 24-25, 27, 29, 31, 33-34, 36-38, 42-45, 48, 50-53, 78, 110, 112, 123, 125, 137

First Epistle of 50-51, 60, 65, 112
Pharisees, party of 33
Pneuma 95, 105-06, 112
Poor, poverty 37, 47-50, 54, 66, 70-71, 73-79, 80, 81, 84-85, 87-89, 94, 116, 119-22, 133; *see also* Spirit, poor in
Prayer(s), pray 44, 46, 66, 108, 130-32, 133-34; *see also* Lord's Prayer
Preacher(s) 63-65, 70, 85, 97-98, 99, 103, 122
Preaching 20, 21, 29, 44, 45, 49, 51, 54, 57, 60, 63, 65, 70, 74, 76, 78, 83, 84-85, 88, 94, 99-103, 108, 120-21, 126, 128, 135, 136, 138
   of Gospel 124
   by Jesus 84, 100, 106, 111, 136
   of Law, condemnatory 63, 64, 101, 103-04
   office of 107
Predestination 61-62
Prophet(s) 22, 26-27, 72, 81, 82, 88, 99, 123, 127-29
Protestant(s) 20, 41
Punishment 67

Rabbi(s), rabbinical 22, 26, 29, 38, 44, 49, 69
Rahab 90-94, 136, 140
Ransom 98
Reconciliation 80, 91
Redaction criticism 21
Reformation 20, 45, 141
Regeneration 50, 59-60, 61-62, 139-40
Reicke Bo 100, 102-03
Resurrection 19, 21, 24-25, 30, 32, 33, 37, 43, 44, 45, 51, 55, 61-62, 66, 74, 82, 88, 96, 114, 126, 133, 136
Rich, riches 47-50, 70, 73-77, 78-79, 84, 85, 89, 117, 119-22, 123
Ritual 88-89, 91
   Jewish 29, 31
   peace 89
Righteousness, righteous 53, 54, 55, 64-66, 69, 92, 93, 96, 97, 107-08, 115, 122-23, 132-34, 140
Roman Catholic(s), Catholicism 131-32, 139, 139-40
Roman Empire 25

Sacrifice, sacrificial 26, 48, 59, 140
Salutation 27, 30-31
Salvation 20, 28, 29, 32, 35, 44, 49-50, 54, 57-59, 61-62, 65-66, 69, 75, 78, 88-89, 93, 94, 101-02, 114, 119-20, 126, 129, 131, 132-34, 141
Sanctification 49, 52
Sanhedrin 33-34
Satan, satanic 39, 43, 49, 52, 56, 65, 93, 105-06, 112-14, 116, 129, 130; *see also* Demons, Devil
Saul (Paul) 33, 37, 52, 54; *see also* Paul
Schweitzer Albert 136
Scripture(s), Scriptural 19-20, 60-61, 63, 81-83, 92, 138
Sermon on the Mount 21-22, 23, 41, 64-65, 66-68, 70-71, 74, 83, 86, 88, 91, 98, 99, 100-02, 110-11, 114, 120-21, 129-30, 141

Servant(s) 23, 26-27, 80, 86, 113-14
unforgiving 86
Shalom 89
Shema 29, 90
Sick, sickness 66, 70, 130-34
Sin(s) 55-58, 60, 61, 65, 67, 81, 83, 85, 99-101, 112, 113-14, 116, 133-34
Slave, slavery 26, 67, 113
Son
    of Abraham 140
    of God 27, 46, 59, 61, 75, 96, 90, 107-08, 130
    of man 59, 115, 124, 127
Soul 93-95, 106, 112, 115, 134-35; *see also* Body
Spirit
    Holy; *see* Holy Spirit
    poor in 74, 75
Stephen 28, 36, 42, 43, 53, 54, 69, 77, 84, 110, 123
Suffering(s) 40, 44, 52-54, 56, 59, 71, 91, 110, 112, 122-23, 124, 127-29, 129, 136
Synagogue(s) 33, 73, 77, 79, 89-90, 94, 131
    relationship of church to 25, 29, 110

Teach, teacher(s), teaching(s) 21, 44, 45, 49, 57, 59, 63, 98-100, 103-04, 134-35, 140, 141
Temple 26, 36
Tempt(s, ed) Temptaion (s) 22, 39-41, 42-45, 47, 49, 56, 112-13
Thomas 27
Tradition 24, 36, 44, 74, 107, 120, 126
    apostolic 99
    oral 13, 23, 53, 64, 98
Tribulation 45
Truth 21, 44-45, 47, 49, 60-61, 78, 91, 101, 105, 106, 130, 134-35, 136

Widows 69-70
Wisdom 19, 21, 39, 44, 45, 92, 104-07
Word (of God) 40, 47-48, 49-50, 57-69, 73, 98-99, 125, 138,
    of condemnation 113
World 22, 23, 29, 34, 39, 41, 42-43, 47-48, 56, 58, 71, 74-75, 76, 79, 88, 92, 93, 105-07, 111-12, 115, 119, 124-25, 126-27,
    ancient 84
Worship(ing) 21, 29, 33, 35-37, 39, 73, 77, 78-79, 88-90, 91, 101, 122
Wrath 64, 67-68, 70, 86, 126; *see also* Anger

www.ingramcontent.com/pod-product-compliance
Lightning Source LLC
Chambersburg PA
CBHW070908160426
43193CB00011B/1401